CLARICE CLIFF

THE ART OF BIZARRE

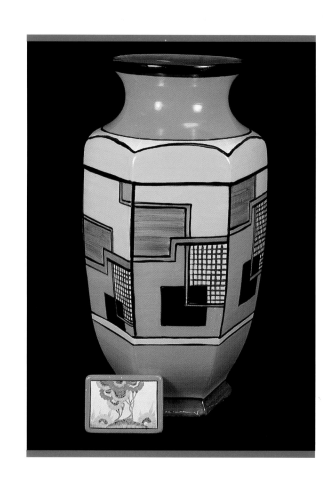

CLARICE CLIFF

THE ART OF BIZARRE

A DEFINITIVE CENTENARY CELEBRATION BY

LEONARD GRIFFIN

PAVILION

To Michael, for everything, forever...

First published in Great Britain in 1999 by
PAVILION BOOKS LIMITED
London House, Great Eastern Wharf
Parkgate Road, London SW11 4NQ

Designed by Nigel Partridge

A CIP catalogue record for this book is available
from the British Library

ISBN 1 86205 219 0

Set in ITC Berkeley Old Style
Colour reproduction in Hong Kong by Asia Graphic Output
Printed and bound in Singapore by Imago

2 4 6 8 10 9 7 5 3 1

This book can be ordered direct from the publisher.
Please contact the Marketing Department.
But try your bookshop first.

TITLE PAGE: Football *on a massive fifteen-inch high shape 37 vase and an* Advertising Plaque *in* Rhodanthe
RIGHT: Luxor *on a fifteen-inch high shape 37 vase and an* Advertising Plaque *in* Blue Firs

CONTENTS

INTRODUCTION

KAY AND PETER WENTWORTH-SHEILDS

The centenary year of Clarice Cliff's birth will be remembered by collectors and admirers all over the world. The commemoration of her life and work will be captured in a unique exhibition at the Wedgwood Museum in Stoke-on-Trent. The celebrations will include a gala champagne party in the famous garden of Chetwynd House, where devotees will meet Clarice's original *Bizarre* 'girls' and reminisce about her life and times. On the other side of the world Clarice Cliff Collectors Club members will remember her with exhibitions and parties in New Zealand and Australia. It will be a year for sharing information about shapes, patterns and prices, meeting dealers and making new friends. But most of all it will be a time to reflect on her incredible life.

During the Brighton Exhibition in 1972 Clarice said that she did not understand how her work 'could be considered interesting'. The modesty of this remark is in startling contrast to what we see today.

Our curiosity started several years earlier when we explored the markets in Bermondsey, Kensington and Portobello Road in London. Saturday mornings found us at Camden Passage where we bought from a stall called High Camp, then run by two enthusiastic girls. Mr Chiou was a favourite stop where we purchased a large job lot of *Crocus*. We became friends with the early pioneers who had amassed huge collections, including a wonderful array of *Conical* sugar dredgers, and bought some fine examples which we had first seen displayed at the now legendary Brighton Exhibition. That show was a revelation; huge plaques, vases, even umbrella stands – the sheer range of colours and shapes was staggering.

A major impact on us was the full colour page of Clarice's ware in the catalogue for the 1971 World of Art Deco exhibition in Minneapolis. The brilliant text was written by Bevis Hillier, who later so generously wrote the insightful foreword to our book, which perfectly balanced a note of lightness and serious interest in the subject. His summation of the quintessential appeal of her work remains unrivalled: 'One tunes in to Cliff pottery as she, every day, used to tune in to The Archers – in confident anticipation of scenes more brightly painted and fantastical than real life, yet recognizably linked to known reality.'

RIGHT: The stunning eighteen-inch plaque from the cover of Peter and Kay's book, with a shape 362 vase in House and Bridge

We were inspired by two of Martin Battersby's books, *The Decorative Twenties* and *The Decorative Thirties*. We met him at a soirée held in the Great Kitchen in the Brighton Pavilion. He was a charming and knowledgeable person who convinced us that Clarice was a true genius and not the 'superficial plagiarist' that some suggested. He was a gifted artist and his love of Clarice inspired his superb poster for the Brighton Exhibition. A high point came when an entry for Clarice appeared in Geoffrey Godden's *British Pottery* and *The Observer's Book of Pottery and Porcelain*. We knew she had arrived as an established and appreciated artist.

Our efforts to unravel the Artists in Industry endeavour proved a fascinating experience. We visited Charleston to see and photograph the Bloomsbury contribution. The house was still a family home where we were greeted by Angelica Bell. We were shown the pieces they owned, rather casually stacked in a kitchen cupboard. We photographed these in the dining-room on a table painted by Vanessa Bell and which as a backdrop had the fireplace decorated by Duncan Grant – who emerged

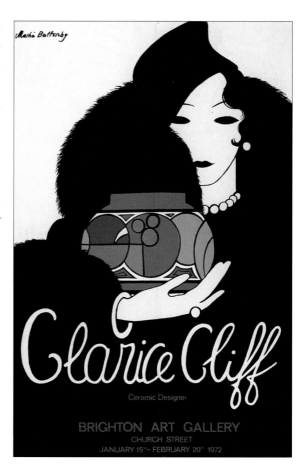

briefly from the Studio. We tracked down the Laura Knight dinner service bought by Gracie Fields and inherited by her niece in its amazing entirety.

We first met Noël Tovey and David Sarel at their stall on Kings Road. We bought and talked Clarice, became good friends and had some heady times together. One evening David was due back from a buying coup in Scotland with boxes of Clarice in his car. We waited with Noël into the night for his triumphant arrival. We were not disappointed. Newspapers flying and with cries of astonishment we unpacked each new treasure, including a fabulous eighteen-inch charger in what we now know is *House and Bridge*! We spent many a spirited dinner either at their flat or ours, gloating over new finds and pondering the depths or shallows of Clarice. Her creations seemed to unlock uninhibited pleasures at many levels. Noël was a gifted cook and many evenings were enriched by a Baked Alaska. He threw fabulous Thanksgiving dinners, with Kay and a friend dressed as 'backless', Puritan maid waitresses! By now Noël and David had opened L'Odeon, their famous shop on Fulham High Street.

When we wrote our book, *Clarice Cliff*, we tried to classify patterns and shapes and were inevitably thwarted by the almost daily appearance of new ones! We pored over the Hanley Library collection of press cuttings and pattern books but the latter were so incomplete that we resorted to inventing names. Getting the book published was a story in itself. No publisher knew or cared who Clarice Cliff was, even though by then Art Deco was a recognized style. (We still think Clarice falls outside the parameters of the term.) Several publishers were enthusiastic but evasive. After much futile editing and vague promises we could wait no longer. L'Odeon had amassed a splendid collection of Cliff with an exhibition in mind to coincide with the book's debut. They decided to publish it themselves!

The L'Odeon exhibition opened on 22 April 1976 and was stunning and beautifully designed, along with Peter's clever recreation of Clarice's *Bizooka*, which twenty-three years later is alive and well. The publicity was outstanding, with posters all over London and very favourable reviews. Amongst these was a half page in *The Times Saturday Review* and an article in the prestigious *Times Literary Supplement*.

We have only recently met Leonard Griffin but over the years have admired the way he has carried the Clarice Cliff torch and inspired an ever-expanding appreciation of her work, even converting a few ceramic snobs along the way. This book is a magnificent tribute to Clarice. With meticulous scholarship, it vividly brings her character and times to life in a unique and personal way. She now has an established place in the history of twentieth-century ceramic art, an unusual achievement for a woman in a male-dominated industry. Her extraordinary talent and business acumen combined to produce an unbelievably diverse range of *Bizarre* artefacts that will be treasured into the twenty-first century and beyond.

RIGHT: Kay and Peter pictured in 1998 with the wooden Bizooka *they created for the L'Odeon* Clarice Cliff *exhibition in 1976*

A JAZZ AGE ENCOUNTER

It was a dark wet night, and every surface reflected the illuminated theatres, picture houses and department stores. Despite the Depression the West End of London was electric. Peering through the glittering raindrops on the cab window, she could feel the excitement of the city she had grown to love in the few years since she first studied in it. She relished her long days at the trade shows and the evenings enjoying all London had to offer. The city was almost a second home to her. At first she had found it overwhelming compared with the Potteries, but now enjoyed her weeks in the capital as much as her quiet weekends walking in the Staffordshire countryside. She was beginning to appreciate her good fortune. The unexpected success of *Bizarre* had opened up her career as a busy designer and she was not going to let her natural reserve interfere with her ambition.

Clarice glanced across the cab at the mature but handsome face of Colley Shorter. In the Potteries he was renowned for his tough approach to business but he had never been able to maintain that façade with Clarice. His works manager had first drawn her to his attention and Clarice had soon become, in his eyes, more than just a designer. Her approach to her work was unlike that of anyone else in Stoke-on-Trent and she had caused him to revolutionize his ideas. Such was the chemistry between Clarice and Colley that, whereas the other potbanks struggled to survive the Depression years, their factory thrived. Inevitably, Colley Shorter had felt drawn to the woman, who was seventeen years younger than him. Their shared success enabled them to go away regularly to London. The promotion of her *Bizarre* ware gave them numerous opportunities to enjoy all the capital had to offer. This evening he was treating her to dinner, and dancing to the Harry Roy Band!

When they arrived at the Café de Paris Clarice was helped from the cab by a top-hatted doorman. She glanced back from Colley to the brightly lit portico of the building. Colley took her arm and steered her through the foyer where the warm aroma of tobacco and scent greeted them. Her fur wrap was taken and she went to the powder room where she adjusted her hair and make-up. Looking at herself in the mirror, she could still not really believe that this was her: Clarice Cliff in London with the boss of the factory she had joined as a lithographer in 1916. She took a small elaborate glass bottle from

ABOVE: A complete set of Clarice's rare Age of Jazz *figures*

her purse, dabbed an oriental fragrance onto her wrists, and then headed back to the foyer. Colley beamed at her as she approached. Being much taller he always seemed so completely confident, and she was glad of his arm on hers as they entered the ballroom.

Tables surrounded the dance floor and the hubbub of conversation and cigarette smoke filled the air. Many of the women were wearing the longer slinky dresses that had recently become fashionable; all the men were in evening dress. A stage with iridescent curtains was at the opposite end of the room. An attentive maitre d' seated them at a 'reserved' table.

Clarice's only trip overseas had been to Paris and her knowledge of the language did not extend to food so Colley perused the French menu and ordered for them both. Soon they were enjoying a cocktail and Colley listened as Clarice talked about her latest ideas. Colley was extremely interested in art and design, and although more conservative in his tastes than his protégé was continually impressed by her ideas. *Bizarre* ware had become a shared passion: for Clarice it provided endless scope for her imagination, for Colley marketing it challenged his promotional skills. By cleverly basing the promotion around Clarice's distinctive name which people now associated strongly with her innovative pottery, Colley's intuitive belief in her work had been totally justified. Their reward was these enjoyable evenings together in a world very different from the canal-side factory in Burslem.

They became aware of a couple approaching their table. Clarice looked up and did not recognize them, but the woman looked at Colley knowingly, and inspected Clarice in a polite way. Always extremely well-mannered, Colley was instantly on his feet, greeting them. Turning he said. 'I do not think you have met Miss Clarice Cliff, but I am sure you have heard of her?' Clarice, was momentarily disarmed. The woman reached out to shake her hand, 'Pleased to meet you Miss Cliff, I'm Elsie Havenhand, and this is my husband Sydney.' And suddenly it dawned on Clarice that Elsie was a friend of Colley's wife, Annie!

Elsie Havenhand had been taken aback to see Colley Shorter when she walked into the room and had for a moment thought it might be diplomatic to leave. However, recognizing Clarice Cliff from photographs she had seen, she could not resist insisting to her husband that there was *no* reason why they should not join the other couple!

More meals and drinks were ordered and then their conversation turned first to the economy. Both Sydney Havenhand and Colley Shorter were in fortunate positions during the Depression. Colley had Clarice's very successful *Bizarre* ware and Sydney was making a fortune from his wireless receiver business. He was in London for a trade show, much like the ones Clarice and Colley organized to promote their pottery, so the two men had a lot in common and were soon talking about finance.

Elsie Havenhand engaged Clarice in conversation. Clarice spoke about her six brothers and sisters who were all still in Tunstall, but she did not mention that she now lived alone in a flat in Hanley. Even in the 'new world' of the thirties such things were still not spoken of in the Potteries. What really broke the ice, though, was when they discovered that they had both chosen the Café de Paris that evening because they wanted to hear the Harry Roy Band! Elsie decided that despite all the rumours about Colley Shorter and his designer she quite liked her.

As they ate, the conversation began to flow a little more easily. Clarice was a great fan of the 'wireless', and already had one in her flat. She listened attentively as Sydney Havenhand described the newest models. Then, looking at an elaborate decoration in the centre of their table, Sydney said, 'Miss Cliff, you should design a centrepiece that reflects the Jazz Age theme of this club!' He knew that she produced many pottery novelties and it struck him as a commercial idea of great potential. Clarice smiled, thought for a moment, and said, 'What a jolly good idea! Actually, Mr Havenhand, your company might also benefit from such a novelty, perhaps as a display item beside wireless sets to catch the eye of shoppers!' They were all highly amused by the idea of Jazz Age ornaments, and before they realized it, they were all talking animatedly together.

As they finished their meal the compère appeared on stage to introduce the band. The curtains parted to reveal a pianist, a small brass section, guitarists and a drummer, all splendidly bedecked in evening dress. Soon both couples were on the polished wooden dance floor and Clarice had resolved the idea for a set of figures dancing to a Jazz Age quartet…

Later in the cab returning them to their hotel, Clarice and Colley were busy discussing the next day's work. Clarice noted the names of potential new buyers Colley had invited, and then excitedly explained her idea for a set of *Age of Jazz* figures to display by a wireless. He liked the idea very much but his attention was distracted by the fear that Elsie Havenhand would almost certainly mention their chance meeting to his wife, probably even before he returned to Stoke. He decided to handle that problem if it arose, and gave his full attention to Clarice. She was suggesting that the figures should be flat-sided! He knew instantly that once again she had struck a novel idea that was bound to keep his profits buoyant. He had already decided to make her art director of the factory and her constant flow of new ideas only convinced him even more that he was right with this decision, 'even though she was a woman'. He reached out in the darkness of the cab and squeezed her hand. She received the beam of admiration from him and smiled back.

One of the romances of the pottery trade has been that of Miss Clarice Cliff who a short time back was a modeller for a pottery firm in Stoke, before she conceived the idea of brighter pottery for the home. Now she spends her days designing gay, many coloured fantasies, that are painted on ordinary cream pottery by over 100 girls, paintresses as they are called locally, who quickly learn her designs by heart.

Daily Mirror, June 1930

Clarice Cliff's astounding emergence as the premier ceramic designer in the Staffordshire Potteries in the thirties, is a story as fantastic as her pottery. Daring enough to create ware in unique and diverse styles, Clarice's prolific output between 1927 and 1939 left a trail of pieces all around the world.

Today, these entice, intrigue, bewitch and mystify collectors. When this *Bizarre* treasure trail was first rediscovered in the sixties, delighted collectors rose to the challenge of trying to assemble the seemingly endless variety of pieces. Since then, the legendary high prices, tales of unique pieces being bought for just a few pounds, and the intriguing true stories behind the pottery, have made Clarice Cliff a charismatic icon.

After the first retrospective of her work at Brighton Museum in 1972, Clarice's reputation continued to grow as more and more of her work came to light. In the last ten years much new information has appeared which means we need to re-evaluate her work, and its importance for twentieth century ceramics. Whilst this volume seeks to answer many factual questions, it also asks that the reader to use their imagination. Stories of events that happened seventy years ago, recalled by Clarice's friends and colleagues, are inevitably sometimes cloudy. Using a little artistic licence I will recount some of them as fiction, but they are based on fact. Hence the story of Clarice and Colley and the evening she had the idea of her *Age of Jazz* figures! The tale is true, as Elsie and Sydney Havenhand did indeed surprise them that evening as Elsie later related to her son. To bring to life just another everyday event in the life of Clarice and Colley I gave it dialogue and used a little imagination – something Clarice Cliff used a lot, and often!

It was Clarice's imagination that helped make her the best-known ceramic designer of her generation. Yet, only fifteen years ago many people still referred to her as 'Clarence Cliff' or 'Who?' Her rise to international fame has been stunning. Yet it is merely a direct repetition of the impact her ware had originally, when as the first woman art director in the Potteries, she uniquely controlled both the shapes and patterns of her ceramics.

As well as celebrating the centenary of her birth, the reason I find myself writing a fifth book on Clarice Cliff is that her output was so complex that I am only now able to document it more fully. The earliest, the L'Odeon book in 1976, was written by Kay Johnson and Peter Wentworth-Sheilds, which is why I am delighted that they have contributed the introduction to this book. Their pioneering volume fired my interest and prompted the research that led to *Bizarre Affair*. When it was published in 1988, the new information, mixed with Louis and Susan Meisel's glorious colour feast of Clarice's best pieces, introduced *Bizarre* to a whole new generation. It also triggered another wave of information as more people who played a part in the *Bizarre* years contacted me. This response was not just from Britain, but from Australia, New Zealand, North America and South Africa; all the countries to where Colley Shorter had so successfully exported Clarice's ware.

You cannot explain Clarice Cliff's ceramics in a cold 'museum label' way. This is why she was the first ceramicist to 'escape' the museum system and be celebrated in exhibitions, often spontaneous, that made up for in flair what they lacked in academic gravitas. It was almost a case of '*Bizarre* on the road', when from 1984 onwards exhibitions were staged in town halls, libraries, theatre foyers and shopping centres, in Warwick, Hertfordshire, Hampshire, Stratford, Manchester and, naturally, several in London. Oh, and along the way her devotees also prompted displays in museums in America, Australia, New Zealand and Holland… Clarice Cliff had arrived, for the second time. And so it was to be in the nineties that the true significance of Clarice as an artist, and her amazing contribution to the Potteries' economy in the thirties finally became fully apparent.

In two of my earlier books, *Taking Tea* and *Fantastic Flowers*, I covered specific aspects of Clarice's life and work, which allows me now to record her unique contribution as both an industrial designer and ceramic artist. Her primary role was that of a designer who focused the skills of over one hundred *Bizarre* decorators. Clarice's unique *Bizarre* shop was staffed by eager and skilled young minds and hands, through which she expressed her art on pottery. Nowhere else in the world was there a factory blending studio principles with production line techniques. Clarice's designs utilized a massive range of decorating techniques: on-glaze enamels, the glorious *Latona* and *Inspiration* glazes, the wildly splattered *Patina* and *Delecia* ranges, highly modelled *My Garden* and *Scraphito* ware. This artistic diversity represented the most comprehensive output of any one designer in the Potteries in the thirties. To fully understand it today collectors need to learn about processes and skills that are long gone, so new devotees will find the *Glossary* not just useful, but essential.

BELOW: Clarice and her Age of Jazz figures in September 1930

Previously I have told Clarice's story chronologically but she was so prolific that the ware she created in her heyday does not lend itself to neat dating. Indeed, whereas we believed *Bizarre* ware was launched in September 1928, I can now show that the true date was a year earlier, and her work as a modeller actually began in 1922. Therefore, whilst these new dates are important, *The Art of Bizarre* looks at the various expressions of her art, allowing us to follow their development and appreciate her greatest pieces more fully. The Clarice Cliff Collectors Club has fortunately brought me into contact with collectors as enthusiastic as myself and I cannot over-emphasise the importance of their observations. Two, Doreen Jenkins and Dr Phil Woodward, *have* to be singled out. Doreen's insight helped capture the essence of Clarice the woman. Phil's astute detective work proved beyond doubt her pre-eminence in the thirties, and finally answered the intriguing question at the root of the Clarice Cliff story – why *Bizarre*?

Looking at a glorious selection of Clarice's major shapes we can see that she captured a style no one else was to equal. No other Staffordshire designer created such delightfully different shapes: vases, bowls, dozens of tea and coffee shapes, face masks, smoker's sets, endless fancies, and Art Deco icons such as the *Age of Jazz* figures and *Lido Lady Ashtray*.

What has until now been perceived as Clarice's biggest mistake, dropping her *Bizarre* tradename, was with hindsight probably her best decision. Like other talented creative artists who were largely self-taught, she did not have grandiose ideas about the importance of her own work. She pursued a goal, achieved it, and then saw no point in perpetuating that achievement, so left the talented team she had assembled to fuel the creative fires at her factory. She left us wanting more…

Because Clarice Cliff achieved what she did by rejecting the dictates of the establishment, even today she is regarded as a rebel by some, hence the mass of spontaneous exhibitions. It is, however, fitting that in her centenary year, Clarice's *Bizarre Art* is celebrated not in a dull Victorian museum, but on a green field site at Barlaston where Wedgwood built the most modern 'pot-bank' in Britain in 1939.

Wedgwood inherited Clarice's name when they absorbed the factory where her pottery had been made, and now reproduce hand-painted copies of her work. Her art is also readily available for everyone as others have created Clarice Cliff tea towels, mugs or biscuit tins, with a sound commercial eye Colley Shorter would have admired. Her unique style has made Clarice Cliff an icon of the twentieth century. This still surprises her detractors, as even today her work is avant-garde. Yet as early as 1932 an Australian *Bizarre* stockist commented:

There is nothing more typical of this age of simplicity in design than Clarice Cliff's work, and it is safe to say that early twentieth century design will be inseparably associated in the minds of collectors of the future with the name of Clarice Cliff.

Clarice's art made her name one that meant a great deal in the thirties. Having bewitched the world she retired artistically and physically, though just her name continued to sell ceramics for a further twenty-five years. But from the moment she was inspired to create her stunning *Age of Jazz* figures she had secured her place as the innovative ceramicist of the thirties. The fact that she 'married the boss', moved into his Arts and Crafts house, and then toured the world with him, only enhances her appeal. There are few designers, past or present, who have Clarice Cliff's charisma. The ceramic spell she cast in the thirties is a force as potent now as it was then.

Leonard Griffin

COLLEY SHORTER

The Clarice Cliff legend, so rooted in the thirties, was actually conceived by a man born in 1882. Long before the term 'Art Deco' had been coined, Arthur Colley Austin Shorter, the eldest son of Arthur Shorter, was born in the wealthy suburb of Wolstanton near Stoke-on-Trent. The large house was home to Colley's four sisters, and his younger brother Guy, born in 1884. They lived a typical, privileged Victorian home life, captured in many photographs by Arthur Shorter whose passion for photography was to be passed on to Colley.

After a good schooling where he excelled at sports, Colley left aged sixteen and as was expected of him went to work at his father's large earthenware works in Burslem. The Shorter family had owned the A. J. Wilkinson Royal Staffordshire Pottery since 1894, Arthur Shorter having previously married Wilkinson's sister Henrietta. The vast site by the Trent-Mersey canal at Newport was covered with a mass of Victorian bottle-ovens, kilns and shops and employed nearly 400 workers. It made earthenware of a superior quality to that of most other potbanks in the area, but artistically there was little to distinguish its products.

Colley Shorter was immediately called 'Mr Colley' by his father's workers and threw himself enthusiastically into learning how to manage a potbank. Two years later Guy left school and trained as a manager at the original family factory, Shorter & Sons in Copeland Street. Arthur Shorter was a serious man who expected much of his sons and was pleased when Colley showed a flair as a salesman. From 1907 Colley started to undertake trips to vital overseas markets and visited major dealers in both Canada and America. He also learned the art of promoting the company at trade shows and represented Wilkinson's at Ghent where ceramics by the art director John Butler won an award. Butler had joined

BELOW: Colley Shorter aged twelve in 1894, with two of his sisters

Wilkinson's in 1904 when he was thirty-eight and his work was of high quality but traditional in style. Meanwhile, Guy Shorter supervised production at the Shorter & Sons' factory whose products at this time were limited mainly to large, traditional jardinières and vases in majolica glazes.

In 1910 Colley Shorter went to a ball at the Trentham Gardens Pavilion near Newcastle where he was introduced to Annie Rogers who was just twenty-two, six years younger than him. He immediately started courting her; they married shortly afterwards and moved into a small farmhouse near the village of Clayton. In 1912 their daughter Margaret was born.

At the start of the First World War, Guy Shorter was temporarily marooned near the German border, but made his way to Lucerne in Switzerland, and then home. He enrolled in the army, and served in the trenches, unlike Colley who did not enlist. Exactly why is unclear but this later led Arthur Shorter to change the way the factories were managed. Although he made his sons joint directors of Wilkinson's in 1915, when he retired to Llandudno in 1918 it was not Colley who was given the senior position but his younger brother Guy. However, Colley and Annie were given the family home, Chetwynd House in Wolstanton.

In 1920 Colley Shorter decided to continue his work at Wilkinson's and also establish his own factory. He did not need to look far, as immediately next to Wilkinson's was the run-down Newport Pottery, owned by S. W. Dean. As its site was only separated from Wilkinson's by a wall it was the ideal location. A contemporary aerial photograph shows the canal, with the white scar of the shard ruck tip in the foreground. Wilkinson's, with a mass of giant bottle ovens is on the left. Newport, although smaller, was tightly packed with buildings and facilities dating from 1840, including an anonymous disused building, on the corner of the site next to the canal, which would soon become very active.

Colley's problem was that he could not afford to buy Newport Pottery. That same year Annie Shorter had given birth to their second daughter, Joan, and with the added expense of his enlarged family he found that he simply did not have the funds. Fortunately his wife's father was prepared to lend him the £5000 necessary and a formal agreement was drawn up between them. The loan was to be a good investment.

ABOVE: Colley Shorter (right) with his younger brother Guy in 1912

BELOW: The Trent Mersey canal at Newport Wilkinson's is on the left and Newport Pottery on the right

Colley Shorter's first priority at Newport Pottery was to improve the quality of the product, and as well as making vitrified hotel ware he wanted to add new lines of quality earthenware. The existing ranges were all made with Japanese-style prints covered in lustre glazes or aerographing. Nearly every Stoke factory produced ware in this style and he knew it was a shrinking market. He also realized that the marketing needed improving and in September 1921 employed Ewart Oakes who became the premier salesman representing the three family factories for the south of England. Colley knew that if he was to improve sales he needed to produce new lines, which is perhaps what prompted him to prompted him to promote a young woman to be an apprentice modeller in 1922. Clarice Cliff was first drawn to his attention by Jack Walker, the works manager. Unlike the other young female staff, she paid considerable attention to her work, and was interested in the practical aspects of the potbank. Gradually, she was given more responsibility. Throughout the twenties Colley Shorter cultivated an overseas dealer network in Australia, New Zealand, South Africa and North America. Travel to these countries was a long and difficult process, so he spent weeks on such trips, but he knew how crucial personal contact was in securing overseas orders.

BELOW: Wilkinson's ware from 1920 to 1926 in aerographed and lustre finishes

Colley's new affluence enabled him to buy a larger home for his family in 1926, near the farm they had first lived at in Clayton. The Goodfellow House had been built on an open hillside by architects Barry Parker and Raymond Unwin in 1899. It was named after Charles Goodfellow who had commissioned it but Colley renamed it Chetwynd after the family home in Wolstanton. Colley was now forty-four years old and his youthful passion for sport had been replaced with antique collecting and his role as a freemason. He bought many of Goodfellow's antiques and his collection of Chinese blue and white porcelain. Colley was to spend a lot of time and money changing the house and almost the first thing he did was to ask John Butler to embellish the Italianate landscape in a long panel over the inglenook. Butler added knights in armour on horseback, and this was to re-appear a few years later as the *Knight Errant* design.

ABOVE: The inglenook at Chetwynd House

Passionate in his work and belief in his products, Colley organized stands at all the major British trade shows, where he used the company's most prestigious ware, such as John Butler's *Tibetan* and *Oriflamme,* to attract attention to the everyday products. Notable amongst many overseas shows was Philadelphia in 1926, where a large Wilkinson's stand was dominated by *Tibetan* ware. Observing how the Americans organized these shows on a huge scale, with eye-catching displays, gave him the ideas that were to surprise his competitors. They were to become well aware of his flair for marketing and promotion, later a major asset in establishing Clarice Cliff as his designer.

Colley mixed pride in his youngest daughter Joan, with sound commercial sense, when he used her as a designer! A range initially called *From a*

LEFT: A.J. Wilkinson's stand at the 1926 Philadelphia Exposition in America, including a Boy Blue *milk and* Humpty *sugar jug*

Child to a Child was launched in May 1928. Each piece, marked 'Joan Shorter aged 8', showed matchstick people drawn in a child-like manner. Colley created tremendous interest by offering journalists interviews with Joan. A story from *Home Chat* gives an idea of how Joan's ware was sold in 1928.

'It certainly was very sickening', said eight year old Joan when I asked her to tell me about it. 'You see I was so busy with my painting that I quite forgot that it was terribly late and long past bed time. And daddy came home and was so cross and he didn't even look at my lovely postcards, and I had done them specially for him to see. But daddy got quite sorry and when he came up to say goodnight – what do you think? he said that he loved my paintings and gave me an extra hug, because he was so sorry he'd been angry, and he promised me that he would have my paintings put on some cups and saucers for me. He makes cups you see so it's rather lucky isn't it?

'I had such a lovely dream about them, but in the morning when I asked if the cup was ready for breakfast, daddy did laugh, and then he took such a long time – quite a month – to do them, that I began to think that he'd forgotten. Then they came, and Betty and Jane, they're in my form at school – came to tea – and weren't they jealous.'

BELOW: Joan Shorter inspecting her ware

Colley had seen Joan drawing at home and taken her drawings into the factory where he arranged for Clarice to evolve a children's tableware range. As well as the pieces based on Joan's drawings Clarice modelled some innovative shapes; a teapot of a globular man wearing an apron, *Bones the Butcher*, a *Boy Blue* milk jug and a *Humpty* sugar clearly inspired by Humpty Dumpty! The most unusual addition to the range both in style and name, was a *Subway Sadie* comport, which had Sadie's head and body as the handle.

From a Child to a Child was hand-painted at Wilkinson's by a small team of female decorators who were just fourteen so they were only six years older than Joan! To cope with demand the range was moved to Newport and simplified by using prints which were enamelled by the paintresses, who found they had suddenly become *Bizarre* 'girls'. Further designs were issued as *Kiddies Ware* from 1930 and as late as 1933 Joan was still used to publicize them when she was thirteen! Ironically, many years later Joan herself remembered the matchstick ware but had completely forgotten *Bones the Butcher*.

The real significance of the Joan Shorter ware made Colley realize how much publicity could be attracted by linking a person to a product. Adding Clarice Cliff's name alongside *Bizarre* on the ware was to give the factory a personality they could promote with the pottery, and for the first time ceramics were designed by a woman to appeal to women!

MISS CLIFF

When Colley Shorter asked Clarice Cliff to develop the ware marketed under his daughter's name, she was probably extremely pleased to be able to assist the factory owner in this rather prestigious task. The interest he had taken in her work since he had given her a new Indenture of Apprenticeship as a modeller in 1922 had allowed her to gain considerable experience. In 1928 Clarice was unique in the Staffordshire Potteries in that the role of modeller in a potbank had previously been a male domain, but she was now also allowed to design patterns for her shapes! This was all an amazing achievement given her very ordinary background.

Clarice had been born into a typical Potteries family in 1899. Their small terraced house in Tunstall was home to Ann and Harry Cliff and their seven children. Clarice's childhood in the first ten years of the twentieth century was almost identical to that of a child born forty years earlier in Staffordshire. Poverty and deprivation was everywhere as work was limited to the mines, the iron works or the potbanks. Few people had any real hope of escaping from this life. Ann Cliff took in washing to make extra money, and Clarice's father and one of her brothers worked at Fuller's Ironworks whose factory was at the bottom of their road. Her aunts worked as hand-paintresses at local potbanks in Tunstall, where Clarice was known to linger after school and during school holidays. The hand-paintresses in the local factories were not encouraged to have original ideas; their work was basically to fill in printed patterns with enamels, or use a wheel to band and line tableware with gilt. Worse still was the job of a lithographer, whose skill was limited to mechanically placing printed designs accurately onto ware. These visits would have made Clarice aware of the limited opportunities once she left school.

ABOVE: The earliest known photograph of Clarice Cliff (right) from 1917, with friends from work

As the family grew they had to move to a slightly larger house in the adjoining Edwards Street. Clarice's childhood was tempered with a strict church-going regime, and all the Cliff children attended two or three times every weekend. This included Sunday School, where the stories told by the teachers fascinated Clarice, and inspired her later to become a teacher there. When electric lights were installed in the church in 1909 it was a novelty for the children as the Cliff family home was lit by gas and candles.

When Clarice joined the Summerbank Road school in 1909 her sisters went to another school and this early separation may have led to her later artistic individuality. At school her interest and skill in modelling meant she was given the task of making relief maps out of papier mâché for use in geography lessons. From an early age Clarice was seen as being different from her siblings. Whilst they were happy to play in the streets with other children, or take part in plays at the Sunday School, Clarice was more of a loner, and happiest with her own company. She became a prolific reader, and her sister Ethel recalled that she could be kept quiet for hours by being given a lump of clay to model. However, whatever creative juices these solitary interests stimulated, Clarice had no real chance to develop them, as her schooling was simple, with just half an hour a week devoted to art.

When she was just thirteen Clarice left school and became an apprentice hand-paintress at Lingard Webster in Tunstall. Joining the firm in 1912 she was to experience the last few years of the lingering influence of the Victorian age on a typical potbank. Men earned a great deal more than women, who were regarded as being less efficient, weaker and were certainly not allowed to design! In the same year the Miner's Strike over low pay severely affected Staffordshire. Whole families dug on abandoned pits to get some of the coal

BELOW: Clarice's father Harry in 1928

essential to warm their homes, and emergency food centres were set up to feed children. The Cliff family was insulated from this but it was surrounded by the hardship it caused.

The start of the world war just two years later was one catalyst that prompted Clarice Cliff to re-evaluate her life. Suddenly, many of the male workers went off to fight, as did one of her brothers, and others were sent to work in factories supplying the troops. Clarice changed jobs, and joined Hollinshead & Kirkham where she learned lithography. Her parents were worried that her hand-painting skills would suffer but fortunately she had won a scholarship to attend the Tunstall School of Art. Like all the young artists who attended these institutions, Clarice was initially stimulated by the classes, but in later years she commented derisorily 'drawing from plaster casts and vases of honesty were the sum total of tuition'. The principal of all the schools of art in

Stoke-on-Trent was Gordon Forsyth, who also did freelance designing for lustre ware made by Pilkingtons. His own work was heavily steeped in the William Morris style, with busy foliate designs executed in dark lustre colours. He was influential in the Potteries and so this style still predominated in the art pottery issued by some of its factories even into the twenties. As fate was to show, Clarice, unlike her fellow students, was to learn that there was a great deal more to art than the philosophy that permeated the local art schools.

When Clarice's brother Harry was seriously wounded and invalided out of the army in the middle of the war, she took to travelling down to London with friends to visit him and other soldiers in military hospitals. It was her first experience of the capital. In 1916 she decided to change jobs once again because, as she later recalled, 'I decided I would like most to learn the various branches of pottery decorating.' This is probably why she moved to the A. J. Wilkinson factory several miles away at Newport in Burslem where she was recruited by the works manager Jack Walker. On her first day at work, much to her embarrassment, she arrived without the apron she was meant to provide. Jack Walker apparently made sure one was found for her, and this rather kindly man supported Clarice as she settled in.

ABOVE: *Clarice's brother Harry in 1914*

The significance of Clarice joining Wilkinson's was that it was a great distance to travel to work. There was limited public transport and her journey there six days a week (workers did a half day on Saturday) involved a tram ride and then a walk through Middleport Park, in all weathers. Although this is seen as no great distance now, at the time it was almost unheard of for someone to travel so far.

When she joined Wilkinson's, Clarice was intrigued by the vast site and had soon investigated every department during her lunch break or after work. Her fellow workers noted that as they left she would often stay behind and model figures from clay, so Clarice inevitably arrived back home in Tunstall long after her sisters. She began to see less of them though she was still close to Ethel. The youngest, Dolly, two years younger than Clarice, was the most extrovert. She became well known for her ballroom dancing and later a family member recalled, 'she made her own gowns, and had a treadle machine in the parlour which Ann Cliff was not happy about. Dolly had a friend who was a widow, so left home to have space to do her dress-making.' Dolly joined Wilkinson's a few years after Clarice. The oldest sisters were Hannah and Sarah Ellen, known as Nellie, who left home when she married.

The earliest known photograph of Clarice (shown on page 22), taken in 1917, shows her with some of her fellow workers near Wilkinson's. At eighteen she was a pretty young woman, with rosy cheeks and thick hair that she later grew very long. All her paintresses recall that few photographs ever truly did her justice. Clarice's frock is in a very bold pattern so was probably made for her by Dolly Cliff. Her fellow workers are both fashionably dressed so this may have been a social event, but she generally chose to stay at home. At weekends when her sisters went out socializing, she preferred earning a little extra money, baby-sitting. Clarice and a friend, Alice Frith, often spent an evening minding the children of the Nixon family, who lived in Ricardo Street, Middleport, barely a hundred yards from Wilkinson's. On several occasions Clarice got thoroughly soaked giving the youngest, Elsie, a bath. Their paths were to cross again years later.

Gradually, Clarice became quite well known at the Wilkinson factory as unlike most of the workers she was always exploring the factory lingering in different departments to learn from what she saw. She made friends of many of the other workers, particularly Lucy Travis who she travelled to work with on the tram, and Minnie Rowley who worked alongside Clarice in the lithography department. In 1919 Reg Lamb joined Wilkinson's, and working on the 'clay end' of the factory he was able to purloin special modelling clays for Clarice to take home to practise modelling in the evenings and at weekends.

The works manager Jack Walker was the first person to note Clarice's enthusiasm for all the practical aspects of pottery manufacturing. The decorating shop was one long room holding both the lithographers and the hand-paintresses. Minnie Rowley recalled that one day a paintress doing the outlining let Clarice decorate some pieces. Jack saw her doing this and was so impressed that he showed the pieces to Colley Shorter. Clarice's potential was formally recognized in September 1922 when she was given a further apprenticeship as a modeller working with John Butler. The employer's signature on her indenture was not that of Guy, but Colley Shorter. Starting a further apprenticeship aged twenty-three was rather unusual but Clarice was clearly valued by the company as her wage was two guineas a week, seven years before the *Bizarre* 'girls' were paid six shillings a week; Colley was not usually known to be so generous. He had a reputation for being a tough business man but as the factory staff noticed he started to mellow when Clarice was around.

Clarice was now put in charge of 'keeping the pattern and shape books up to date' and worked with John Butler producing *Tibetan* and *Oriflamme* ware, which were used to gain recognition for the company at prestigious shows where the main products were printed tableware. Butler was a skilled artist so nurtured Clarice's hand-painting skills and as early as 1924 asked her to work on a special exhibition piece of *Tibetan*. She spent many days intricately

LEFT: *John Butler's* Tibetan *on a shape 342 vase and* Storm *on a shape 120*

BELOW: *John Butler, the Art Director at Wilkinson's*

outlining a massive ginger jar with gold. Impressed with her work he allowed her to add her own signature in gold to the base, so it was the first time her name appeared on production ware. The ginger jar was then exhibited widely at tradeshows at home and abroad, and is visible in the photograph of the Wilkinson's stand at Philadelphia in 1926. It was one of the few pieces of her work that Clarice was later to feel nostalgic about.

Clarice was now able to work as both a paintress and modeller. Butler involved her in decorating a quality tableware range with a hand-painted pattern of fruit. Simultaneously Clarice modelled vases, bowls and jugs to extend the range of shapes for Butler's designs. Between 1922 and 1927 shape numbers 186 to 341 appeared, and these were mostly traditional shapes as Butler's taste predominated. Clarice also worked with Fred Ridgway, an elderly designer who had been an important artist at Birks Rawlins creating much of the *pâte-sur-pâte* ware that Queen Mary collected. After an illness he had joined Wilkinson's on a freelance basis producing Japanese-influenced designs of dragons or fish on lustre pottery. Clarice added the gold highlights on these and the record of Ridgway's ware in the Wilkinson pattern books is in Clarice's distinctive, fluid handwriting.

BELOW: *The base of the* Tibetan *ginger jar Clarice Cliff decorated and signed in 1924*

Clarice started to show her individuality at Wilkinson's as early as 1924 when she modelled some distinctive handmade figurines. She sculpted them in solid clay, and hand-painted them on-glaze in bright colours. Some of these were then made into production pieces. A bookend of a cottage against an L-shaped support was modelled with intricate detail. Fred Ridgway had produced a series of vases and plates called *Cries of London* and Clarice modelled two figurines, an orange-seller and a pin-seller. She was allowed to add her embossed signature on the side of these. A more characterful figurine of a 'cockney' man, with exaggerated features, wearing a waistcoat and flat cap, was one of the first pieces to have the hallmarks of her later modelling style.

Clarice was still living in Tunstall, but the house had become rather crowded because when Nellie Cliff's husband died after the First World War, she had moved back with her daughter Nancy. Clarice often babysat the three-year-old and later became very close to her. Even after a long day at work Clarice still did modelling at home, and worked on a bust of her sister Ethel which was stored in the basement covered with a damp cloth. However, her work at the factory meant that she had no time to complete this piece and it was found, disintegrating, many years later.

BELOW: A Rustic cottage *bookend, a* Tut Tut *head, a* Cockney man *figurine and* Mrs Puddleduck

Colley Shorter was so impressed with Clarice's modelling that he asked her to sculpt several special pieces, including a bust of Arthur Shorter who had died by this time. Fellow workers recalled her spending long hours modelling several close friends of the Shorter family which Colley commissioned as presents for special occasions. These pieces may explain why Clarice's aspirations to be a sculptress grew. A recently discovered figurine from 1925, in Doulton 'crinoline lady' style, inscribed with Clarice's full signature on the base, indicates that by the middle of the twenties she was extremely proficient at modelling in a traditional style.

Some of Clarice's earliest modelling work on art pottery, as it was called then, was in 1925. *Davenport*

ABOVE: Davenport ware which Clarice modelled in 1924 and 1925

ware featured fruit and birds modelled in bands around the pieces which were then enamelled or gilded. At the same time she modelled jampots with fruit handles, such as the shape 230, the *Apple* and the *Orange*. As Clarice developed her modelling skills her pieces were influenced by the Arabian themes John Butler designed for Wilkinson's earthenware. Clarice's figures

LEFT: A Seated Arab figurine, a Girl flower block, the early version of the Arab boy candlestick and a Kookaburra flower block made for the Australian market

ABOVE: Clarice's Laughing Cat *figure and a 1932* Cat *bowl*

impressed Butler, and some were produced commercially as hollow cast figures. The *Seated Arab* was sold mounted on a wooden base as bookends, and the *Arab boy* candlestick also appeared. The factory already had a large range of flower blocks, featuring realistically modelled birds, to display flowers in bowls. Clarice created one modelled as a young, naked woman sitting on a rock. A similar female figure was modelled as a candlestick, kneeling and holding a bouquet that is the sconce.

The first manifestation of the sense of humour which became a hallmark of Clarice's work in the thirties was an amusing, stylized standing duckling, vibrantly hand-painted on-glaze in yellow, with a curly orange worm at his feet! Clarice called him *Mr Puddleduck*, perhaps reminiscing about the Jemima Puddleduck character in the Beatrix Potter stories, which were published when she was a child. *Mr Puddleduck* soon appeared as a male duck wearing a top hat, a female duck in a night-cap, and an amorous pair, smooching, which she called *Friday Night Ducks*! Clarice also designed a simple cruet set with shapes based on peg dolls, a concept she later evolved for the Joan Shorter ware.

One piece which was not Clarice's work was the *Laughing Cat*, based on an original designed by Louis Wain. The early examples are aerographed in black with just a little hand-painted enamel colour for the detail, but the Clarice Cliff versions are humorously decorated in spots or hand-painted all over in orange! Aerographing involved spraying a thin layer of colour on ware, often next to a printed pattern band. It was the most economical way of applying colour but the dull finish had an industrial look. Nevertheless, it was the standard technique used on many fancies during the twenties. The *Drum* shape jampot, the *Sabot* and milk jug demonstrate how these pieces looked before Clarice added her *Bizarre* magic to them a few years later.

The pieces Clarice modelled in 1924 and 1925 were created at a time when she regarded her work as a stepping-stone to being a sculptor. However, the *Exposition des Arts Decoratifs et Industriels* held in Paris in 1925 was to change her plans. The abbreviated title of the exhibition was eventually given to the style of ware it showcased, *Art Deco,* though at the time, the French called it *L'Art Moderne*. It seems likely that Clarice and Colley visited the exhibition together, secretly. Colley saw it as an opportunity to expose Clarice to new artistic influences, as in the depressed market Newport Pottery urgently needed new products to increase sales. Certainly, within a few years her work showed influences of shapes displayed at the exhibition. Some of Clarice's *Bizarre* abstract patterns suggest she must also have been impressed with the work of Robert and Sonia Delaunay. However, the greatest significance of the trip was that it may have been the start of their *Bizarre* affair.

Clarice kept the Paris trip confidential until an interview with a newspaper journalist in the thirties when she related that she had only been abroad once, to Paris. The trip may also explain why Clarice created some very modern shapes long before the ones she made in the 1928 series 366 to 370, which are now classified as Art Deco. The triangular, flat-sided vase 200 dates from around 1926 and yet it is clearly the predecessor of the same shape as a shallow bowl which Clarice issued as shape 499 in 1931.

BELOW: A shape 200 vase in the later Appliqué Blossom design

One can only fully appreciate how different Clarice's new role was when one remembers that she was still living at home in Edwards Street. Clarice's mother spent most of her time at home or shopping in the local streets. She only needed to walk a few yards to the grocer, Billy Evans, and a Mr Davis called once a week with vegetables on his horse-drawn cart. Ann Cliff always gave the horse a drink of water in a bucket, so it did not want to stop anywhere else, and all the neighbours were amused when the animal scraped the pavement with his hoof until he got the water! Also nearby was Mrs Eardley who sold sweets, chocolates, biscuits, cigarettes and, at Christmas, even cigars! Clarice's niece Nancy soon became the family errand-runner and in the hot summer months was sent out to see Mr Nixon who always stopped his bicycle-propelled, mobile ice-cream cart outside their back gate. Nancy recalled that, 'It was a fatal attraction, we were always customers, for an ice-cream or "hokey-pokey" as we called water ices then, Clarice included!'

As the fascination with her work and responsibilities grew Clarice spent less and less time at home. She realized she had the potential to live a life very different to the one that awaited her if she ever 'settled down' in Tunstall. She also still harboured a strong desire to be a sculptor. However, the effects of the Miners' Strike and the Jarrow March of 1926 made it a financially difficult time for all potbanks in Stoke and restricted her from fulfilling her ambition. Fortunately, Colley, as the factory's main salesman, had always encouraged her to develop new sales opportunities whilst being economical, and it was this that prompted her to suggest a simple idea to him early in 1927. The Newport Pottery warehouse held a large stock of ware inherited from Deans which was virtually unsaleable because it was poorly glazed and had surface defects. Clarice recalled that, 'this huge stock had always interested me and presented a challenge!' She met that challenge when she suggested that it could be made saleable if it were decorated all over in bright enamel colours painted on-glaze. Colley thought this was a brilliant idea and gave her a small studio at Newport to do some samples.

Clarice at last had the chance she had waited for to use bright colours! However, her love of colour had already manifested itself in her bedroom. Nancy vividly recalled that, 'When Clarice decorated the bedroom in bright colours, I was the muggins who had to paste all the paper. It was gold paper and Clarice was up the steps sticking it on the ceiling in squares – everyone else just had white-washed ceilings! We painted the bedroom walls cream, and the window frames, doors, and furniture, black and orange, and we had a good time doing it!' Clarice's neighbours in Tunstall already thought she was a little unusual, and Ann Cliff did not know what to make of her daughter's taste in home decoration, but for Clarice it was just a small start. The orange and black were to be used to even greater effect in the next few months, but on pottery!

In March 1927 Colley moved a hand-paintress from Wilkinson's across to Newport to work under Clarice on the experimental ware. Gladys Scarlett was just sixteen and had joined the previous year, after some training at art school. In the small studio, Clarice first experimented with covering the old shapes all over in banding in bright colours which was simple to apply on a potter's wheel. She then outlined simple patterns of triangles on the old shapes and Gladys filled these in with orange, green, yellow, blue and purple enamels. Clarice encouraged Gladys to exaggerate the brushstrokes to make it obvious the pieces were hand-painted. Colley Shorter visited the studio every morning, and as he entered would say, 'Top of the morning girls!' Gladys was a slim, blue-eyed blonde, and made her own clothes, often in vivid pink. She enjoyed painting but was never happier than when she went to the dances at the local art colleges where she was renowned for wearing the most dazzling outfits! 'Occasionally Colley would take in bunches of flowers, one for Clarice and one for Gladys. But when he called Gladys his 'little girl in pink' one day, Clarice clearly disapproved. However, soon Gladys

ABOVE: Clarice's banded designs on an Isis *vase and shape 278 vase which were also marketed as the* Liberty *pattern*

was left to work on the ware alone – from March 1927 Colley arranged for Clarice to study at the prestigious Royal College of Art in Kensington, on two one-month courses. By this time there was some rivalry between Gladys and Clarice, and Gladys recalled many years later that when Mr Colley suggested she might also go to Kensington, Clarice objected.

When she arrived at the Royal College of Art on 14 March 1927, Clarice realized she was rather older than most of the other students. She did not look twenty-eight, but conscious about her age she gave her date of birth as 1900. She studied 'modelling the head and figure from live models, figure composition, and life drawing' under Gilbert Ledward, a gifted sculptor.

Touring the shops and galleries in her free time, Clarice came across much of the avant-garde art that was later to so influence her work. The biggest impact on her was not what she learned at the college, but the realization that British pottery lacked *colour*. Her ceramics were to incorporate elements of colours and forms from Picasso, Mondrian, Modigliani and the Delaunays. Although few were actually direct copies, her awareness of their work was clearly an inspiration for a woman from Stoke-on-Trent where art meant something totally different. Clarice was also almost certainly impressed with

BELOW: Clarice's first paintress Gladys Scarlett is the 'belle of the ball' in an outfit she made herself

some ceramics by Austrian designer Margarete Heymann-Loëbenstein displayed at Heals Store in Tottenham Court Road. Another designer influenced by these was Shelley's Eric Slater, as we will show in *Taking Tea and Coffee*. Slater was later to become art director at Shelley Potteries in Stoke.

Clarice returned to Stoke in late May, and her tutor Gilbert Ledward reported on her studies in a letter to Colley Shorter: 'There is little doubt she has native ability, I consider that the figure she has just

modelled shows a surprising advance on her work of two months ago, and if financial circumstances had not to be taken into account, but only the development of her talent considered, I should say, go on studying for two or three years.' It has recently become known that Clarice *did* study further. She later recounted how she went to the Central School of Arts and Crafts in Bloomsbury 'because it was considered the most advanced'. The fact that Clarice attended this avant-garde institution does help explain her inspired rejection of the artistic heritage of the schools of art in the Potteries.

By 1927 Clarice's observations on the lack of colour on ceramics being offered to the public had crystallized her ideas and even before *Bizarre* was launched she put her new ideas into practice. She modelled a series of flower holders: *Gaiety* and *Elegant* were based on large handled wicker baskets, and the third was a *Viking boat*. Each of these held a flower block to support the blooms. However, when they were launched in August 1927 the *Pottery*

BELOW: Original Bizarre on candlesticks and a plate

Gazette and Glass Trade Review noted, 'One of the newest decorations for this type of novelty – and novelties such pieces undoubtedly are since there was nothing like them in the trade until they were modelled by this house (Wilkinson's) – is executed in black and yellow.' The article illustrated the pieces, which were covered in just wide bands of alternating colour. Significantly, although Clarice was still having to create traditional shapes she chose to decorate them in just two bright colours. The *Gaiety* and *Elegant* flower baskets probably represented Colley Shorter's idea of commercial shapes but Clarice's idea of how they should be coloured. She was not specifically mentioned, but the article shows that even before her name appeared on ware, her ideas for bright colour had been realized and were catching people's attention.

ABOVE: An Elegant flower basket and Viking *boat from September 1927*

A young woman joined Newport Pottery in 1927 who was to play a significant supporting role to Clarice and become a life-long friend. Hilda Lovatt was just fifteen when she joined to work in the warehouse but her first duty of the day was to clean the offices and so she saw Clarice every morning, before reporting to Len Hulse the warehouse man.

August 1927 was a significant month in Clarice's career. Already endowed with a remarkable awareness of art, she was now to discover the key to a novel concept for marketing and naming her new ideas. Her inspiration was not the work of a living modern artist, but the genius of one born in the seventeenth century. A collection of rare prints was donated to the British Museum in August 1927 by Campbell Dodgson, a wealthy entrepreneur. These were the work of a little known Italian artist called Giovanni Batista Bracelli. The set of prints were from original ink drawings done by Bracelli between 1624 and 1649. These featured incredible figures made from everyday objects to resemble human or animal forms. Looking through the images

BELOW: One of the images by Giovanni Batista Bracelli from his Bizarrie *prints*

one is instantly reminded of the *Bizooka*, the pottery horse which Clarice first created as an ink drawing in 1928. We might have assumed it was just a coincidence that the *Bizooka* resembled the figures in Bracelli's drawings. One simple fact makes it abundantly clear, however, that it was no coincidence: Bracelli called the creatures in his prints, *Bizarrie*…

THE BIRTH OF BIZARRE

He was extremely tired. His area covered Land's End to Southend, and from Birmingham down to the south coast, and in the last five days he seemed to have travelled it all. Once, he had calculated how many thousands of miles he travelled by train each year. He had then consoled himself with the thought of the one and a quarter per cent commission Mr Colley and Mr Guy paid him. He of course realized that they paid this annually, in arrears, to keep him working for them. Even though he protested mildly about this, it was a double bluff, as in truth he enjoyed his work. His case was more than usually full, as many major stores had given him substantial orders for Christmas delivery. His treat for his hard work was that he could look forward to Saturday afternoon when Port Vale Football Club were playing at home!

As the train approached the Potteries the smoke from its funnel, previously grey, assumed more of a shade of white as it mingled with the millions of flecks of soot from the hundreds of bottle ovens that studded the area like a jet necklace. These coal-fired ovens were active all year apart from Christmas Day so, except on the warmest days, the sun failed to break through the mantle of smog. As he walked up the steps from the station he noted that today was no exception. Mr Colley's chauffeur, Herbert, was waiting in the Armstrong Siddeley, and greeted him jovially. It was a short ride to Burslem, but the car travelled at just twenty miles an hour as the road was congested with trams and horse-drawn vehicles. As they entered Newport Lane, Ewart Oakes could see a group of children playing in the gutter; many were shoeless. The strikes of the last few years meant that the security of a job such as his was rare in 1927. He knew he had Mr Colley to thank for this as when he returned from the war in 1919 within two years he had been appointed home trade representative for the south of England. Realizing they needed each other, the two men had a strong working relationship. Ewart would never have invited Mr Colley to watch Port Vale with him as knew he was far happier drinking with the owners of other factories at his club, The Leopard, in Burslem. Ewart was strictly teetotal…

BELOW: Ewart Oakes and his wife outside their family home in Wolstanton

His daydream was broken just as the car entered the factory gates. He nodded at the watchman, and the chauffeur parked in the reserved space under the works canteen. Ewart crossed the cobblestone yard and headed toward the canal where the office was located. He ascended the open wooden steps into the long, narrow offices, and greeted Miss Wordley and Miss Browe who looked after much of the work on the ledgers and order books. He was about to try to get a cup of tea from them, when Virginia Browe said, 'Oh, I just remembered. Mr Colley said that when you arrived you were to go and see him.' Ewart wanted to go home as soon as possible, but any request from Mr Colley was actually more of an order. 'Mr Colley is in Clarice's studio,' volunteered Agnes Wordley, although this information was hardly necessary as when he came across every afternoon from Wilkinson's Mr Colley was invariably with Clarice. His only other time at Newport was spent on a curt but thorough inspection of the order books. Mr Colley was a stickler for formality, so Ewart checked his jacket and tie in a rusting mirror hanging by one of the Victorian ledger desks, and then headed towards Clarice's studio.

Clarice had been a friend of Ewart's for quite a few years and they often chatted quietly together. Since she had become a modeller her friendship with Mr Colley had made her a great deal more confident. Knowing Mr Colley was in her studio he naturally knocked before entering. 'Good afternoon Mr Colley, Clarice.' Colley gave him a perfunctory greeting; Clarice smiled warmly and gestured Ewart to take a chair. Instantly, she was pouring him a cup of rather strong tea from an *Athens* teapot.

'Another good week, I trust, Ewart?' inquired Colley.

'Excellent, Mr Colley, I have many more Christmas orders this year than last year.'

Clarice quietly observed, 'It couldn't be as bad as 1926', and Colley nodded in agreement.

'Now', said Colley, never one to let polite conversation intrude upon business, 'We', he paused and beamed knowingly at Clarice, 'have something rather special to show you.' He leaned forward. 'You may have heard that Clarice has been producing some pieces rather hush hush? Well, we have them ready to be tried out on the stockists, but I must stress that even now I want to keep them away from prying eyes.'

Ewart was aware that Clarice had been doing trials for a new line, which were secretly taken to and from firing in the enamel kilns, but he had no idea what this new ware was. Mr Colley rose from his

BELOW: The Newport and Wilkinsons office staff in 1933. Virginia Browe is on the left in the back row, Eric Grindley is on the left in front, next to Stanley Critchlow

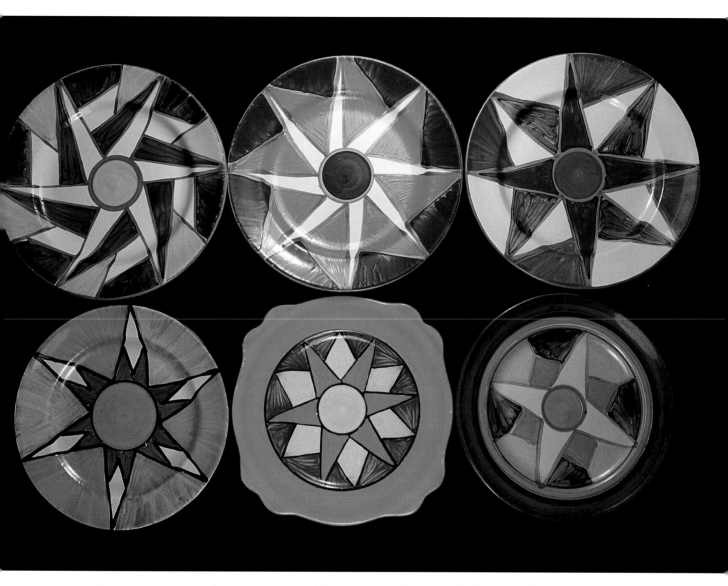

ABOVE: Variations on Original Bizarre from 1927

chair, and motioned Ewart to the other side of Clarice's studio. A curtain hung across the room which kept a jumble of modelling equipment out of sight. Clarice never wasted valuable creative time tidying up; the curtain was a far more efficient way of keeping things neat! Mr Colley un-hooked the curtain and let it fall to the floor.

Ewart was so surprised by what he saw that he started up from his chair and stood for a moment before walking across the room. A display of ware covered in brashly coloured triangles was arranged on a piece of cloth. His first thought was that it was colourful, in fact *very* colourful! Ewart ran his eyes along the rows of pieces, but over and over again they were caught by the forcefulness of the colour. Every bowl, candlestick, vase and jug was covered from top to bottom. He had *never* seen anything like it before!

'Well…?' said Mr Colley.

Ewart paused to phrase a response, as the colour had so taken his breath away. He had just realized that all the pieces were old Newport and Wilkinson shapes – but they looked so different! This was his response to Colley's question. 'But do you *like* the decoration?' Ewart picked up a large jug and inspected it. The enamel colours covered the entire surface and had been well fired. He knew how difficult it was to apply large areas of enamels as they tended to flake during firing if painted inconsistently. He saw Clarice looking at him from across the room and replied cautiously, 'It is *extremely* colourful!' He turned the jug upside down, and on the base, hand-painted in a rust colour it read *Bizarre, Newport Pottery*. 'Why is it marked *Bizarre*?' Ewart asked.

Clarice joined him and Colley at the display. 'I called it *Bizarre* because it is intended to surprise people. There is so much dowdy ware made in the Potteries that I decided to offer brightly coloured pieces for the young housewives who I'm sure want something different!'

Ewart said, 'It is certainly a clever idea to use up all this old stock!'

ABOVE: Original Bizarre on a 358 vase, a ten-inch plate, a 195 vase, and two miniature vases which were also used as tradesmen's samples

'Exactly', said Colley Shorter, 'and *you* are going to have the first chance to sell this ware. You can have my chauffeur and the Armstrong Siddeley for the whole of next week while you try it out on some stockists.'

A few minutes later, as Ewart descended the wooden steps from the office a man passed by with a board covered in a mass of the Japanese-style orange lustre ware Fred Ridgway had designed a few years earlier. It had not been selling well, but clearly there was still more being manufactured, so he knew he would have to continue encouraging retailers to take it. Well, if nothing else, Clarice's vividly coloured pieces would be an amusing diversion for his customers. Now, what would be the score at the Port Vale game on Saturday?

In 1973 Ewart Oakes recalled his response on seeing *Bizarre* for the first time in a letter he wrote to the authors of the L'Odeon book: 'To be candid, I didn't like it – it was so extreme. But after my first call in Oxford at William Barker & Co., who took a lot of goods from the car and gave me a nice order for delivery on 1 February 1929 I felt quite at ease.'

Ewart's memories were accurate except in one respect. It was actually in October 1927 that he first saw *Bizarre* ware, not 1928, and so the delivery in Oxford was for February 1928. We know these dates are correct because the advertising campaign for *Bizarre* began in February 1928, and the dates the first *Bizarre* paintresses joined Newport Pottery. Ewart Oakes sold all the *Bizarre* ware in his first week and the Newport office staff were most surprised when he returned with further orders. Clarice's simple idea was a resounding success! It was the birth of *Bizarre*, which could have remained just the trademark for a line of ware covered in triangles and banding, but it was to be used to represent a far wider range. In the following eighteen months the possibilities that hand-painted ware offered were to multiply.

The *Bizarre* revolution really started in October 1927 when a corner of the Newport showroom was cleared to make way for a small decorating shop devoted to making the ware. There was a ready supply of young paintresses in a shop run by Dolly Cliff at Wilkinson's and at Colley's suggestion Clarice took some of them, which apparently caused friction between the sisters. In just a few weeks the team consisted of Annie Beresford, Mary Brown, Cissy Rhodes, Vera Hollins, Nellie Harrison, Florrie Winkle, Clara Thomas, Phyllis Tharme and Nancy Liversage. They were all just fourteen or fifteen years old.

Initially Clarice herself taught them and they were all soon able to execute the simple outlines of the

BELOW: Variations on Original Bizarre from 1928

triangles and then exaggerate the brushstrokes as they filled in with enamel colour. Clarice emphasized that this was to make it obvious that the ware was hand-painted, a strong selling point as most ware at this time was aerographed. The final stage of the decorating process was to apply banding in two or three colours. The *Bizarre* name was then hand-painted on the back of the ware, generally in the rust colour, next to the underglaze *Newport Pottery* backstamp that was already there.

ABOVE: The first hand-painted Bizarre *mark used from September 1927 to early in 1928*

The paintresses were paid just six shillings a week while they learned to execute the *Bizarre* designs but this was increased to ten shillings as they became more proficient. However, they were still very young and to relieve the repetitive nature of the work when they were not being supervised they sang or played pranks on each other. Len Hulse, who looked after the Newport showroom, was not at all happy when he found spilt turps and powder colour on the showroom carpet!

A rudimentary production system was established, and Hilda Lovatt was responsible for selecting and taking the undecorated glost ware to the shop and then ensuring it was taken for firing. She was also still working in the warehouse and as the paintresses got busier she found herself trying to please two bosses. Clarice realized this was upsetting her so had a quiet word with Colley and he asked her to work just as Clarice's personal assistant. This was the first of many times Clarice protected her workers, and she gained a reputation of being a very fair person to work for.

By January 1928 the new *Bizarre* ware was attracting the attention of the trade press and a journalist from the *Pottery Gazette and Glass Trade Review* visited the factory. His article stated:

BELOW: An early Bizarre *advertising photograph taken by Clarice in the Newport Pottery studio in February 1929*

There has recently been established at Newport Pottery a special department which might also be likened to a studio. It consists for the time being of a single room in which is to be found a group of young ladies working under the personal superintendence of a mistress instructor, who, whilst herself creating new freehand styles of decoration, and applying these direct to pieces of ornamental pottery, simultaneously holds a watching brief over what is being done by her apprentices.

This type of coverage of one single factory's output was unusual as trade journals such as *Pottery Gazette and Glass Trade Review* normally just gave polite coverage to the new products displayed at trade shows. This article was the first to mention the *Bizarre* name in print and it is interesting that,with great foresight, the writer rather accurately predicted what was to happen in the future:

With the elimination of much of the bric-a-brac that was a heritage of the Victorian era the chances are that ornamental pottery with bold and courageous designs treated in vivacious colourings will more and more experience a vogue. It is possible that the Newport Pottery have but succeeded, as yet, in touching the fringe of the field to which the new movement may ultimately lead them.

Production of *Bizarre* grew so quickly that more space was needed and it was moved to a long room on the top floor of a three-storey building overlooking the canal. The factory carpenters hastily constructed rows of simple wooden benches which each held three or four decorators. On the opposite wall were stillages to hold the boards used to carry the ware to and from the kilns. The windows had a depressing vista of acres of waste and shards from Newport Pottery and the other potbanks that lined the canal, but the paintresses were to have little time to inspect the view. All the processes in a potbank have their own production areas, referred to as 'shops' by the workers, so the new decorating area instantly became known as the *Bizarre* shop. Amongst the older male workers, the pretty young paintresses became known as the *Bizarre* 'babes' and as they matured they became the *Bizarre* 'girls'.

With her paintresses now in their own area Clarice was able to retire to the privacy of her studio where she could design and model without interruption, or take the advertising photographs for *Bizarre*. She regularly visited the shop to inspect the ware and advise the 'girls'. Sometimes she painted new patterns onto shapes with enamels, but more often she did them in watercolour on paper and took the design to an outliner who would adapt it on to a selection of shapes. Hilda regularly reported to Clarice on progress in the shop but her only other regular visitor now was Colley Shorter. He generally came across most afternoons from Wilkinson's and they discussed business together over tea in her office.

Clarice was now free to create new shapes for the *Bizarre* range. Initially she developed these cautiously. An early example was the use of *Mr Puddleduck* for an egg cup set. She put the duck in the middle of a plate which held four or six egg cups. This was then decorated all over in bold *Bizarre* triangles. Colley Shorter realized there was a definite market for these novelty pieces, and he encouraged Clarice to develop more. One of her next jobs in April and May was modelling the shapes for the *From a Child to a Child* children's ware, which was launched in June 1928. The story of the ware is recounted in the previous chapter but its significance was that the modelling was her most stylish to date. The pieces were and are amusing, and Colley was pleased with them.

From 1928 onwards Clarice was free to pursue her own ideas, and her workers soon realized that if she wanted to do something her way, she would! Every afternoon when he came across for tea, Colley was astounded as Clarice produced more and more of her extrovert designs and shapes. He realized they had a unique product which had to be sold with the same zest with which it was created, and he decided to tackle this in several ways.

Colley had acted as a salesman for the family's factories for over twenty years and was well aware of the creative limitations of most British earthenware and china producers. Few used any form of image advertising in anything other than trade journals. What now seems an obvious device – advertising directly to the public – was almost

ABOVE: At the Waring & Gillow exhibition, Nellie Harrison and Florrie Winkle are on the left, Gladys Scarlet and Clarice Cliff are seated on the right

unheard of then. However, Colley's travels to North America had introduced him to new techniques for promoting and marketing ware. He also began to arrange in-store painting demonstrations using the young paintresses to show how *Bizarre* was produced. He was not the first person in Britain to use this method, but he was the first to do it effectively and regularly. He 'had an eye for the ladies' as his colleagues observed, and it was no coincidence that he ensured that only the prettiest *Bizarre* 'girls' were sent on the demonstrations!

Clarice and Colley planned their strategy, and the first painting demonstration was in August 1928 at Waring & Gillow in London. This prestigious store was only too pleased to provide space in the foyer. The *Bizarre* 'girls' were understandably excited as they travelled down on a Yellow Way coach as none of them had been to London before. For a whole week Gladys Scarlett outlined, Nellie Harrison enamelled and Florrie Winkle banded. The press were invited to the event which naturally aroused great interest: three pretty young women hand-painting in a shop was very much a novelty. Clarice joined them briefly when the journalists and photographers arrived but after-

BELOW: Clara Thomas using a wheel to demonstrate banding at a London store in 1929

wards left with Colley to visit other *Bizarre* stockists. She was still rather shy and Colley used these opportunities to build her confidence. When Gladys, Florrie and Nellie returned to Burslem they told the other 'girls' of their adventures, going to the cinema or big stores. They also enjoyed relating how Clarice and Colley went off together each day and this became the subject of some whispered speculation. The prospect of visiting big cities to work meant that all the 'girls' were delighted when they were selected to go on these demonstrations.

Along with many other Staffordshire factories Newport Pottery exhibited new products at the

ABOVE: Original Bizarre *on a* Tankard *shape coffee-set*

British Industries Fair every February, but they were just one of many factories present. Clarice and Colley decided to stage trade shows exclusively for the products of Newport, Wilkinson's and Shorter & Sons. Ironically, as they planned these innovative marketing methods, some of their competitors who were not doing as well, advertised that they had to *cancel* their stands at tradeshows! In contrast, interest in *Bizarre* was so strong that within a year of its launch it was being exported to North America, Australia, South Africa, Brazil, Cuba and Holland. We know that Clarice's early pieces had reached Australia by 1928 as a *Tankard* shape coffee set decorated in an early *Bizarre* pattern still has the 'Thomas Webb & Sons Melbourne' retailer's label underneath.

Another significant event in 1928 was when Clarice decided to add a floral pattern to her *Bizarre* range. She experimented with painting free-hand flowers on ware. One design was of lupins, but it required too many brushstrokes and looked clumsy. However, she had been taught by John Butler how to create very natural looking crocus flowers by doing three or four downward strokes which came together at the base. Butler used this motif briefly for expensive art pottery with white and blue crocus flowers on lustre ware, but it had not proved successful. Clarice, had a strong sense of colour balance, and painted simple clusters of crocus flowers in her favourite vibrant orange and blue, with a few small purple ones. What gave the design its lasting appeal though was the simple banding; yellow above, which Clarice said represented the sun, and brown below for the earth. She showed Colley the samples and he was enthusiastic.

To see if it was possible to paint *Crocus* at the speed needed for commercial production Colley took a young Wilkinson's paintress, Ethel Barrow, across to Newport Pottery where Clarice showed her a cup in the design and asked her to copy it. The natural brushstrokes needed to produce the *Crocus* flowers were easy for Ethel, and the fine leaves were individual strokes in the opposite direction so she swiftly completed the piece. Clarice then got Ethel to produce a sample range on a variety of shapes for test marketing. Clarice wanted to promote this new line as *Crocus by Clarice Cliff*, but Colley knew that the *Bizarre* name was already gaining a reputation, and was memorable, so he insisted they use it as the umbrella title for all her designs. Therefore, it was launched as *Crocus Hand Painted Bizarre by Clarice Cliff*, and all her subsequent ranges were billed in this style.

Ethel became the *Crocus* 'girl', painting the flowers, and Nellie Webb or Winnie Pound did the leaves, and Clara Thomas the banding. On the early pieces Winnie hand-painted the design name in green on the ware, but soon a custom *Crocus* backstamp was made. As more and more orders poured in Ethel trained teams of *Crocus* 'girls', consisting of two or three doing the petals,

ABOVE: Crocus *paintress Ethel Barrow aged twenty-one*

LEFT: An early colour advertising photograph by Clarice for her Crocus *and* Gayday *designs*

ABOVE: The Arabesque *design on a* Tankard *coffee-set. It was inadvertently sold with a milk jug in* Picasso Flower

a 'leafer', and a bander. The teams totalled twenty girls in all who were grouped together in a dedicated *Crocus* shop on the floor beneath the *Bizarre* shop. The original *Crocus* colourway was the most successful and, combined with later variations such as *Sungleam* and *Spring Crocus,* thousands of pieces were sold each year through until 1964, making it Clarice's signature design.

The factory was now so busy that a further twelve girls were recruited by the end of 1928. With so many new paintresses Clarice could no longer personally train them so she employed Lily Slater, who was a skilled paintress herself, as the 'missus' to train and supervise them.

As Clarice took on more and more responsibility she gradually started to assert herself and distanced herself from most of the workers with the exception of her 'girls'. Office boy Stanley Critchlow recalled that not all the staff liked the *Bizarre* designs, and one day when some of the typists were inspecting and criticizing a sample, Clarice overheard them and said sharply, 'Since it sells, it doesn't really matter what *you* think!' On another occasion when a warehouse-woman asked her, 'What should I do with this, Clarice?' she replied sternly, 'Don't you think it's time you started to call me Miss Cliff?' From that day on almost everyone at the factory, including her *Bizarre* 'girls' referred to her as 'Miss Cliff'.

Stanley also recalled how protective Clarice was towards the younger staff, including himself. He was rather small and still wore short trousers and

Clarice took to measuring him to reassure him that he was still growing. He also recalled some of her zany promotional ideas. For one trade show she created a whole football game of *Mr Puddleduck* figures. She decorated the teams in two different 'strips' and glued them to a board painted as a football pitch. Stanley remembered this distinctly because it was left at the factory and he had to take the cumbersome board to a London tradeshow on the train!

Several Isnic-inspired designs appeared late in 1928 and 1929. The original version of *Persian* was hand-painted. The intricate pattern was quite striking but proved too time consuming to produce cost-effectively. As a result, Clarice later simplified it for her *Inspiration* ware. The *Arabesque* design was similar but simpler and probably only issued for a few months. The Persian-inspired scrolls in coral were startlingly different to the simple *Bizarre* triangles.

Clarice's first major modern shapes appeared in 1928 and were to sell throughout the *Bizarre* years. As a paintress herself she knew that vases with surface ornament or handles were difficult to band, so she designed some simple vases in six- and eight-inch sizes that were perfect to take design panels with banding above and below. The 342 was the earliest, and she then evolved a vase with a globular body and ribbing at the top, shape 358. Another simple vase was the 360 which had angular horizontal faceting. She then realized that by inverting these shapes she could make other vases! The 358 inspired the 362 which had the ribs at the bottom, and the 360 became

ABOVE: Diamonds *on a 358 vase,* Kandina *on an* Athens *shape jug, and a 342 vase in* Football

the 365! She then produced a spherical vase, shape 370, which was to prove popular for over five years. Decorated in *Double 'V'*, the example shown is a variation from the standard design having three stylized leaf shapes in blue, green and orange, rather than simpler shapes. The shape 365 vase is in *Sharks Teeth* which Clarice based closely on an abstract motif by Edouard Benedictus. Some of these new shapes were inspired by Robert Lallemant's ceramics which Clarice had seen in *Mobilier et Décoration*. The new vases were issued in a refined version of the standard Wilkinson glaze, which had one per cent iron oxide added to give the body a pale warm 'glow'. It was called honeyglaze and was to prove the perfect background for Clarice's designs.

BELOW: Sharks Teeth *on a 365 vase, a 370 Globe vase in* Double V *and a miniature vase in* Sunburst

Just a year after she introduced *Bizarre*, Clarice created a new range of designs for the September 1928 trade show which introduced a range name. *Fantasque* featured outlined patterns, originally numbered in a series starting from 100, but later the designs were named *Tree*, *Cherry*, *Broth*, *Lily Orange*, *Lily Brown*, *Pebbles* and *Kandina*. Every one of the new designs featured bold shapes and colours; some of the distinctive elements of Clarice's style were beginning to emerge. *Pebbles* featured oval shapes in bright colours on a zigzag ground. *Kandina* was a busy abstract which seems to have been named after, but not inspired by, Wassily Kandinsky. For *Broth* Clarice took simple massed circles from an earlier John Butler design which she placed between star-shaped forms.

ABOVE: *The first* Fantasque *range featuring* Tree, Lily, Cherry, Broth, Pebbles, Fruit *and* Kandina. *The 365 vase is an example of the original* Caprice

Clarice had originally wanted to call this new range *Fantasy*, and a few pieces are known with this as a hand-painted mark. Staff recall that Clarice and Colley named the designs together during their meetings in her studio, so when *Fantasy* evolved into the invented word *Fantasque*, it was probably partly Colley's influence. At the same time he decided to issue *Fantasque* as a Wilkinson product to split the tax on sales. Therefore, when these pieces were produced each bore an elaborate backstamp, initially stamped in gilt, but replaced shortly afterwards with a stamped black mark; *Hand Painted Fantasque by Clarice Cliff Wilkinson Ltd England.*

Colley decided to launch *Fantasque* alongside *Bizarre* in the *Pottery Gazette* – the 'bible' of the industry. He asked Clarice to devise some inventive copy for a full page advertisement, and being a skilled cartoonist, she executed a pen and ink drawing. The idea was inspired by the Bracelli drawings of creatures made of everyday objects, though Bracelli had not done a horse composed entirely of pottery! When Clarice showed Colley the finished drawing he was impressed with everything about it except her name, *Miss Bizarre*. When the advertisement went into print in October 1928, the horse had become the *Bizooka*.

RIGHT: Pebbles *on a shape 360 vase*

BELOW: *The gilt* Fantasque *backstamp crediting Newport Pottery was only used briefly in 1928*

From the earliest days of *Bizarre*, a shape that was to become indelibly associated with Clarice Cliff was

LEFT: Fantasque Butterfly *on a double-handled* Lotus *jug*

BELOW: *The* Archaic *backstamp from 1929*

the *Lotus* jug. This had been designed by John Butler in 1919 and issued by Wilkinson's as part of a jug and bowl set. As it had a handle it attracted less tax because it was classed as functional, and it proved popular as a flower holder. Confusingly for collectors, variations on the original single-handled twelve-inch version were introduced late in 1929. These comprised six-, eight-, ten- and twelve-inch sizes with one or two handles, or no handle, and the shape was renamed *Isis*! As the original version with a handle had *Lotus* impressed underneath, collectors now call handled shapes *Lotus jugs*, and non-handled shapes, *Isis vases*.

Some of the early variations on *Bizarre* were heavily influenced by Colley Shorter. Together they evolved *Archaic* ware early in 1929 which was based on decorations of Egyptian temple columns illustrated in *The Grammar of Ornament* by Owen Jones. Clarice copied the columns as a series of vases, shapes 373 to 377. Each had an elaborate backstamp detailing the location and date of the column. Having a very regular design they had to be produced with a printed outline filled in with bright enamels. Colley's advertising slogan for the ware was, 'Nothing new under the sun'. However, ware

BELOW: *An* Archaic *series 375 vase*

reproducing ancient designs during the *Jazz Age* was not the correct way to evolve *Bizarre*, as the poor sales proved. This probably prompted Colley to let Clarice pursue her more modern ideas.

Clarice constantly returned to her first love of modelling, and next sculpted some fancies that were to capture the imagination of her customers and their children – her *Teddy Bear* and *Golly* bookends. An early example of the Parisian influence on her work can be seen in the stylish and practical *L'Oiseau* bookends. These featured a stylized bird on an angular base, and it could be painted in many different ways. These pieces were marketed alongside the Joan Shorter children's ware and other nursery items such as Clarice's *United Services* cruet set, which consisted of a guardsman pepper, a sailor salt and an airman mustard.

The variety of shapes and designs that appeared in the first two years of *Bizarre* show that Clarice Cliff clearly absorbed a great deal more in London than previously believed. Unlike her contemporaries in the Staffordshire

BELOW: A pair of shape 409 L'Oiseau bookends, a Golly pencil holder and United Services cruet set

Potteries she was able to incorporate many of the principles of colour and line of modern art into her work. However, she tempered this with a mix of traditional production methods and classical design skills she had absorbed from all the staff at Wilkinson's.

Clarice's artistic capriciousness was perhaps best manifested in her *Delecia* ware, launched late in 1929. The vision of sixties art, when a painter literally threw pots of vividly coloured paint over a canvas, is a stereotype today, yet Clarice Cliff did exactly this in 1929! *Delecia* was produced by mixing bright enamel colours with turps, and then these were consecutively allowed to run down the ware. This process was a great deal more controlled than the results suggest, as the paintress had to make the runnings stop anywhere except at the bottom! Thoughtfully moving her paintresses to a room away from the now tidy *Bizarre* shop she encouraged them to create the colour effects. The process of doing this meant they virtually became *Delecia* 'girls', often covered in enamel colours! To launch *Delecia* Clarice used many of her new shapes and, innovatively, colour advertising. *Delecia* was not just a whimsical, avant-garde line – from 1931 she developed the idea of putting *Delecia* runnings alongside floral and fruit designs, and these were to sell well. From

the artistic experiment came a commercially marketable result.

As the many decorators produced the same designs there is often a vast difference between pieces painted just weeks apart. The two *Umbrellas and Rain* shape 342 vases pictured below are both from 1929 and yet the panel of 'umbrellas' between the 'raindrop' panels, and the top and bottom banding, are coloured completely differently. This is another factor which makes Clarice's ware so appealing as in this respect the pottery resembles the product of a studio rather than a factory.

Bizarre ware was soon being sent throughout the British Empire. None of Colley's competitors had either the contacts or products to exploit as many markets as he did. In 1929 colour adverts for *Bizarre* and *Fantasque* appeared in Australian trade journals. *Bizarre* was sold by Hill & Everitt of Cape Town as

ABOVE: A vast range of Delecia *on a display stand Clarice designed and registered*

early as 1929, whereas in comparison Clarice's only real competitor, Susie Cooper, did not appoint her South African agent, Dancer & Sons, until 1939. Susie Cooper had produced hand-painted ware in *Bizarre* style for Grays in 1928 and early 1929, but did not then regularly produce ware until 1931 when she established a small decorating shop at Woods. However, when she

RIGHT: Umbrellas and Rain *on two rather differently painted shape 342 vases*

LEFT: A 1929 advertisement from an Australian trade journal

added her signature to the backstamp it prompted Colley to state in his trade adverts 'Your customers want the best, so look for the original signature *Bizarre by Clarice Cliff*.' At a time when the Depression was affecting sales greatly, it was Clarice Cliff's ware that pioneered the overseas markets for the new style ware. As the export market grew during the following decade the staff at Newport increased to 280, although Wilkinson's was still the major factory with around 430 workers.

It is the most idiosyncratic pieces that are perhaps the most appealing now. Among the old Newport Pottery shapes Clarice inherited was a cheese dish and one of the most fantastic of these is an example which seems to have been produced in two patterns. The lid is in *Umbrellas and Rain* whilst the base is in *Sunrise*! This is apparently exactly how it was made originally and this exotic combination of *Fantasque* designs on a traditional shape is what makes this period of Clarice's work so unique, but also confusing, for collectors.

Having asserted herself artistically Clarice now showed her independence by learning to drive. Colley's chauffeur Herbert Webb taught Clarice in 1928, and as there was no test she was quickly confident enough to buy herself a car. Together they went to Holland & Hollinshead in Alsager where Clarice chose an Austin Seven. It cost £60, a fortune

BELOW: Umbrellas and Rain and Sunrise on a traditionally shaped cheese dish

compared to the six or seven shillings a week her 'girls' were earning. Clarice's niece Nancy recalled how her aunt immediately named the Austin 'Jinny'. Nearly every weekend Nancy found herself being treated to a trip into the Staffordshire countryside. 'We used to cover a radius of about thirty miles around the Potteries. There was little traffic so as we went past people would say, "Oh, there's a woman driving that car!" We travelled miles in it.' Not surprisingly, when the Newport Pottery staff saw Clarice arriving in 'Jinny' and parking in a reserved spot in front of the works canteen, yet more tongues started to wag!

'Jinny' enabled Clarice to move from the family home to a flat above a hair and beauty salon at 20 Snow Hill, in the middle of a Victorian terrace, opposite St Mark's Church. It consisted of a lounge, bedroom, bathroom and small kitchen with a dining area. Clarice's assistant, Hilda Lovatt, was a firm friend by this time and remembers helping her find some shiny yellow and black paper from a storeroom at Newport which she used to decorate the bathroom ceiling. Clarice painted the walls black, and used one of her own bathroom sets banded in yellow and black to match. Later, office boy Eric Grindley did some odd jobs, and recalled the *Bizarre* decor: 'In the lounge the chimney-breast and adjoining wall were decorated with a striking hand-painted mural in orange, red, blue, black and green, which depicted what could only be described as a *Bizarre* forest scene with huge leaves, Lotus flowers and fruits. The other walls were covered in a bright red wallpaper with big scrolled motifs, the doors were vivid red with the panels picked out with black. The walls were adorned with "Picasso" type pictures, and vases and lamp bases were Clarice's own shapes, banded in orange and black!'

BELOW: A letter sent to Ewart Oakes by Colley Shorter in 1931

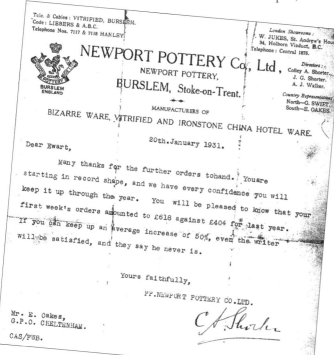

Colley Shorter was known to visit regularly, but apart from her family Clarice invited few of her workers to her new home. Her move to Snow Hill was around the same time in 1930 that she was promoted to art director of Newport Pottery. The birth of her *Bizarre* ware had in a few short years given her a career, her own home, a great deal of artistic independence and an enviable business which successfully rode out the Depression.

LATONA AND INSPIRATION

Muttering, he led them through a dark shop alley with wooden crates stacked high on either side. The walls were caked in soot, wet from the April rain which had soaked them just on the short walk from the Newport site. They came to an open wooden staircase and climbed it until they reached a platform that led to two doors. Mr Wildig went into the farther one, and beckoned Austin Walker and Jim Hall to enter.

A wooden bench ran along one wall and on it were laid rows of tiles in various colour glazes. 'These are the trial tiles here', said Mr Wildig, 'and I wanted to show you this one.' He held up a tile with a matt white glaze decorated with simple doodles in a copper blue. 'This tile glaze should be fired at 1050° but instead I fired it at about 760° and then added these copper oxide colours and, as you can see, they are absorbed into the ware, which is then fired again.'

Austin Walker inspected the tile and admired the waxy feel of the rich blue glaze, and he could see that the streaks of copper blue running through it were actually part of the glaze; the absorption of the colour by the soft glaze before the second firing had created a unique effect. 'I'm impressed', he said

LEFT: Inspiration *and* Latona *ware at a trade show in 1929*

ABOVE: Clarice's water-colour design for the early version of Caprice *in 1928*

turning to Jim, and passed him the tile. Jim had learned a lot about glazes from Austin and recognized the unique qualities Mr Wildig had captured. 'And how much of this glaze do you have available now?' asked Jim.

'I can let you have the four tins over there.' Mr Wildig pointed into the darkness where the large tins sat on the floor. 'Then, if you need some more I can make up the glaze in about a week.'

Austin Walker said, 'I'll speak to Mr Colley and I'm pretty certain we will then take the tins to do some trials. We are looking for some new glazes to use on some art pottery Clarice wants to do.'

Mr Wildig smiled at Austin and Jim, and as it was nearly break time invited them to the lodge for a cup of tea. He also wanted to find out more about what they were doing at Newport Pottery, as he was very surprised to see the kind of ware they were now producing and apparently selling in large quantities. Malkin's Tile Works were extremely slack and had laid off workers twice that year already. This was why he was so pleased to sell batches of the glaze, as it would at least ensure he was kept busy!

It was early in 1929 that Austin Walker, son of the works manager Jack Walker, and his assistant Jim Hall visited the Malkin's Tile Works factory, which adjoined Newport Pottery. A few months later the batch of tile glazes they bought was to lead to some entirely new ware in the *Bizarre* range, which Clarice imaginatively called *Latona* and *Inspiration*.

Clarice produced some trial pieces, decorating the 'soft-fired' glaze with oxides of copper. These were applied in a watery state, and this together with the firing gave a mottled blue-green background to the ware. On this Clarice devised designs that were outlined in brown, using other oxide colours in rich blues, mauves and purples for the detail. The broader brushwork needed to execute the designs on to the absorbent glaze meant some simpler, flowing images were needed and Clarice devised new floral patterns, and adapted the *Caprice* landscape which had previously been produced in on-glaze enamels. The surface glaze finish made the ware unique. Clarice and Colley liked the results very much and at one of their afternoon meetings in her studio decided to call it *Inspiration*. The name proved a well-chosen one as the qualities of the ware attracted a great deal of publicity when it was launched. Colley Shorter's press release at the time declared:

Inspiration has created tremendous interest unveiling the secret (which was lost for centuries) of reproducing in a superb matt glaze that gorgeous colour peculiar to

Ancient Egyptian Pottery, known as the Scarab Blue. This colour was inspired by the Scarab Beetle, the Egyptian sacred symbol of immortality.

Because the glazes were volatile, a separate *Inspiration* shop was set up and Clarice trained a team of girls. The copper sulphate details were painted by Ivy Stringer, Marjory Higginson and Edna Becket. The outlining was skilfully done by Ellen Browne whose handwritten mark distinguishes the early pieces: *Inspiration Bizarre by Clarice Cliff Newport Pottery Burslem England.*

ABOVE: The handwritten Inspiration *mark in Ellen Browne's writing*

The most popular design in the range was *Caprice*, which featured impossibly tall trees, in lilac, blue and brown, with a bridge. When Ellen Browne outlined *Caprice* she painted the bridge in various ways and in some examples it is very ornate. Just a few are known where there are overhanging branches and leaves, or a castle. This variation probably came about because it was technically much harder to decorate than using enamels on-glaze, and this diversity makes it true art pottery.

A series of Isnic-influenced patterns called *Inspiration Persian* were the most exotic designs in the *Inspiration* range. *Inspiration Persian* was extremely detailed, dominated by the lilac shade, and the designs were repeated radially around plaques. They seem to have been produced only in 1929 and part of 1930.

Inspiration ware soon appeared in a large range of designs, but because of the fluidity of the colours many of the floral ones look confusingly similar. These included *Inspiration Rose*, *Delphinium*, *Nasturtium* and *Lily*. The most unusual *Inspiration* design was *Knight Errant*, a scene of a knight on horseback in front of a castle battlement which had been designed by Clarice's former boss John Butler in 1926. Colley Shorter had asked him to embellish a landscape mural in the inglenook at Chetwynd House and *Knight Errant* was the result. The scene was then used on both *Inspiration* and *Latona* ware. The *Knight Errant* image was also used for an advertisement in *Pottery Gazette* in 1931, a puzzling choice of publication in which to advertise Clarice's ranges as it was neither *Bizarre* nor 'moderne'. The medieval caption, 'Holds Miladyes Favours Against all Comers', shows that Colley Shorter was still influential in how *Bizarre* was marketed.

The *Inspiration* range was certainly the most prestigious line produced for *Bizarre*, but it was expensive as it was difficult to fire. Many pieces were lost as the watery glazes caused the ware to stick to kiln furniture during firing.

ABOVE: Inspiration Persian *on a plaque and shape 265 vase*

RIGHT: Inspiration Caprice *on a plaque, two miniatures in the 188 series and a* Puff Box

The kiln firemen gradually perfected the technique, and later pieces can be distinguished as they have a printed *Bizarre* backstamp with *Inspiration* or *Persian* painted above. *Inspiration Garden* is a simple scene with just a stark tree against a blue sky and small flowers, and the colours are thinner as this was produced a little later, in 1930. Occasionally this design is found on stunning later shapes, such as the unique *Stamford* teaware.

ABOVE: Marigold *on a shape 186, a Globe 370 and a shape 204 vase*

LEFT: Inspiration Garden *on* Stamford *teaware*

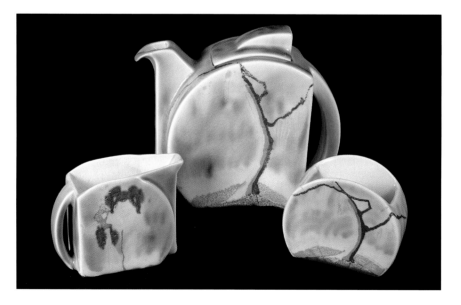

ABOVE: Inspiration Tresco *on an* Isis *vase,* Inspiration Persian *on a double handled* Lotus *jug and a* Yo Yo *vase 379 in* Inspiration Delphinium

The most colourful use of the *Inspiration* glaze was when Clarice combined the deep underglaze blues and purples with on-glaze colours. This resulted in two ranges. *Marigold* combined the *Inspiration* ground with vivid orange and yellow flowers that were skilfully etched where the ware had been left plain during the first firing. The *Marigold* technique was almost the same as that used for *Clouvre*, which had a darker, thicker ground, with an Indian-ink blue, and was produced in more stylized designs such as *Clouvre Tulip*, *Butterfly* and *Water Lily*.

As with all of Clarice's ranges there are rarities in *Inspiration* ware. A bold floral pattern with huge bulbous amber and yellow flowers is called *Inspiration Tresco*. A landscape known from a single example features a river scene with trees similar to those found on *Caprice*, but in the foreground is a deep blue river with an Arab dhow. This design has been given the name *Inspiration Bazique* in memory of the collector who first found it.

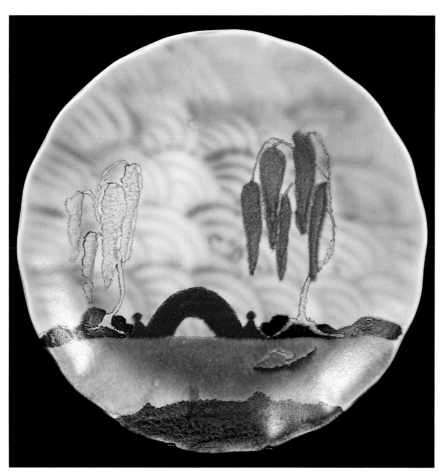

RIGHT: Inspiration Bazique, *a design known from this one example*

The last major range of *Inspiration* ware was pictured in the *Daily Sketch* in December 1931. The photograph was taken in the Newport Pottery show-room and shows that the range included a *Flying Swan* flower holder, shape 450 and 452 vases, and even Clarice's *Friday Night Ducks* executed in *Inspiration*! By the middle of 1932 though there were few orders for *Inspiration* and it was discontinued that year.

Interestingly, the *Inspiration* techniques were briefly used by John Butler who had remained as Wilkinson's art director when Clarice took on that role at Newport. As late as 1929 he was still producing dark lustre ware such as his *Storm* pattern, but he was able to utilize the techniques evolved by Clarice's team and produced some strong landscape images in a range called *Tahiti*.

BELOW: John Butler's Tahiti Regatta *on a charger*

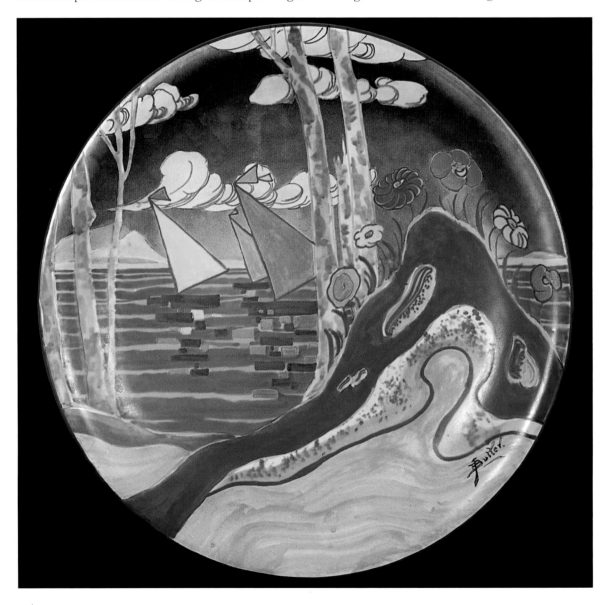

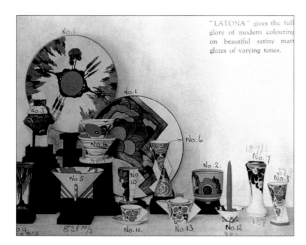

"LATONA" gives the full glory of modern colouring on beautiful satiny matt glazes of varying tones.

ABOVE: An advertising leaflet for Latona *ware from 1929*

BELOW: Latona Tree *on a* Mei Ping *vase 14 and a* Conical Early Morning *set*

These skilfully blended *Inspiration* with on-glaze enamels and the most successful patterns were *Foam*, a coastal scene with stylized flying birds, and *Regatta*, which featured a fantastic coastal scene with triangular-sailed yachts. Large pieces for tradeshows were painted by Butler himself but the designs were too detailed to produce *en masse*. These pieces are now highly prized by many Cliff collectors as they resemble her style and are by a man who influenced her early years.

John Butler worked on early *Appliqué* ware for Clarice in 1930, but with some of her shapes and patterns now being produced at Wilkinson's to satiate demand, Colley Shorter no long needed two art directors. Shortly after this John Butler became art director at the nearby Wood's factory. He was apparently much happier in his new role and ironically a few years later was again working with a young female designer, but this time it was Susie Cooper. Sadly, he was killed by a bus in a freak accident in 1935 when he made way for a lady to board. Susan was then made art director. Shortly after this his daughter, Joy, became her assistant, and even designed some patterns with her, having absorbed some of her father's skills.

Shortly after Clarice evolved *Inspiration*, another version of the tile glaze from Malkins was developed. A milky white glaze was created by mixing the factory's standard honeyglaze with tile glaze creating a semi-opaque surface that gave a chic look to the pottery. Taking her cue from the matt, milky coloured glaze, Clarice decided to call it *Latona*. The new glaze was perfected by June 1929 just after Clarice's *Conical* shape ware first appeared, so naturally she combined the two, as the smart white glaze was perfect for the new shapes.

In order to let the glaze and shapes speak for themselves she developed a series of simple patterns that left whole areas clear to show off the glaze. However, she found there was a much better response to the range when it was decorated in the more colourful all-over freehand designs. One of the earliest was *Latona Tree*, which featured multi-coloured foliage and a bold black trunk. This design does not always have banding on vases and bowls. Tea-sets sometimes have the full pattern on the saucers, but the *Conical Early Morning* set shown has blue banding.

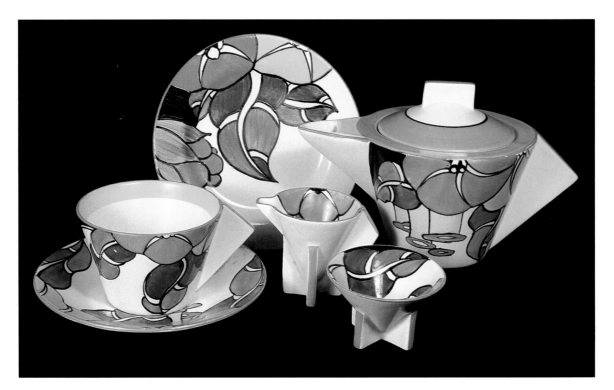

The majority of the *Latona* patterns were floral. Early ones such as *Bouquet* were available on *Conical* teaware and represent the more sophisticated side of Clarice's output. *Latona Bouquet* has bold pendent flowers, totally unlike the small, printed roses Clarice's competitors were decorating their ceramics with in 1929. Indeed, when Clarice used the rose as a motif for *Latona* ware, she produced what is perhaps the ultimate floral Art Deco pattern. *Latona Red Roses* featured black leaves and coral red blooms executed freehand to give a stencilled effect, and it brought an entirely new style to stockists' shelves in 1930. Today we are used to seeing Charles Rennie Mackintosh-style roses, but Clarice is unlikely to have been aware of his work in 1929 as he had died virtually unknown and uncelebrated in 1927.

ABOVE: Latona Bouquet *on a* Conical Early Morning *set*

BELOW: Latona Red Roses *on a* Conical *coffee-set*

Inevitably some new designs issued in *Latona* ware were only produced briefly. Notable amongst these is *Latona Thistle*, a stunning pattern again mainly using red and black, but this time outlined. Often low production designs were only sent to a few dealers before they were discontinued, and most examples of *Thistle* seem to have gone to Australia and New Zealand. *Blossom* featured large flowers on a trellis, and was later revived for the *Appliqué* range. Office boy Stanley Critchlow believed that Clarice was inspired by peering into a kaleidoscope when

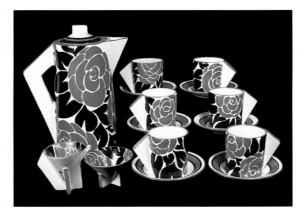

ABOVE: Latona Thistle
on a 392 candlestick,
a Hiawatha *bowl in*
Blossom, *a 177 series*
miniature vase in
Thistle *and a bowl in*
a partial Latona *design*

she created the *Latona Stained Glass* design. He thought this device inspired several of her early designs, and looking at the more advanced *Bizarre* geometrics, this might easily be true.

Latona Dahlia was very popular, combining a blue geometric form with bold outlined flowers. It has been found on complete six-person tea-sets and many other shapes, and even on full original sets there is quite a lot of variation, the flowers sometimes being orange. This is just another charming feature typical of individually painted ware as opposed to rigorously produced industrial tableware.

Most *Latona* pieces have a standard printed *Bizarre* backstamp with *Latona* elaborately hand-painted above, but a few later examples have a full *Latona* lithograph mark. The *Latona* glaze was discontinued during 1932, although some of the designs survived and were later produced on honeyglazed ware. Certainly teaware in *Red Roses* is known to have been produced briefly in 1935. It was ironic that the matt white *Latona* glaze disappeared in just a few years as it was ahead of its time; Wedgwood were to sell a mass of their stylish Keith Murray ware in the similar *Moonstone* glaze throughout the thirties.

Both *Latona* and *Inspiration* were successful in overseas markets. Numerous examples of *Inspiration* are now found in Australia and New Zealand and some *Latona* patterns were produced solely for stockists there. As early as September 1929, Robert Simpson's store in Toronto was stocking pieces and the *Canadian Homes and Gardens* magazine pictured items in *Latona Tree* and

RIGHT: Latona Dahlia
on a Mr Puddleduck
Sandwich *tray,* Latona
Knight Errant *on a*
Hereford *biscuit barrel*
and a Latona Red
Roses *cigarette box*

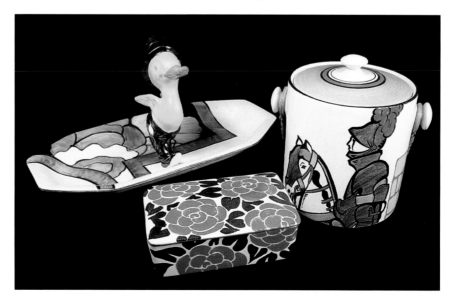

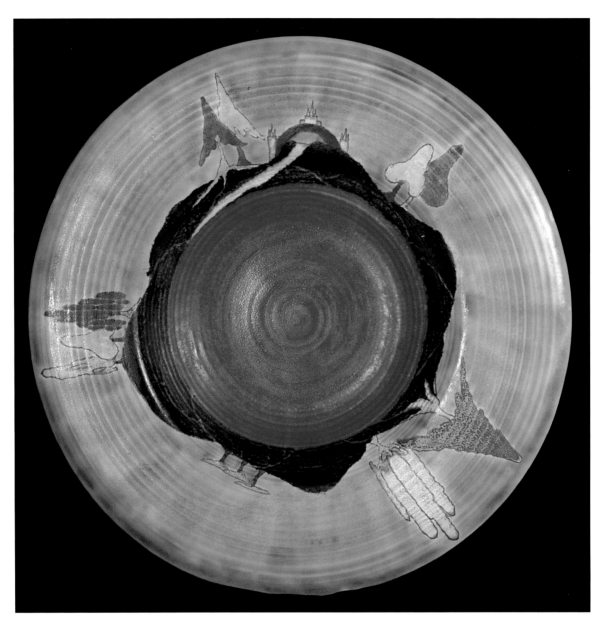

Inspiration Caprice. It described a large charger in *Caprice* as having, 'a touch of fairy tale modernism'. Unfortunately, although Clarice Cliff pottery was to sell in most parts of the world, the Wall Street Crash that happened a month after this article was published was to blight potential sales for the first half of the thirties. This is why Clarice Cliff collectors in North America have a dearth of the true *Bizarre* patterns.

ABOVE: An Inspiration Caprice *radially decorated charger*

DRAMATIC ART DECO

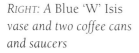t was not until 1928 that Clarice was able to make use of her impressions of the *Exposition des Arts Decoratifs et Industriels* as an inspiration for ceramics that were Art Deco in both style and shape. The triangular shape 200 vase that appeared in 1926 is an early example of the new style but it was only issued in traditional patterns at the time. Clarice was still several years away from having full control over her work.

The *Bizarre* designs of 1927 and 1928 are too simple to be classified as pure Art Deco. They have more in common with its Egyptian roots. Most significantly, though, when Clarice did finally produce patterns and shapes

RIGHT: A Blue 'W' Isis vase and two coffee cans and saucers

in the Art Deco style in 1928, even though it was three years after the Paris exhibition, she was still the first British ceramicist to do this. Indeed it might be argued that if she had not embraced the style, it might never have appeared in British ceramics. Much of the Art Deco style ware produced in Staffordshire during the thirties can be shown to have been inspired by her shapes three or four years earlier. Many Staffordshire potbanks were still using watered down elements of the style as late as 1936, eleven years after the exhibition.

It can be argued that Clarice Cliff's pieces are not truly Art Deco. Having so much bold, brash colour many do not conform to the more stylish, industrial, European idea of Deco that prevailed in the twenties. Our perception of Clarice Cliff as an Art Deco designer has perhaps come about because of the image of her portrayed in the popular press in the last ten years. If we believe that some of her pieces are truly Art Deco, then surely we should give them a distinguishing definition, such as Colourist Art Deco.

BELOW: Castellated Circle on a 369 vase, a pair of 465 bookends and a cigarette box in Football

Art Deco was of course the very essence of the *Jazz Age*, and the jazziness of the designs was the first element which Clarice was able to produce. This style appeared, incongruously, on some traditional shapes. The tall *Octagon* candlestick shown seems an unlikely object to be defined as Art Deco but the pair in *Circle Tree* seem to have all the *joie de vivre* that was characteristic of the style. The freehand circular forms on the stark black branches may have been inspired by the work of Sonia Delaunay which was on show at the 1925 exhibition. Delaunay was an independent, modern painter but it might be presumptuous to call her work Art Deco. Regardless of how we classify *Circle Tree*, the fact remains that Clarice introduced this avant-garde pottery into people's homes for the first time. The plaque behind the candlesticks is an early variation on *Original Bizarre* in the *Mondrian* design and reveals the influence of Cubism on Clarice's work. It is important to point out that the *Mondrian* name was given retrospectively to classify the design – Clarice's original name is lost.

The simplest early designs based on overlapping geometric forms included *Diamonds*, *Circles and Squares*, and *Castellated Circle*. These were generally brashly painted in bold outline with the enamels brushed brusquely in-between. Stylistically, we can attribute their introduction to between January and June 1929. Conversely, the more developed *Blue 'W'*, *Cubist*, *Football*, *Lightning*, and *Orange Battle* appeared a few months later. With its links to

RIGHT: Circle Tree on a pair of Octagonal candlesticks, and a plate in Mondrian

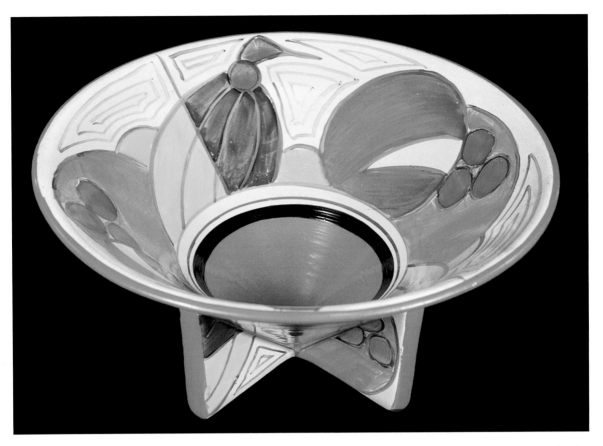

the Wall Street Crash we may date the classic *Sunray* design to October or slightly later.

Clarice's designs from this period are very varied and are the product of a mind teeming with new ideas for blending contemporary art with ceramics. Her first shapes in the geometric Art Deco style were the round-tiered vase shape 366 and shape 392 candlestick. Square, tiered shapes included the 367 bowl, the small *Fern pot* shape 368 and the shape 369 vase. Whilst these were innovative, they presented the decorators with problems as the tiered surfaces made it difficult to apply the outlining consistently. The first Art Deco shape that was both practical and commercially successful was the *Conical* bowl. This was an original shape and one which Clarice's technical staff tried to convince her it was not possible to make. She had disagreements with both the casting manager, Bill Lunt, and the modeller, Joe Woolliscroft, over its production. She wanted the four triangular feet to run to the edge rim but this caused it to warp when fired. Eventually, the shape appeared in April 1929 with the feet only going half way to the edge. While the *Conical* bowl was Art Deco in style, however, Clarice almost immediately issued it in her vivid *Bizarre* and *Fantasque* designs. These florid patterns are not really Art Deco and clash with the shape; yet it is this strange interaction that makes her ware unique.

ABOVE: A Conical *bowl in* Melon

As well as the *Conical* bowl with triangular feet, versions were made with a round foot rim, shape 382, and the equally rare *Conical* bowl shape 381 had just a round foot with no triangular supports. However, shape 383, with the four triangular feet, proved the most popular. It inspired a complete range including a *Conical* candlestick shape 384, a *Rose bowl* shape 400 and a *Conical* biscuit jar shape 402. The shapes were so extraordinary when launched in April 1929 that they naturally attracted many new customers to the *Bizarre* name.

One of the most *Bizarre* variations on the *Conical* theme was the *Conical Double Decker*, which had one inverted cone above another and so held water at two levels to display flowers. The superb shape was, however, not an easy one for the factory to fire and seems to have been produced only in limited quantities until about 1933. The example shown is in the early landscape *Orange House*, and the pattern is imaginatively painted on the outside of the lower cone and inside of the upper one! Such *Bizarre* combinations of shape and design are the ultimate manifestation of Clarice Cliff's art as far as collectors are concerned.

Two vases which appeared at the same time as the *Conical* bowls were the shape 379, catchily called the *Yo Yo*, and the single version, the 378. These were loosely based on silver goblets by the French designer Desny which Clarice had seen in *Mobilier et Décoration*. The *Yo Yo* vase was produced in one piece, thanks to the skills of the modeller Joe Woolliscoft and his team. The top cone is hollow, whereas the lower one has a solid base with just the small circular hole necessary as part of the casting process. Within a few months of designing these very pure forms

BELOW LEFT AND RIGHT:
A shape 380 Conical Double Decker *in* Orange House

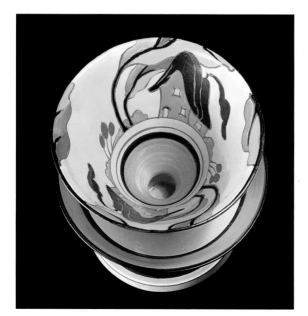

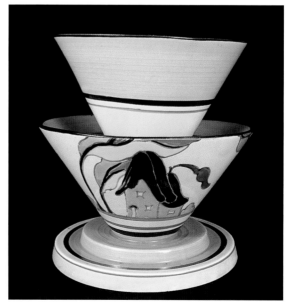

Clarice issued them in her jazziest patterns. The example pictured is in *Broth Red* which is rather sharper than the standard orange colourway because it is outlined in green, and this is a perfect example of what we can classify as Colourist Art Deco.

The success of the first *Conical* shapes led Clarice to create the space-age *Conical* teapot in July 1929 with its solid triangular handle and a pyramid-shaped spout! Even the cups had solid handles! A miniature *Conical* bowl served as the sugar, and the milk jug had four triangular feet, one of which was extended to make the handle. Such shapes were unheard of in British ceramics at the time, and when she added her new outrageous designs to them, such as the stunning *Cubist*, the media instantly acknowledged her as an original. Under the heading 'Cubism in a Teaset', the *Daily Express* reported, 'The teaset does not look like a teaset, it looks like a Russian ballet master's nightmare solidified!' The manager at Lawleys Regent Street store in London was quoted as saying:

This pottery has become enormously popular. We have been showing examples of it in the window and demand is so great that we can hardly keep up with it. Young

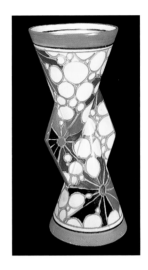

ABOVE: Broth Red *on a shape 379 Yo Yo* vase

BELOW: Cubist *on* Conical *teaware*

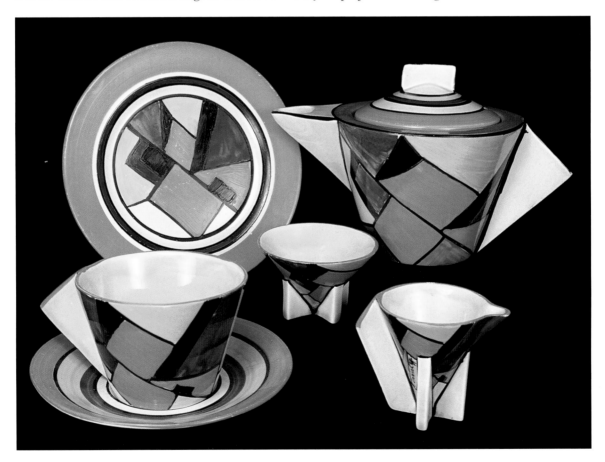

ABOVE: Sunray on Conical teaware

people particularly who are furnishing and decorating their homes in the Cubist style are keen about it. Other people like it for their early morning tea as they say it is so cheerful to wake up to, and one bowl or vase of this kind in a room can make a great difference.

In London, the *Evening News* covered *Conical* ware when it was shown at the exhibition at the British China and Glass at Chesham House, Regent Street in November 1929. The article said, 'A girl artist, Miss Clarice Cliff, is responsible for the most striking feature of the show, pottery she has named *Bizarre*. The cubes and scrolls of her patterns are incorporated with the new ideas she has created for teacup handles, candlesticks, vases and dishes.' A few days later the newspaper published an interview with Clarice which began by saying she was 'pretty, dark haired and very shy about talking about herself'. Clarice's comments reveal a considerable insight into her understanding of the market for her ceramics.

I think a woman knows best the kind of ornaments and articles for use in the modern home which the average woman of up-to-date ideas wants. Women's homes are changing. The housewife nowadays demands more individuality about the articles she handles and sees about her, yet each thing must be as useful as it is colourful.

She has more choice about originality in colouring and we work toward giving her greater freedom in this way.

The interest in Clarice's *Conical* wares was so strong that the factory was unable to keep up with demand. Certainly in late 1929 and early 1930 many stockists had to be content with the new style designs on traditional shapes, as is shown in photographs of shop window displays. This may be one reason why new designs were still being issued on traditional shapes. For example a freehand pattern featuring Cubist forms in bright colours that has the attributed name *London*, which would have been perfect for the *Conical* shapes or the geometric ones, has only been found on traditional ones such as the shape 353 vase. Customers would have been aware of how innovative the design was, and so the shape was not of such importance. Nowadays a *Conical* tea set in this colourway would be a highly desirable item because of the rare combination of design and shape.

ABOVE: A display of Bizarre, Fantasque *and* Latona *ware in the window of Haven's, Westcliff-on-Sea, in December 1929*

Spurred on by the public's interest in the design, Clarice issued yet more *Conical* shapes including the coffee set in February 1930. The gently tapering cone of the coffee pot had a massive open triangular handle balanced by a pyramidal spout. Most examples are in Clarice's vivid landscapes, which by 1930 had taken over from the earlier designs based on modern art. The full range of tea and coffee shapes is more extensively detailed in the *Taking Tea and Coffee* chapter.

LEFT: London *on a shape 353 vase, and a single handled lotus jug in* Red Melon

ABOVE: Café *on a shape 452 vase*

ABOVE RIGHT: Yoo Hoo *on a plate and a* Conical *bowl shape 383*

BELOW: Café *on a* Stamford *shape tea caddy or biscuit jar*

In September 1930 Clarice issued some of her most striking Art Deco pieces at the annual Holborn Hotel show. The stunning *Age of Jazz* figures attracted enormous publicity, but it was the *Stamford* teaware launched alongside them that was to sell so well. At the same show *Yoo Hoo* appeared for the first time, chic tableware in a shiny black aerographed glaze with just a touch of coral detail to the rims, handles or feet. This was the epitome of smart tableware at the time, when other manufacturers were still marketing dainty china with small floral motifs.

The stark colours of *Yoo Hoo* may have given Clarice the inspiration for a magnificent pattern called *Café*. The mix of red spots on a black ground, with oblongs in black, coral and grey, echoed some of the intrinsic motifs of the *De Stijl* movement in Holland. This severe Cubist design, with a mass of straight edges, must have been difficult for the decorators to execute in the fluid paints, and is a tribute to their skills. If Clarice had executed the design in her favourite vibrant egg yellow and orange it would have lacked the impact and lost the Art Deco feel, so she knew exactly how to use colour. Unfortunately, Clarice's incredible productivity meant this startling design was just one of dozens available then and like many others it was overlooked in the rush to the most commercial patterns so remains rare. *Café* has been found on few pieces apart from an *Eton* shape coffee-set, a *Stamford* biscuit jar and a shape 452 vase.

Even rarer than *Café* is another Clarice Cliff abstract which shares a limited colour palette and modern art images.

Sunspots was again a freehand pattern, with blocks and spots of colour, but it also incorporated bold, wavy black lines and circular forms. In distilling modern art into this commercial form Clarice produced the most avant-garde ceramics made in Britain at this time. The lack of examples of this stunning design suggest that it was too bold for the market then, but it led to the much more commercial *Tennis*.

The *Stamford* teapot, with its flat sides, was a perfect 'canvas' for the decorators to execute her patterns on, and it is found in a mass of designs dating through until 1936. *Stamford Early Morning* sets proved immediately popular and were made in relatively large quantities in *Fantasque* designs such as *Trees and House*. However, perhaps the most successful combination of design and shape was the *Stamford* teapot in *Tennis*. It combined a mixture of squares and curvilinear lines in bright colours, and proved particularly popular on teaware. To make the *Stamford* shape available at a slightly cheaper price, floral patterns with a printed outline and hand-painted detail were issued such as *Nemesia* and *Solomon's Seal*. These were decorated at Wilkinson's but they were certainly Clarice's work as they are recorded in the pattern books in her handwriting. It was because she used the decorating shop at Wilkinson's to produce lines that involved printing with hand-painting that she sometimes mentioned she had 150 staff working for her – there were of course an average of about sixty in the actual *Bizarre* shop.

Apart from their innovative product range, Clarice and Colley pioneered many new methods of marketing ceramics, some of which still sound

ABOVE: Picasso Flower *on a plaque, and a* Stamford *teapot in* Gardenia

RIGHT: Sunspots *on shape 358 and 186 vases*

LEFT: Tennis *on two* Stamford *teapots and an* Isis *vase*

advanced today. The *Daily Mirror* reported that they organized training sessions for the sales staff at London stockists.

Hundreds of London girls who sell china and pottery in the big stores and smaller shops have just been attending a series of lectures explaining the technicalities and intricacies of the production of the ware they sell. The London shop girl is tremendously keen on knowing the ins and outs of her job, and these lectures have been a great success. The idea originated with one of the biggest manufacturers of pottery in Staffordshire, A. J. Wilkinson of Burslem, who were the pioneers of the modern pottery – that gaily coloured ware which appeals so strongly to the modern housewife. In connection with the display of their latest designs they have been having these talks at a London hotel.

The *Daily Mirror* reporter was intrigued about *Bizarre* and asked how Clarice had thought of using so much colour:

'I decided to take a course of colour work at the Royal College of Art in South Kensington, and I used to take a busman's holiday viewing all the china shops in London. I thought how drab the old china was, and how ugly the few examples of modern work were. When I got back I persuaded the works to try out some of my designs. To our surprise, the first pieces were an enormous success.'

From 1931 onwards Clarice issued fewer patterns that we might now define as Art Deco but the influence of the style on her work remained. It can be seen in *Apples* where the multi-coloured fruit and leaves are contrasted with some vertical black 'piano keys', and as late as 1934 in *Xavier*, a freehand geometric pattern executed on a shape 515 bowl certainly conforms to the style.

LEFT: Picasso Flower on shape 405 bookends and a shape 365 vase in Apples

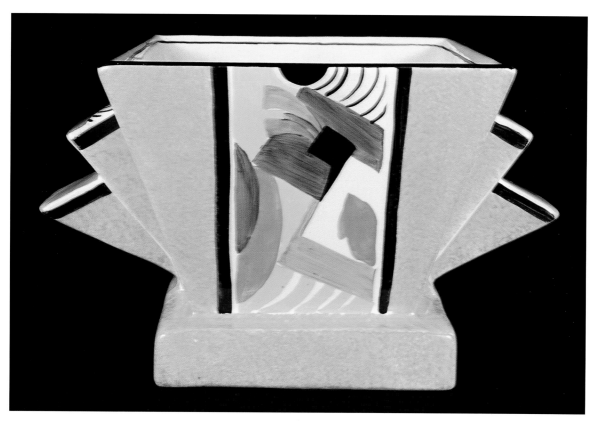

ABOVE: Xavier *on a shape 515 bowl*

We can more fully appreciate the impact of Clarice's work by examining the products of her contemporaries in the Staffordshire Potteries. Managers at other factories had always been keen to follow any new trend and were aware of her style as the British Industries Fair at Olympia was dominated every spring by her stand. By 1936 it was clear how strong Clarice's influence had been. At the fair Price Brothers of Burslem had a jug with a triangular handle, and also a tiered vase and even the name of their *Mattona Ware* range acknowledged the link with *Latona* ware. The Soho Pottery of Corbridge showed their *Burlington* shape with open triangular handles, Hancocks of Hanley used the same handles in their *Corona* ware range, as did Cartwright & Edwards of Longton who incongruously named the shape *Empress*. Also from Longton was Thomas Forester who had several items that were clearly inspired by Clarice Cliff shapes; a vase had triangular feet, as did a bowl which was similar to the *Conical* bowl. A cigarette box issued by Crown Devon was an almost identical copy of the 1933 *Biarritz* tureen. The Globe Pottery of Shelton showed a lamp base in their *Renaissant Ware* which had the semi-circular lobes of Clarice's shape 464 and 465 vases from five years earlier, and a footed bowl clearly inspired by the shape 475 *Daffodil* bowl.

However, little of this ware can really be considerd as Art Deco, as simply putting triangular handles onto traditional shapes was an unsatisfactory design solution. Nor had any of them linked their products to a designer's name: as late as 1936 the marketing advantage Colley Shorter had gained in making Clarice Cliff's name the focal point of his factories' products had still not been capitalized upon by all of the other Staffordshire potbanks bar one. Only Susie Cooper recognized the value of the designer's name. In September 1931 she had finally established her own business within Wood's factory and used her name on the backstamp. Most importantly, Cooper never produced Art Deco teaware as her first shapes did not appear until 1933. The *Wren* and the *Kestrel* teapots were basically egg-shaped, which the name she gave them clearly alluded to. These have been championed as examples of good design in recent years, yet in 1933 the influential *Studio* publication commented of the *Kestrel* shape: 'The rather dumpy appearance has been cleverly neutralized by the employment of cross hatching'. In 1936 Cooper issued a flower

trough set of curved and square sections, which were identical in concept and shape to Clarice's 1931 *As You Like It* set. In contrast to the numerous articles in the press about Clarice's shapes and patterns in the early thirties, there were very few on Susie Cooper's ware. The whole matter is investigated by Dr Phil Woodward in the *Clarice Cliff – Myth and Reality* chapter.

ABOVE: *Some of Clarice Cliff's tableware shapes: a* Bon Jour *tureen and gravy boat, a* Biarritz *plate and a* Stamford *tureen*

Ironically, in the same year that Susie Cooper launched her *Kestrel* shape some of Clarice's best shapes in the pure Art Deco style appeared. These were the *Bon Jour* coffee and tea ware, and the *Biarritz* tableware. *Biarritz* was created from an eye-catching mix of oblong and square plates, with vessels combining square and semi-circular edges with flat sides. These shapes were issued both in busy *Bizarre* patterns, and with simple motifs, in small cartouches, or with a flourish of black and gilt on one corner. The ware became amazingly popular, particularly as wedding gifts, as the marrying couple's monogram could be hand-painted on each piece as the sole decoration.

The *Biarritz* range now represents the best Art Deco tableware shapes made in Britain, yet it took Clarice until 1933 to make the pieces – eight years after the exhibition that launched Art Deco. These technically advanced shapes may have been impossible to create earlier, and certainly none of the other Staffordshire factories were able to copy them. Sadly, *Biarritz* ware is, of course, never found in the early Moderne or Cubist patterns: only in our imagination can we see a *Biarritz* plate in *Blue 'W'* or *Sunray*. Such was the accelerated output of Clarice's designs and shapes that many of her total design ideas never saw the light of day.

THE BIZARRE 'GIRLS'

ABOVE: Kathy Keeling being given a piggy-back by Nora Dabbs by the canal at Newport Pottery

*We are the gay Bizookas – happy girls are we
With dabs of paint we're decorating
And for work we're always waiting
Then the stampers will not stamp it
Naughty girls are they
And so we sit and suck our thumbs
Until that great big order comes
So now you know why we're all chums
We're happy girls and boys.*

We will never know how many times the song the *Bizarre* 'girls' sang resounded around the white-washed walls of the *Bizarre* shop! Several of them had adapted it from the 'Ovaltinies' song they had heard on the wireless installed in the shop by Clarice. The reference to 'Bizookas' was not alluding to Clarice's pottery horse, but was a name the male staff at Newport Pottery had bestowed upon some of the more voluptuous 'girls'. The 'stampers not stamping it' was a light-hearted reference to the fact that the *Bizarre* backstamp was added on glost ware before the 'girls' decorated it, and this sometimes caused delays. Long before the song was written the team spirit was all pervasive in the *Bizarre* shop. The

RIGHT: Gibraltar *on a 194 vase, an Octagonal plate and an Athens jug*

older 'girls' who had worked for Clarice from 1927 were joined by the new apprentices who were all just fourteen or fifteen years old. It was normal to take apprentices straight from school, but a department full of them was unusual, so the *Bizarre* 'babes' name bestowed on them by the older workers was rather fitting.

At this time most factories in Stoke were laying off staff, but the 'girls' found that working for Clarice Cliff meant they were busy from 8am to 5pm on weekdays, and 8am to 12.30pm on Saturday. Their wages were around six shillings a week, but many of them gave all but one shilling of this to their parents as they came from large families. Despite this, none of the 'girls' ever felt they were 'short' of money, and they fondly recall having a night out for a penny or threepence, at the Coliseum in Burslem, the theatre, or even dancing at the Grand Hotel in Hanley.

The first 'girls' to work on *Bizarre* ware were trained by Clarice to adapt the patterns, making them tall for a candlestick, low for a bowl, or cleverly wrapped around the handle and spout of a teapot. Phyllis Tharme, one of the first banders, recalled that the newer girls had to learn to mix the paint. 'We had a tile with powdered colour on and had to grind it for ten to twenty minutes with a palette knife and mix it with turpentine until it was smooth, and then add fat oil.' The girls remember fat oil as an 'unpleasant substance' but it was a stabilizer and much needed for Clarice's beloved orange colour. Mary Brown became a bander, and the factory was so busy that when Clarice asked her to go to London she had to demonstrate hand-painting alone. To make up for this Clarice showed Mary the sights of the capital from an open-top bus and took her for a meal at a Lyon's Corner House. Mary enjoyed going on demonstrations and later went to Lance & Lance in Weston-super-Mare, Spooners in Plymouth and Pauldon's in Manchester.

Annie Beresford had worked at Wilkinson's with Dolly Cliff for just three weeks when Dolly said she did not need her any more and took her across to her sister Clarice. Annie later recalled, 'I was just mixing paint at first, but after a while I became an outliner. First of all we had the great big ewers (*Lotus* jugs). Clarice would do two lines around them, and then show me how to do the diamonds between the lines. Later, my favourite pattern was one with a cottage. I did not really like the modern shapes but I thought Miss Cliff was clever designing them. She used to sit with us and help us, and we thought the world of her.'

ABOVE: Sunrise and Swirls on Octagonal candlesticks

BELOW: Outliner Annie Beresford in 1930

ABOVE: Bizarre 'girl' Nellie Thacker relaxing with her boyfriend at the weekend

As orders for *Original Bizarre* poured in, Clarice advertised in the *Evening Sentinel* in September 1928: 'Girls wanted to learn freehand painting. Apply Miss Clarice Cliff, Newport Pottery.' When fourteen-year-old Marjory Higginson applied she was almost too late. 'I was seen by Clarice Cliff herself. I remember her now in a blue georgette dress, she was very smart. She wore high heels because she was small, and had her black hair pulled back in a bun. I thought that she was only twenty-two and was surprised to find she was twenty-nine!' Clarice had already filled the vacancies but impressed with Marjory's enthusiasm, recruited her to join the team.

Other new paintresses included Annie Cotton, Gertie Love, Mary Moses, Sadie Maskrey, Nellie Thacker, Lucy Travis, Ada Cornes, Winnie Davis, Agnes Durber, and May and Kathy Keeling who were not related. May Keeling's memories of first going into the shop are evocative:

You were hit by the smell of aniseed and turpentine. We were sat at the back, given a bowl or a plate, and taught the brushstrokes; thick-thin-thick-thin. Within a week we were allocated a colour to fill in the triangles and squares. You had to buy your own paintbrushes, from Travis, a little shop at the back of Burslem Town Hall. They had a selection on a tray and you'd choose the ones you wanted. They cost between two and six pence each.

BELOW: Harold Walker, one of the four boy outliners in the Bizarre *shop*

Marjory Higginson recalled how they worked on the orders. 'When I first started to paint, tiny orders used to come in, perhaps just one *Early Morning* set. It came on a scrap of paper and a description of what was wanted. Nothing had pattern numbers and we had to work out what it was. I used to stand up and say "Does anybody know how we did this?" and someone would say "Oh yes, I do." The pattern books started later, when orders got bigger.' Had Clarice employed mature paintresses things might have been very different. What makes the pieces unique is the simplicity of Clarice's designs, combined with a charming individuality in how each of the 'girls' painted them.

In July 1928 the *Bizarre* shop staff increased again when three talented boy artists joined. John Shaw, Harold Walker and Tom Stringer were recruited from the Burslem School of Art. In 1927 Colley had received a letter from the British Pottery Manufacturer's Association saying that, 'Twenty boys and twenty girls aged fifteen to sixteen, who will have completed a two year course, will be available for employment in various branches of the Pottery industry.' Colley selected the boys, and also a young girl called Ellen Browne, as outliners. This proved to be a sound move as the outlining on *Bizarre* improved dramatically, and Clarice was able to create more elaborate designs.

Clarice and Colley realized that the *Bizarre* 'girls' also gave them a strong promotional tool. The success of the first Waring & Gillow event in August 1928 meant demonstrations were held throughout the year at stores in England, Scotland and Wales. Many of the 'girls' even now recall the stores, and which of their fellow paintresses they went with. They regarded these trips as adventures as most of them had never left the Potteries before.

As orders for *Bizarre* grew, *Fantasque* was introduced, and more staff were transferred from Wilkinson's as enamellers, or banders and liners, including Nancy Lawton and Sadie Maskrey. Three other paintresses, Elsie Devon, Hilda Peers and Harriet Rhodes, were recruited from Adam's of Tunstall where Clarice's sister Nellie was the 'missus'. It was probably quite easy to persuade these experienced paintresses to move to the more secure work at Newport. A fourth boy outliner, Fred Salmon, joined from the Newcastle-under-Lyme School of Art and along with the other boys was to be responsible for outlining many of the *Fantasque* designs. Ellen Browne was to outline most of the *Inspiration* pieces in 1929 and 1930 and later spent many months on *House and Bridge*.

Elsie Nixon, who had soaked Clarice many years earlier when she babysat her, joined the *Bizarre* shop straight from school in 1929. Elsie's mother was still a close friend of Clarice's, and so as was traditional in the Potteries, where whole families might work for one factory, Clarice employed her daughter. The Nixons rented their Ricardo Street home from the Shorter family who owned many of the terraced houses surrounding the factory. Elsie learned the skills of hand-painting but Clarice also trained her to assist in the photographic studio where Clarice took the publicity shots for *Bizarre* ware. These included the photographs to record the new shapes for the salesmen's sheets, or grouped selections for press pictures. Clarice used what resources she had to 'dress the photographs'; vases were filled with flowers or dried leaves, or she arranged the pieces on a mirror table. Clarice used very bright lights, which created quite fierce shadows giving some of her photography an almost *cinema-noir* quality. Nearby she had a darkroom where Elsie processed the films and printed the black and white shots.

During 1930 demand for *Bizarre* grew dramatically, so Clarice took on yet more 'girls' including her sister Ethel who became a bander and also did some enamelling at Wilkinson's. Fred Ridgway's daughters Beryl and Audrey joined, as did Marjory Higginson's sister Dorothy, Jessie MacKenzie, Gladys Birkin, Nora Dabbs and Alice Andrews. Later in the thirties, Alice became the

BELOW: Bizarre 'girls' Alice Andrews (left) and Betty Henshall (centre) with a friend in the summer of 1935

ABOVE: A collection of Lotus *jugs and* Isis *vases: top row,* Bobbins, Blue 'W', *and* Orange Roof Cottage, *bottom row,* Orange House *and* Autumn Red

'missus', but initially she was put in charge of making the tea, whilst learning how to enamel with Lily Slater. She remembers Clarice wandering around the shop in a white overall which she never fastened.

By 1930 Clarice had around sixty decorators, and their teamwork by this time was superb as, being paid on a piece-work basis, the speed with which they co-ordinated the outlining, enamelling, and the banding was crucial. All the paintresses remember having to paint the large 'ewers' as they called the *Lotus* jug shape. These were quite heavy to hold steady as they painted. They were a nightmare for the banders who had to complete the banding at the top around the handle; being large and having no handle, the *Isis* vase version theoretically had nowhere to hold it once the banding was applied!

Colley Shorter worked intensely in 1930 to ensure all the London stores stocked *Bizarre*. Major stockists such as Barkers, Gammages, Harrods, Lawleys, Selfridges, Bentalls, John Lewis, William Whitely and Liberty were all sold exclusive ranges. In return he supplied teams of 'girls' who spent every day demonstrating hand-painting, and they always attracted fascinated shoppers. The pieces could not be fired, so they had to clean every item with turpentine to use them again the next day! Clarice appeared at many of the promotions to meet the press and the public for a few hours a day. A typical event, staged at Lawleys in Regent Street, was publicized in the *Daily Mail*. Sadie Maskrey, Gladys Scarlett, Ellen Browne and Annie Beresford all bought new outfits to wear in the evenings when they were chaperoned by someone from the store who took them for a meal and to the cinema. They stayed at the Russell Square Ladies Club in Kensington where no male visitors were allowed.

ABOVE: The Bizarre Skool *float in 1930*

The *Bizarre* shop was so established by 1930 that Clarice persuaded Colley to let her team have their own float in the annual 'Crazy Day' parade when companies raised funds for the local hospitals. As her 'girls' were still very young Clarice called the Newport float the 'Bizarre Skool'. The boy outliners helped decorate the float but did not want to take part. However, the 'girls' enjoyed dressing-up as teachers and pupils and it was clearly a riotous event.

Paintress Vera Hollins, an enameller working on the *Appliqué* range, was often seen wearing wonderful hats as her father ran a hat shop in Burslem. For her the highlight of the summer of 1930 was the *Bizarre* outing Clarice organized to Llangollen in Wales. The 'girls' travelled there on a charabanc and Clarice provided everyone with a lunch box of sandwiches, slab-cake and lemonade. They all wore their best frocks as by this time their wages allowed them such luxuries, and some were skilled seamstresses. Influenced by the clothes Clarice treated herself to in London, they were noted for dressing well. Vera noted that Clarice and Colley did not go on the coach but travelled behind in his Armstrong Siddeley car. Vera took the family camera and as everyone strolled across the fields she captured shots that caught the atmosphere of the day. Colley, unusually relaxed, lay in his suit in the short

BELOW: Clarice's girls relaxing during the trip to Llangollen. Dolly Cliff is sitting directly in front of the girl standing wearing a jacket

grass, and Clarice looked splendid in a fashionable dress and a cloche hat. Vera took a group shot of some of the *Bizarre* 'girls' which is interesting as Clarice's sister Dolly was amongst them and there are few photographs of her. Clarice's experience of Sunday school outings came to the fore as she organized one-legged and egg and spoon races!

A family atmosphere evolved in the *Bizarre* shop with the slightly older 'girls' training and looking after the newer ones. Several clubs were started, occasionally, a dancing club was held at lunchtimes and there was also a 'chocolate club'. Phyllis Tharme

ran 'the rainy day' club, a way of saving money for holidays. Every day the 'girls' would pay in to it; a half penny for a fine day, a penny if it rained, or two and a half pence if it thundered! It was paid on the Friday before the holiday and ran until 1938 when the factory introduced holiday pay.

In the thirties all the Staffordshire factories took the same 'potters holiday' of just one week in August. A favourite location was Colwyn Bay, where outliners Ellen Browne and Sadie Maskrey stayed in a chalet, and the coast at Rhyl and Blackpool was also popular. Later in the thirties, now used to travelling around Britain, groups of the 'girls' ventured to the Isle of Man and the Isle of Wight. Their photographs of these holidays record the carefree camaraderie among these young women.

A new recruit in 1931 was pretty, petite Rene Dale. Rene was a family friend of the Cliffs and Clarice had promised her that if she passed her art exams at school she would find her a job. Rene was rather disappointed by the austere surroundings in the *Bizarre* shop; the only decoration was photographs of stage and movie stars. At first she tried to sneak off and hide in the factory, but soon she started to enjoy her work.

ABOVE: A bevy of Bizarre *'girls' holidaying in North Wales, from the left, Ellen Browne, Beth Evans, Betty Hollingsworth, a friend, Sadie Maskrey and Vera Hollins*

When I joined I sat behind Ethel Barrow and spent six months learning 'strokes'. As apprentices we arrived before everyone else and cleaned all the paint pots out for the 'girls' and put clean newspapers on their benches. We also had to grind the colours with a sharp knife on a tile. I still have a cut visible on my finger which I had to go to hospital with! Later they got a grinding machine and we just had to put the mixed paint into tins. As I learnt, one job I was given was the lids on Beehive honeypots. You were given a pile of a hundred and just painted the eyes and the wings!

When Clarice created a real *Bizooka* in 1931, the pottery horse she had first drawn for an advertisement, it gave her the idea for the Newport Pottery float in the 'Crazy Day' parade, 'Help your Hospital, Save the Race'. The paintresses and other workers went in fancy dress, Gladys Baggaley was a gypsy dancer, Clara Brindley was Al Jolson and warehouse worker Lizzie Evans wore a cape and fur hat.

Even in the early thirties many of the 'girls' were still just fourteen or fifteen so, although they were working in an adult world, when the opportunity came for a break they resorted to pranks in various parts of Newport Pottery. It is strange but amusing to think of Kathy Keeling, who artistically outlined thousands of pieces of *Gibraltar*, being given a piggy-back by bander Nora

Dabbs, who added the blue, pink, mauve and yellow banding! The original *Crocus* 'girl' Ethel Barrow was always first to get involved in mischief and when the men from Oliver's Flint Mill started to use an impressive lorry to deliver the raw materials rather than a horse and cart, she and other *Crocus* paintresses soon clambered all over it. Enameller Phyllis Woodhead accidentally broke the prow off a *Viking Boat* flower holder Clarice had asked her to decorate in *Crocus* for a special order. Phyllis was so worried she might get into trouble that rather than put it in the 'breakages box' she threw the boat through the window of the *Bizarre* shop into the canal!

Late in 1931 *Bizarre* ware attracted yet more publicity. A photo-spread covered the back page of the *Daily Sketch* on 4 December. Captioned 'How famous *Bizarre* ware is made at Stoke' it showed warehouse staff taking ware from the saggars arriving from the ovens, and girl assistants posing by a display of ware in the showroom. The picture was captioned, 'Some examples of *Inspiration* ware designed by Miss Clarice Cliff, the only woman art director in the Potteries.' Colley Shorter capitalized on this by buying 1000 copies of the paper and sent one to every pottery retailer in the Britain!

Outnumbered, the four boys in the *Bizarre* shop generally kept to themselves. John Shaw and Harold Walker were thought to be 'quiet' by the girls, Tom Stringer was 'a loner' and only Fred Salmon joined in the pranks when Clarice was away and Lily Slater was not watching. He was known to chase the 'girls' around the shop with dead mice and on one occasion swung across the canal on a crane to impress them, but fell in which cost him half a day's wages. The boys had expected to be trained as designers under Clarice but instead they found themselves doing endless outlining. Rene Dale also became an outliner and she and Annie Beresford outlined *Honolulu* when the boys were inundated with orders. Rene remembers that her 'sweetheart at the time' was warehouse worker Ben Simpson and she was photographed in his arms by the steps at the side of the *Bizarre* shop.

By 1931 the *Bizarre* 'girls' were regarded as an élite group, both at Newport and in the area generally. With their steady income they enjoyed a rather privileged life. It is hard not to romanticize the weekend hiking at Trentham, tennis at Wolstanton or Newport Park, swimming at the baths, picnics and regular visits to church. But they were surrounded by deprivation; Elsie Nixon remembered that groups of shoeless children begged at the factory gates, shouting, 'we want cake missus, not bread', and Rene Dale sadly noted there was a period when the police regularly 'pulled suicides out of the canal next to the shop'.

Mollie Browne, the younger sister of Ellen, worked in the trouser department of a tailors and did not like 'having to measure gentlemen', so Ellen got her a job in the *Bizarre* shop. Mollie was a fun-loving person and soon became

ABOVE: Crocus 'girl' Ethel Barrow commandeers a lorry with some fellow paintresses

BELOW: Outliner Rene Dale with Ben Simpson by the Newport Pottery steps

RIGHT: Conical *sugar dredgers in* Umbrellas, Pink Roof Cottage *and* Apples

a popular member of the team. 'I remember we had to practice in the rust enamel colour as it was the cheapest, and I used to get covered from head to toe – everybody laughed!' Mollie was soon a proficient bander but remembers she had problems with the *Conical* sugar dredgers. 'When you rotated them on the wheel to band them sometimes they were all wibbly-wobbly at the top. If you did not get the banding right you had to wipe it off and start all over again!'

During 1932 some staff left. Fred Salmon wanted to do more traditional hand-painting so joined Burgess & Leigh whose factory was just a few streets away. Phyllis Woodhead and May Keeling had painted *Crocus* for over two years and were persuaded by their night-school teacher to join Richardson's in Tunstall to produce a pattern he had sold them called *Firefly*. This work only lasted briefly, so May then moved to Radfords and Phyllis later worked as an enameller for Charlotte Rhead. Gladys Scarlett had never really been happy to accept Clarice as her boss and, unable to get the wage increases she thought she was worth, joined John Steventon in Burslem. Her hand-painted designs were issued with a custom backstamp *Royal Venton ware Hand Craft by Gladys Scarlett* but after two years the range was discontinued. However, when Rene Dale went for an interview with Susie Cooper at the nearby Wood's factory, Clarice found out and rang while she was there and told Miss Cooper to send Rene back! Duly chastised, Rene stayed in the *Bizarre* shop but she recalled she did then get the pay rise she wanted!

The one thing all the 'girls' disliked about Clarice was her officious attitude to time-keeping. She insisted they clocked in with their overalls on, at

8am. Occasionally she waited in the shop to see if anyone was not sticking to her rule, and would dock an hour's pay from any paintress who dared to break it. However, Clarice was always sad to lose her staff and is only known to have sacked one paintress, Kitty Oakes, who applied the enamels too thickly on a large order for *Blue Chintz*. The whole batch was ruined and Clarice explained this was why she had to dismiss her. Many of the paintresses recall her as being very kind, but Clarice could be strict and when Nora Dabbs dropped a whole tin of expensive powder colour in the storeroom, Clarice sent her home without pay.

No matter how busy she was, Clarice would always go through the *Bizarre* shop at least twice a day to inspect the work. If she was not satisfied she would make the 'girls' rub the paint off and start again. She always remembered how a pattern was first executed and was quick to spot that almost imperceptibly some of the paintresses were changing the outline. She would invariably notice and ask them to do it the original way. It was, however, essential that the 'girls' were able to adapt the designs to fit various shapes.

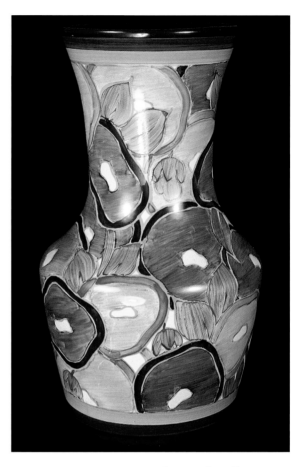

ABOVE: Blue Chintz *on a shape 386 vase*

Teamwork in the *Bizarre* shop was vital. If a piece was poorly outlined, no amount of careful enamelling could improve its final appearance. Conversely, a piece well outlined, but then poorly enamelled, would not look good. If Clarice rejected a finished piece the 'girls' had to paint it again and, as they were paid on a piece-work basis that would have cost them money, so they worked at speed but with care. Some decorators, such as Nancy Liversage, were day waged as they just did sample pieces which were painted very carefully. Nancy would both outline and enamel the pieces; only the banding would be done by another decorator. These pieces are exceptionally well painted, but usually a little more restrained than the more swiftly executed production pieces. Experienced collectors can discern such sample pieces, and they are particularly desirable.

Despite the Depression that was seriously affecting the world economy, business remained good in 1932. Marjory Higginson and Elsie Nixon were fortunate to be sent to demonstrate by the seaside that summer. They were on a large *Bizarre* stand at the British Empire Exhibition in the Kursall in Southend. One visitor to their stand was the High Commissioner for India.

Marjory was pleased when he paused to watch her dextrously band a plate, and he commented, 'How nice it is to see something being really hand-done.'

Every Christmas Clarice and Colley had a party for the 'girls', generally at the Co-op in Burslem. Each had to pay two shillings and sixpence for this but it was subsidized and was a way of thanking them for their hard work. In December 1932 they got an extra present when Santa Claus appeared in the shop. In the outfit was Mr Colley, wearing a red coat and white beard! He gave each girl a bakelite powder bowl as a Christmas gift, a most untypical gesture of generosity. What the 'girls' did not know was that the bowls had been taken by 'Santa' in part payment of a debt to Wilkinson's. Nevertheless it shows that Clarice and Colley undoubtedly appreciated that the workforce was an integral part of their success.

BELOW: Pictured at the end of Newport Lane in 1931 are (back row) Edna Becket, Florrie Robinson, Gertie Love and Ethel Barrow, (front) (unknown), Lily Barrow, Betty Henshall and Phyllis Tharme.

Further coverage of *Bizarre* was carried in the national newspapers in 1933. A press photographer visited Newport and captured a group of Clarice's 'girls' being shown how to paint *Windbells*. On the left is Lily Barrow, younger sister of Ethel Barrow the *Crocus* paintress, and next to her is Nancy Liversage, who did many samples for Clarice. In the centre is Ivy Tunicliff, who had just joined in 1932 as a bander and liner, as had Lily Dabbs, who is next to her. The 'girl' with a kiss curl is Elsie Nixon. Top centre is bander Marjory Higginson who always thoroughly enjoyed her work with Clarice.

Marjory realized the 'girls' were fortunate in having so much work, and one day in the early thirties decided to explore the factory to see exactly how many decorators worked on the site. She added up the workers in the *Bizarre* shop, those in the *Crocus* shop, *Ravel* shop and other areas at Newport where printed and enamelled patterns were produced, and found that the total of decorators was over *eighty*!

Surprisingly few of the *Bizarre* 'girls' married until late in the thirties. Amongst those who did were Annie Beresford, who married Chris Clowes a packer she met at Newport, and she left in 1934 to start a family. When *Bizarre* 'girl' Annie Cotton married Walter Downes in 1934, Dolly Cliff made her dress, and Annie used her skills as a decorator to hand-paint flowers directly onto the material. The majority of the 'girls', however, did not feel compelled to 'settle down' as they had job security and an independence not enjoyed by their mothers.

While the 'girls' rushed away from the works to enjoy the good times their jobs enabled them to have, Clarice diligently devoted herself to her work. Making the factory her 'home', and the paintresses her extended 'family', was

IT ALWAYS LOOKS EASY when the expert shows you. Miss Clarice Cliff, the pottery designer, instructing some of her pupils at the Royal Staffordshire Potteries, Burslem.

a key factor in her success, but it also meant she forsook having a family of her own. However, Clarice's income was now a great deal higher than her sisters, and her niece Nancy recalled, 'She spent quite a bit of money on clothes, and wore 4711 eau-de-cologne, that was her favourite. At Christmas she always bought her mother something special, a dress, coat, cardigan, or hat.' Clarice's sisters and brothers had all married and had children. Her brother Harry, who had been invalided out of the war and married, had two children, Stanley and Clarice, so his daughter's full name was Clarice Cliff! Although she was a devoted aunt, instilled with a keen business sense by Colley and well aware of the value of her name, she told her brother 'She will never be able to use it commercially you know!'

Clarice's only free time was on Saturday afternoon and Sunday when she often stayed at her flat in Snow Hill, which she had made very cosy. Colley Shorter undoubtedly visited her during the week but weekends had to be spent with his family. This may explain why she occasionally drove the forty miles to Nottingham to visit Gerty Langford, a friend of hers who was also the main china and glass buyer from Griffin & Spalding in the city. If Clarice stayed in Stoke, she would occasionally still go round to the family home in Edwards Street at weekends. The neighbours were most intrigued at her arrival, driving herself in a motor car! She would have Sunday lunch with her mother, her sister Nellie, brother Frank and Nancy.

Clarice was extremely fond of Nancy and after lunch they would drive off into the Staffordshire countryside. Nancy's memories of the trips, over sixty years later, revealed another side of Clarice's personality, for she was happiest going on simple walks through the woods and fields. This gave her the chance to teach Nancy about nature, whilst she found new ideas for her floral patterns, as recorded in *The Fantastic Flowers of Clarice Cliff*.

Back at the factory, to replace paintresses who left, more new apprentices joined in 1934 including Doris Johnson and Edna Cheetham. Doris warmed to Clarice, recalling, 'She had no airs and graces, you could talk to her straightaway.' Edna's first impression of Clarice was that, 'She was charming and had a quiet dignity. The *Bizarre* shop was always "abuzz", but as soon as she walked in it would quieten right down. I never heard her tell anybody off, or raise her voice. She had a charming smile; I am not surprised that Colley Shorter was charmed by her.'

BELOW: My Garden vases, sugar dredgers and a Girl candlestick

Edna soon became friends with the 'girls' who painted *My Garden* ware with her, Katie Hulme, Vera Parr, Vera Hollins and Connie Hodgkinson.

When Rosa Rigby joined in 1935 aged fourteen she soon got bored doing the repetitive brushstrokes the learners had to master. So instead she found herself watching, fascinated, as Winnie Davis applied the *Delecia* runnings to *My Garden* ware. This was done on a wheel to run the colours and create gentle runnings. Rosa was so absorbed that she did not hear someone come up behind her. 'Haven't you got anything to do?' demanded Clarice. Rosa went back to her strokes but shortly afterwards was delighted when Lily Slater asked her if she would like to learn to work at the wheel. Rosa always felt that Clarice had acted upon what she had seen, and really did look after her 'girls' individually.

ABOVE: Bander and liner Rosa Rigby in 1935

As they sat together painting, many of the 'girls' struck up lifelong friendships, such as Edna Cheetham who became a close friend of enameller Dorothy Higginson as they painted *Rhodanthe*, *Viscaria*, *Aurea* and *Pink Pearls*. The memories of working in the *Bizarre* shop are still fresh for many of the 'girls'. Edna recalled, 'The smell of turpentine was all pervading – a stranger could find his way to the *Bizarre* shop by his nose! Our clothes, hair and skin must have absorbed a great amount. This we could cope with, but it was imperative that hair was washed before going out to a dance. One whiff of turps and romance was killed stone dead!'

BELOW: A Bizarre 'girl' on the road, Annie Cotton in 1935

By 1935, many of the 'girls' were 'ladding', and headed for the Staffordshire moors at the weekend with their boyfriends on motorbikes. Enameller Annie Cotton and bander Mary Brown enjoyed these jaunts in the traffic-free lanes, although it is likely that their parents did not know they were riding on the bikes, an act of which they would have disapproved. Some of the younger 'girls' were content with more placid pursuits, and Mollie Browne and Edna Cheetham regularly played tennis with their boyfriends on the Middleport courts.

The theme of the 1935 Newport Pottery float, to celebrate the Jubilee of King George V, was 'Jubilee Babies'. Doris Johnson was a nurse and the smallest *Bizarre* 'girl' Ethel Timmis was the baby, and clung precariously on to the pram she was in as the lorry lurched along the route. The money was raised that year for the Hayward Hospital in Burslem, where just a few months later Clarice was to experience a personal tragedy.

From the middle of the thirties Clarice started to delegate more of the design work. She gave Harold

Walker and John Shaw the job of modelling the pieces the best-selling *My Garden* range was cast from. However, still disillusioned as they had not been allowed to develop as designers, they decided to leave in 1935. Their loss certainly affected the style of hand-painting as they had outlined many major designs since 1928. The matchings of early thirties designs produced after this are noticeably different to the originals, and of the original boys just Tom Stringer was left.

All the 'girls' had memories of the difficult time around the abdication of Edward VIII. They were divided as to whether or not he should marry Wallis Simpson, and spent so much time debating this as they painted, that production slowed down noticeably. Clarice questioned them as to why this was, and with her personal situation with Colley being very similar, she apparently empathized with Wallis Simpson!

From the middle of the thirties Clarice responded to the public's changing taste as moulded ware became more fashionable. Heavily embossed ranges such as *My Garden* soon led to *Raffia*, *Corncob* and, later, *Harvest* and *Fruit and Basket*. These needed many hours of skilful modelling to develop so she took on Betty Silvester, Nancy Greatrex and Peggy Gibbons as apprentice modellers from the Burslem School of Art in 1936 and 1937. Being just fifteen or sixteen they tended to stick together, so did not regard themselves as *Bizarre* 'girls'. Peggy Gibbons later became a renowned modeller at Doulton under her married name, Peggy Davies. All three of the recruits did a lot of the modelling for new ranges based on Clarice's designs, and as their skills developed Clarice also encouraged them to produce original pieces.

BELOW: Bizarre 'girl' Mary Brown with her son Michael

Peggy Davies occasionally worked with Edna Cheetham, and both were surprised when they were sent on a painting demonstration to Dundee by Clarice. Edna assumed it was because none of the older 'girls' who normally did these were available. 'We were painting at Lawleys, Dundee, and we were very young and rather green; it was a wicked city. On our day off we went to the local lifeboat station and met the crew, and they *all* turned up at Lawleys the next day, all these big, burly Scotsmen, to say "hello" to us again. Lawleys staff were horrified, and we were whisked away to the supervisor's house!'

In the late thirties, the *Bizarre* 'girls' started to leave the shop to get married. Clarice seemed upset whenever one of them left, and some of them believe she felt a little betrayed. She took on new paintresses to try to preserve the hand-painted ware, including May Booth in 1937 and Ray Booth and Marianne Holcroft in 1939. Then, in the first eighteen months of World War II, one by one, nearly all the paintresses were recruited to help the war effort.

ABOVE: Lily Barrow and Nancy Dale demonstrating hand-painting at James Colmer's store in Bath, in February 1936

The *Bizarre* shop, where a total of over 100 decorators had enjoyed a unique camaraderie, became a dull storeroom as it had been commandeered by the army for storage.

Clarice had been both 'the boss' and also a friend towards her 'girls' right from the start and many were to spend the whole of their working lives with her. Clara Thomas worked for Clarice right through until 1959 and they became good friends, so she was one of the few 'girls' invited around to Clarice's flat. Mary Brown left in 1938 to have her son but then returned after the war to work right through until Clarice retired. Rosa Rigby remained at the factory long after Midwinter took over, finally retiring in 1980. Florrie Winkle and Cissy Rhodes were amongst the longest-serving *Bizarre* 'girls'; having joined in the late twenties they worked with Clarice until 1964. Clarice had given her paintresses such security, and such a pride in their work, that they *never* ceased calling themselves the *Bizarre* 'girls'.

THE ART OF COLOUR

Women today want continual change, they will have colour and plenty of it. Colour seems to radiate happiness and the spirit of modern life and movement, and I cannot put too much of it into my designs to please women.

Clarice Cliff in 1930

She walked up to the shop to where Lily Slater was standing in a fresh white overall. 'Good morning Lily – I'm sorry you had to work late last night but Mr Colley was insistent that the *Ravel* order was finished for firing before we went home. I simply had to go into Stoke to see Lawleys, so could not help you. Arnold tells me it was finished and will be out of the kiln by four this afternoon.'

Lily nodded. 'Yes, they were very good, Miss Cliff. Even the ones who had not painted *Ravel* before managed to match the pattern well. They were pleased to stay behind as they can all do with the extra wages!'

'Harold and John finished the samples of the new *Fantasque* pattern, Miss Cliff. They are on the stillages just over there.' Lily Slater followed Clarice across the shop towards a vase, a large plaque and some teaware, all decorated with a balloon-shaped tree, and a cottage half-hidden amongst some bushes. These had a little black and green detail but the rest of the pattern was a mass of vivid coral red. 'I do love this coral colour; it's a shame it is so difficult to apply', said Clarice, admiring the thick layer of enamel. The plaque had been finished in a broad red band of coral, and Clarice thought to herself, 'It's a symphony in red!'

She walked down the shop to where Harold Walker and John Shaw sat together, their heads bowed over plates they were outlining in *Melon*. 'I'm pleased with the way you both outlined the new landscape, who did the enamelling on them?'

'We did it between us Miss Cliff. As you know the coral is hard to apply but we did our best', said Harold.

'Well, I love the effect, but I think we will probably have to do the trees in simpler colours, such as blue, green and yellow…' said Clarice, who noticed the boys' brushes had not stopped moving. They were concentrating so hard on their work that they carried on painting as they talked to her.

On the front row of the *Bizarre* shop Eileen Tharme was trying out a new colourway of *Crocus*. Clarice paused by the bench and smiled encouragingly as the seventeen-year-old built-up the flowers with skilful strokes. Then Eileen turned the vase upside down and selected a brush with fine bristles, which

RIGHT: Autumn Red *on a thirteen-inch plaque*

she ran lightly across a tile covered in a dark green. She then drew thin lines over the flowers to create the fine leaves. A retailer in Yorkshire had asked Clarice for an exclusive version of the design, which had been his best-selling pattern on teaware for nearly two years. Eileen passed the vase to Clarice who inspected it and admired the flair with which it had been painted. Clarice carried the vase carefully to save smudging the flowers which were drying to the matt finish they would have until the piece was fired. She took it to Nora Dabbs who was sitting in the third row from the back of the shop putting vivid red, yellow and black banding on the new *Appliqué* samples. Clarice had created a design of a caravan under a tree heavy with red and orange fruit and Sadie Maskrey was painting the sample pieces which Nora 'finished off'.

'Nora', said Clarice, 'when you have done that plate, could you just add blue and black banding to the top and bottom of this vase for me?'

'Certainly, Cla… Miss Cliff.' Nora had almost addressed Clarice by her Christian name. She knew the girls had been told that they were not to do this anymore. Nora 'spoke as she found' and could not understand what all the fuss was about. Clarice was only from Tunstall! Why did they have to call her Miss Cliff? She removed the finished *Appliqué* plate from her wheel by slipping a knife under it and placed it carefully on her bench. Then, smiling at Clarice, she carefully took the vase from her.

Clarice knew that Nora was an excellent bander, so left her to decide how to paint the vase. She walked up to the end of the shop and saw that Annie Elsby, who had joined just a few months earlier, was putting too much colour onto her brush. 'Annie dear, just run your brush *gently* over the colour, and cover a smaller area on the vase when you apply the enamel – like this.' Patiently, Clarice took the piece and applied swathes of egg yellow onto the geometric pattern. She knew she was a great deal slower now than her 'girls' but she could still get the right finish – when she tried! Annie took back the brush and vase and did as Clarice had instructed. Satisfied, Clarice walked back up the *Bizarre* shop through the L-shaped extension, past the darkroom and headed towards the haven of her small but cosy studio. She was looking forward to having a cup of tea with Mr Colley.

Recreating a glimpse of life in the *Bizarre* shop gives us an insight into the teamwork and skills Clarice had cleverly brought together. At the beginning of the new decade she found herself in the enviable position of having a whole factory dedicated to producing shapes and patterns stamped with her signature – a unique feat no other Staffordshire designer had achieved. Newport Pottery had been rejuvenated with the success of her *Bizarre* ware, and whilst she relied on Wilkinson's for some of the technical processes, Clarice nevertheless had her own factory with a team of sixty talented decorators whose hand-painting skills she could channel into any style she wished.

Clarice's use of bright enamel colours, applied in broad swathes, was almost unique for the first years of *Bizarre* ware. Her paintresses learnt to apply the more difficult colours thinly to stop flaking, and the Newport Pottery kiln firemen perfected the techniques of firing this style of on-glaze enamels. Several other factories tried to copy the technique of applying broad swathes of enamel colour on-glaze but encountered problems. John Guildford's *Arabesque* ware for Barker Brothers was produced in enamels that fired dull and wore quickly; Susie Cooper's four abstract designs for Gray's between October 1928 and June 1929 were prone to paint flaking and used a blue enamel which often fired dull.

The fusion of new techniques for perfecting on-glaze enamels combined with Clarice's larger colour palette were soon used on a series of mainly landscape designs in the *Fantasque* range, and exotic scenes in the even more colourful *Appliqué*. Both these ranges were about colour: brighter colour, more colours, more skilfully applied. In 1928, Clarice's *Caprice* landscape had introduced the idea of fantastic scenes. Trees, and rolling hills, in dreamlike colours, were to be the trademark of her new style. Clarice adapted *Caprice* for *Inspiration* ware, which became a popular pattern. This was the final magical ingredient that inspired the 'cottage and trees' style, as with a

BELOW: Trees and House *on a selection of traditional and modern shapes*

twist of smoke coming out of the chimney, the image captured the comfort and security of the English countryside. This was the style that Clarice Cliff was to make her own and be identified with forever.

The new style first emerged when Clarice put the ingredients together definitively for *Trees and House*. A prototype line-drawing in similar colours had been produced in May 1929, and from it evolved the simple pattern of a cottage and trees which is now so quintessentially Clarice Cliff. Early trials were executed in coral, green and black with a brown outline. The initial response indicated there was a good market for stylized landscapes and in September 1929 Clarice experimented with a colourway where the trees were lilac, green and orange, the ground yellow and the clouds blue. In total, the *Pastel Trees and House* colourway had seven colours. Later designs were to feature this quantity of colours but the *Pastel* colourway was deemed too complicated at the time and was produced only for a bried period. All the trial pieces were sold, but *Pastel Trees and House* mainly went to Australia and New Zealand, so is now a sought-after colourway.

When *Trees and House* was issued as a production pattern it was in coral or orange colourways. It was

ABOVE: Pastel Trees and House *on a* Tankard *coffee-set*

BELOW: A Dutch advertisement for Bizarre *ware in 1930, note the European-style covered* Conical *sugar*

THEESERVIES VAN ROOMKLEURIG AARDEWERK
Landschapdecor, in zwart, rood, groen — 15 deelig f 30.—
MEYJES & HÖWELER
AMSTERDAM-C. — DAMRAK 19-20-21-22 — Vraagt Prijscourant

RIGHT: Trees and House Orange *on a* Coronet *shape* Lemonade *set*

produced in a number of styles, as at least four outliners simultaneously painted it to satisfy demand, including Annie Beresford and Ella Hopkins and two of the boys. The earliest examples in coral are quite finely outlined, yet by 1930 the 'wedge tree' and 'bubble tree' were being drawn more vigorously. It is possible to find the design on an Art Deco style *Conical* shape teapot, or a traditionally shaped *Athens* one, and the way in which Clarice's decorators adapted the design to these shapes affects their relative collectability. *Trees and House* became the 'signature' design of Clarice's landscape ranges from 1929 to 1932, and was sold on every conceivable shape, leaving a mass of collectable ware for today's enthusiasts.

By 1931 *Trees and House* was painted in the brasher style as shown in the *Lemonade* set which comprises a *Coronet* shape jug with six beakers. Inevitably, as with all work emanating from the *Bizarre* shop, some rarities escaped, a few examples are known where the grass is blue, and two pieces have a colourway of just orange, yellow and blue. *Trees and House* set the tone for Clarice's landscapes and established *Fantasque* as an entirely separate range from *Bizarre*. Although the two were painted by decorators sitting side-by-side in the *Bizarre* shop, it was to be *Fantasque* that was to really distinguish Clarice artistically.

Clarice devoted many hours to designing new landscapes on water-colour paper, experimenting with the various colours to decide how to balance the design. She would then take her ideas to an outliner who would adapt the design on to a group of ware Clarice had selected from the glost warehouse. The enamellers and banders would then carefully finish these. After being fired in the enamel kiln, the pieces were taken to Clarice's office where she and Colley decided which should be test marketed. This system meant that sometimes less than a dozen pieces of a pattern were produced.

Because Clarice created so many new designs in a short space of time we cannot always accurately date the sequence in which they appeared, but the next significant 'house and tree' theme was probably the amazing *Orange House*. The vividly coloured building had a multi-coloured tree blowing violently over the roof. It was set amidst solid coloured bands, normally in acid green but occasionally in vibrant orange. It is found mainly on *Tankard* coffee-sets, plates, *Isis* vases and *Lotus* jugs as it was produced briefly, so the *Conical* coffee-set shown is a rarity. The design cannot be traced to a particular source, but some collectors feel that the tortuous movement is reminiscent of the disturbing art of Edward Munch. For a simple cottage and tree scene it has considerable depth.

ABOVE: Orange House *on an* Octagonal *plate and an* Autumn Blue Conical *coffee-set*

Towards the end of 1930 Clarice created a new scene that combined the elements of *Trees and House* and *Orange House* with a brighter, wider use of colour. The 'bubble trees' were replaced with bulbous trees with sinuous trunks, and it was to sell as well as *Trees and House*. The concept of the 'cottage and tree' scene had come of age. The trial colourway based on her *Trees and House* range was *Autumn Red*, but almost immediately she produced *Autumn Blue* in which the bulbous trees were blue, yellow and green. On early pieces, vases had red banding above the design and green and yellow below, but soon the pattern was issued with many banding variations. The choice of the name *Autumn* was a strange one for a design that had such sunshine colours!

Autumn was one of Clarice's most successful scenes and in order to supply retailers with unique versions Clarice added numerous colourways. The three *Autumn* trees were painted in combinations of orange, yellow, green, or green, lilac and clear. By 1931 *Autumn Orange*, a version outlined in blue with orange and yellow trees, and *Autumn Pastel*, had appeared. Later examples sometimes lack the half-hidden cottage. A collector seeking just this one pattern in its various colourways might never finish assembling a representative selection!

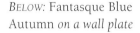

BELOW: Fantasque Blue Autumn *on a wall plate*

RIGHT: *The original* Appliqué *range from March 1930*

RIGHT: *The original* Appliqué *range from March 1930*

ABOVE: *In 1930* Appliqué *ware had the range hand painted above a standard* Bizarre *backstamp*

BELOW: Appliqué Lugano *on a plaque and a* Conical *coffee set*

Clarice created her most colourful landscapes in a range she called *Appliqué,* which was initially influenced by the brilliantly coloured pochoir prints of Edouard Benedictus. *Appliqué Lugano* and *Appliqué Lucerne* both appeared in March 1930. For the first time Clarice created landscapes that had depth and scale, but their unique quality lay in the colours they featured. They were brighter and richer than those used on the standard *Bizarre* range, as Clarice used special enamels that were more expensive. The most striking was a deep, thick, blue enamel used for the sky on *Appliqué Lugano* and the lake on *Appliqué Lucerne.* There was also an iridescent olive green, a thick mustard yellow and a milky blue, seen on few designs except those in the *Appliqué* range. These new colours were the results of trials at companies such as Blythe's Colour Works and Wenger's Colours. The newer colours included more expensive ingredients but, as they achieved a more impressive effect, the factory was able to charge more for the ware. Therefore, *Appliqué* referred to both a decorating style and a higher price range. The owner of Wenger's was Edward Wenger, a life-long friend of Colley's, who was later to give Colley a timely piece of advice…

The style of the *Appliqué* landscapes was different because the outliners produced the design firstly in Indian ink. Enamellers then applied the vivid colours between these lines which evaporated when the piece was fired. This left just colour against colour, and achieved an entirely different finish to the *Fantasque* designs which were outlined.

Appliqué Lucerne featured a castle in the distance and rolling mountain slopes. The castle motif, with a few simple trees composed of green triangles on top of each other, was based on a detail in a Benedictus print. The same landscape composition was used for the similar *Lugano* design which featured a waterwheel. The use of many new, experimental, colours for *Appliqué* meant that inevitably trial pieces were developed which were quickly superseded. These present a challenge for today's collectors and a complex sequence to date. Initially, both *Lucerne* and *Lugano* had blue skies, but whereas the deep blue on *Lugano* gave a strong finish, a different blue used for the sky on *Appliqué Lucerne* was faulty, sometimes firing dull. In June 1930 Clarice issued *Appliqué Lucerne* with an orange sky, and to co-ordinate the range also issued *Lugano Orange*. The banding on the pieces also changed swiftly, but as many examples are on plates with impressed date marks that were used to control stock rotation, we can chart the chronology. Initially, the design was issued without banding and produced as an all-over landscape such as on the *Octagonal* plate. However, the first trials were produced with mainly blue and orange banding, which was almost instantly replaced with black, clear, black banding in April and May 1930. Then, the black, red, black banding style most commonly found on

ABOVE: An Appliqué Etna *plaque and an* Octagonal *plate in* Appliqué Lucerne

BELOW: Appliqué Lucerne *on a* Conical *bowl shape 383, a plate, a small* Conical *sugar bowl and a* Trumpet *vase shape 187*

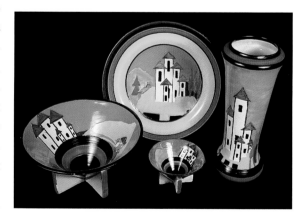

ABOVE LEFT: Appliqué Avignon *on a 386 vase*

ABOVE RIGHT: Appliqué Caravan *on a plate*

Appliqué designs was introduced. This made a strident frame for the designs, softened on some pieces by adding a broad yellow band to the sequence. In the case of tea-sets, it was standard to use both styles, and this sometimes causes collectors to wrongly think they have a 'matched' set.

Clarice's former boss, John Butler, did the Indian ink outlines on some early *Appliqué* pieces but, as the range grew and production pieces were needed, outliners John Shaw, Harold Walker, Eileen Tharme and Ella Hopkins worked on them. Enamellers who remember painting *Appliqué* include Cissy Rhodes, Vera Hollins, Sadie Maskrey and May Keeling.

By June 1930 the *Appliqué* range was selling in moderate quantities, which encouraged Clarice to issue several further landscapes. Next to appear, again inspired by European scenes, were *Avignon*, depicting a lake and bridge scene, and *Windmill*, which featured the building and sails in the vivid *Lugano* blue. The first *Appliqué* seascape, *Palermo*, featured a coast with red-sailed yachts on the bay, and a floral climbing plant in the foreground. *Palermo* seems to have been in production for only about a year from September 1930, although a few later matchings of *Avignon* are known. *Appliqué Caravan* is one of the few of Clarice's designs on which we have Clarice's own comments. She was asked in 1930 how she managed to create so many designs and commented, 'Some weeks are better than others. I got out twelve new designs last week, one of which is just coming out of the kiln. It introduces a caravan under orange trees glowing with fruit against a decorative background.'

Appliqué Red Tree was produced from September 1930 onwards but is rarer than the earlier *Appliqué* designs. Most examples have none of the honeyglaze showing and it is also unusual in that a grey enamel was used. *Appliqué Bird of Paradise* features the exotic yellow and red bird on a branch heavy with black fruit against blue leaves. Just two examples are known, a plaque and a jug. Floral patterns were also produced; *Blossom* from 1930 is an adaptation of a design of blooms on a trellis first used for *Latona* a few months earlier and *Appliqué Garden* has large simple flowers under a stylized tree in dominant blue or orange. This design seems to have been just a sample.

Most of the 1931 *Appliqué* designs were only briefly produced. The volcano and coast scene, *Appliqué Etna*, was painted with various colours for the sky and clouds, and less than twenty examples are known. A unique design that we have called *Appliqué Monsoon*, found on a ten-inch plaque in South Africa, may have been a sample just sent there which never went into production.

The first *Appliqué* designs, *Lugano* and *Lucerne*, were revived in late 1931 but only issued in the blue colourway. They can be distinguished as they have slightly thinner colours, black, clear, black banding, and a lithograph backstamp. The later *Lucerne* has a pale blue sky which gives it a more Mediterranean look. The rarest *Appliqué* pieces are tea-sets and coffee-sets, few complete examples are known, and only one *Conical* coffee-set in *Appliqué Lucerne Orange* has been recorded. Like many of Clarice's designs, matchings of *Appliqué Lucerne* were issued after the main production ceased, and the last piece dates from November 1933.

ABOVE LEFT: Appliqué Garden *on a plate*

ABOVE RIGHT: A Lotus *jug in the 1931* Appliqué Lucerne *colourway*

ABOVE: Red Roofs *on a* Stamford *teapot, a* plate, *a* Serviette holder *shape 468, a* Conical *sugar dredger and a* Globe *vase shape 370*

BELOW: Appliqué Lucerne Orange *on a* Conical *coffee-set*

The range of *Fantasque* scenes was substantially increased in 1931. *Trees and House* continued to be produced on many different shapes and Clarice introduced patterns which had the same theme but with different colour ranges. *Red Roofs* featured a detailed cottage amidst trees and was unusual as it featured a flowering climber on the cottage wall, a fence and, almost surrealistically, a giant flower on the reverse. With the cottage roof in coral, and vibrant orange banding, the design has strongly contrasting colours, and represents Clarice at her best. Several outlining styles can be distinguished on *Red Roofs*. One outliner painted the roof edge overhanging the walls, and curving lines for the roof and buildings, whilst another painted them square and straight. The enamellers coloured the design in various ways, the plate pictured has the foreground just in yellow, but some examples have orange, yellow and green. On a few pieces the cottage wall is painted yellow. The banding is also variable; the standard banding was orange with a fine black line but the shape 370 *Globe* vase has orange, green and yellow banding, and the sugar dredger is banded in blue! This delightful diversity in decoration inspires collectors seeking very individual pieces.

For many collectors the *House and Bridge* design is an ultimate expression of Clarice's art. *House and Bridge* was the first design to incorporate a more detailed scene of rolling countryside with a road

LEFT: Farmhouse *on a shape* 467 Smokers *set, a* Conical *sugar dredger and two plates*

going up a hill, and a river and bridge cleverly incorporated. Unlike *Red Roofs* it is extremely consistent in its colouring and banding; the red, orange, yellow and brown shades were outlined not in brown, but black, giving the design a sharper definition. Ellen Browne was the principal outliner, but as large orders arrived at the *Bizarre* shop other decorators outlined it so several styles can be distinguished. It became famous amongst collectors when it was featured on the exhibition poster, and cover of the L'Odeon book. This was why it was referred to as the 'front cover' pattern until its original name was discovered.

Poplar* and *Farmhouse* both featured a cottage in the distance and flowers in the foreground adding perspective to the designs. *Poplar* is a bright pattern with jade banding whereas *Farmhouse* is in more sophisticated black, brown, orange and yellow. The cottage on *Farmhouse* has small stylized flowers in the foreground in surreal cloud-shaped bushes. By 1931, when these designs appeared, Clarice's shape range had grown larger so they were issued on many more shapes than the original *Fantasque* designs.

The other landscape designs of 1931 took the cottage and tree theme in new directions. On *Fantasque Mountain* the cottage is only a minor part, the pattern is dominated by a giant orange tree, and the main element is a brown mountain with an orange top. With a blue lake and a purple mountain in the

BELOW: An Isis *vase in* Orange House *and a single handled* Lotus *jug in* House & Bridge

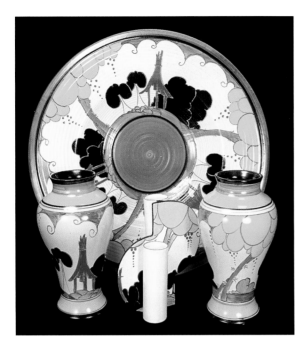

ABOVE: Summerhouse
on a pair of shape 14
vases, a vase 465 and an
eighteen-inch Charger

BELOW: Octagonal
plates in Kew *and*
Mountain

distance, *Mountain* provides another stunning illustration of Clarice's *Fantasque* art. However, perhaps the most successful new landscape in 1931 was *Summerhouse*. The flamboyantly drawn red hut is under a yellow tree, surrounded by black and purple bushes, making it a quintessential Clarice Cliff landscape. The charger pictured is an eighteen-inch diameter example, painted radially. As well as producing plates, plaques and chargers with the design full height for wall hanging, Clarice also offered this rather novel, radial format, which was ideal to display a charger as a centrepiece on a table. The outliners had to be extremely skilful to transform the patterns to the radial format, and Clarice introduced this style of decoration to Staffordshire ceramics for the first time.

In 1932 the landscape range was again diversified, with some fresh elaborations on old ideas, including patterns in entirely new colour styles. *Kew* was based on an oriental pagoda in Kew Gardens, London, and Clarice placed the stylized building between her 'bubble' and 'wedge' trees from *Trees and House*, painted in different colours. The curly blue clouds were similar to those on *Summerhouse* and the pattern was featured prominently at trade shows during 1932. The response to it was encouraging so Clarice simplified it for tableware, as a small motif in a cartouche, amidst fine banding. A customer could buy a vase in the design showing the full image and combine it with much more subtle dinnerware. Clarice had produced her *Moderne* tableware in 1929 with a number of different designs in a cartouche, but this was the first time one pattern was offered two ways.

In 1932 Clarice Cliff thought pink and introduced a new *Fantasque* colour palette, removing her 'signature' orange, and replacing it with pink, lilac, blue, yellow and pale green – more of an innovation than it seems. Pink is an everyday colour now, but in the thirties on-glaze pink enamel was more expensive as it had a high gold content, and was difficult to make. The colour, called Harrison's Pink after the supplier, enabled Clarice to introduce pastel colourways of her most popular designs, such as *Melon* and *Autumn*. For *Autumn Pastel* the design was outlined in blue, and the tree was pastel blue, green and pink. *Melon Pastel* looked totally different to the original, and also the 'contour lines' between the fruit were omitted.

LEFT: Autumn Pastel *on a* Tolphin *flower jug and a complete* Stamford Early Morning *set*

Further new patterns designed around Harrison's Pink were introduced. *Gibraltar*, which was outlined in purple, had the same colours as *Autumn Pastel*. It shows the famous mottled rock face in pastel colours under a yellow sky, with yachts on the blue sea. The banding in blue, lilac, pink and yellow splendidly frames the pattern. The early pieces were outlined by Kathy Keeling but later Rene Dale also outlined it. *Gibraltar* was produced in quite large quantities, as small fancies such as *Sabots*, and ashtrays in *Gibraltar* proved popular with stockists in seaside towns where visitors on their week's annual holiday bought them as souvenirs.

The most important scene introduced by Clarice in 1932 was undoubtedly *Orange Roof Cottage*. It has a dominant central cottage, with green trees in the background and a bridge similar to that on the 1931 *House and Bridge*. The original water-colour showing the paintresses how to outline, enamel and band the design still survives in Clarice's extant pattern books. The popularity of *Orange Roof Cottage* is witnessed by the fact that the page is creased and well-thumbed! As pastel designs were selling well by this time Clarice issued *Pink Roof Cottage* soon afterwards but examples in this colourway are rare.

Clarice appreciated that her pottery had to suit her customer's decor, and developed a range that enabled them to choose any of her designs, regardless of their dominant colours. She introduced *Café-au-lait* which

BELOW: The reference water-colour for Orange Roof Cottage *from the Clarice Cliff archive*

featured her standard patterns executed over a mottled brown or yellow or green background. This was created by using a special stippling brush to cover biscuit ware with all-over colour, it was then glazed and painted in enamels in the usual way. The idea was that the designs took on the dominant colour of the *Café-au-lait* and now harmonized with furnishings. Many of Clarice's landscapes were produced in *Café-au-lait* including *Autumn*, *Summerhouse* and *Trees and House*. Other *Fantasque* designs used included *Bobbins*, *Gardenia* and even patterns from 1929 such as *Orange Battle* were revived.

The last year in which scenes strictly in the *Fantasque* tradition were issued was 1933, but there was a noticeable diversification in style as many even lacked the trademark cottage or house. In February *Windbells* was launched at the British Industries Fair. Outlined in a mustard colour, it had a typical Cliff tree with a sinuous trunk, but there was no cottage and the other main element was a swirling background. For *Solitude*, Clarice used green as the outline colour. *Solitude* was well named as it featured a single tree, from behind which a large coral-coloured bridge arches over a vast grey, green and blue sea. It is illustrated on a *Bon Jour* tea-set, a radially painted charger and some vases. On the tea-set the outliner skilfully blended the pattern on the circular *Bon Jour* teapot, and then used just part of the pattern on the other pieces, giving the design a more impressionistic feel.

RIGHT: Café-au-lait Bobbins *on a* Coronet *shape* Lemonade *set*

The equally strangely named *Secrets* landscape was dominated by a tree with circular foliage and featured two of Clarice's cottages, but this time partly hidden behind the brow of a hill beside an estuary. For collectors of designs featuring cottages, *May Avenue*, issued later in 1933, is an important pattern. As the name suggests it features a whole avenue of red-roofed buildings nestling amongst bushes, with spade-shaped trees. The most dominant feature of the design is again a tree, which is in *Café-au-lait* finish with mottled green and yellow.

The most striking aspect of the 1933 *Fantasque* landscapes is their use of one dominant colour. Whereas earlier landscapes featured a rainbow selection of colours, *Windbells* was mainly orange, *Secrets* was in dominant green, *Solitude* was in yellow and *May Avenue* was blue.

Honolulu, the final major 1933 landscape design, was dominated by a tree with pendulous foliage. Much of its impact came from the fact that it had broad pastel bands overlaid with concentric black lines, so had an almost psychedelic quality. Its alternate colourway, *Rudyard*, was in blue and pink, but lacks the unusual banding style.

The brash outline brushstrokes of 1930 used in early *Fantasque* landscapes soon gave way to scenes which incorporated both more exotic locations and decorating techniques. These came about from 1933 when the 'girls' started using 'pencils', finer brushes which created a more detailed finish. Combined with a move to softer colours, Clarice's landscapes took on a new, more gentle quality as can be seen in *Japan Blue*. Only on close inspection does one realize that this pattern is actually outlined in green! The two

RIGHT: Solitude on a shape 358 vase, a Charger, a shape 464 vase and a complete Bon Jour Early Morning set

LEFT: Honolulu on a thirteen-inch plaque, vase shapes 366, 615 and 202, a Bon Jour vase, Bon Jour candlestick and shape 556 Serviette ring

colours one first notices are blue, and then pink on the leaves and some of the tree trunk. Much of the colour for the sky and the ground was applied with *Café-au-lait* technique. Also, the outline of the lake, and the pagoda roof, do not feature solid colour, but blocks of blue which contrast with the flowing lines of the other elements of the pattern. *Japan* shows how quickly Clarice's designs evolved in both style and colour when compared to the similar subject matter and composition of *Summerhouse* from just two years earlier.

Clarice evolved a number of *Fantasque* abstract patterns at the same time as she created the *Fantasque* landscapes between 1929 and 1933. These followed on from such typical early ones as *Umbrellas and Rain*; indeed that design was still produced occasionally as late as 1932. The most successful *Fantasque* abstract in these years was undoubtedly *Melon,* which appeared in 1930. It was one of the most complex patterns Clarice created, and involved outlining in brown, and the addition in purple of 'contour lines' between the fruit forms. It is one of the few of Clarice's 'all-over' designs produced in quantity for full tableware sets. The fruits

ABOVE: Japan Blue *on* Bon Jour *teaware*

BELOW: Fantasque Melon *on a plate, a shape 14 vase,* Stamford *teaware and a shape 132* Ginger Jar

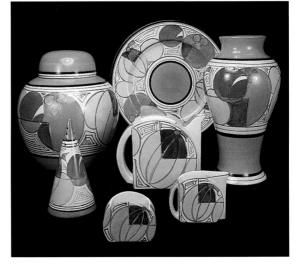

are given a Cubist look by the use of geometric lines bisecting them. The design has a particular style of banding, a broad swathe of orange edged with black, and then a gap and fine brown lines.

The most notable 1931 abstract was *Berries*. Almost as busy as *Melon*, it featured blue and purple leaves, with the berries in orange and coral with a set of diagonal lines in green and yellow. *Apples* was produced the same year but the other *Fantasque* abstracts from this time are mainly floral, *Gardenia* being the most familiar. It was not really Art Deco in style, unlike *Picasso Flower* in the *Bizarre* range in 1930. However, the impact is achieved with both stylized flowers and a mass of overlapping leaves in two shades of green, and black. *Gardenia* is found with the flowers in orange or coral, and a mass of alternate bandings.

The most significant *Fantasque* abstract in 1932 was *Chintz*, which, as the name indicates, was based on a floral fabric style image of overlapping lily pads and flower buds. On first sight it resembles a mass of vividly coloured fried eggs. It is one of the most eccentric of Clarice's designs, and certainly helped earn her the reputation of being a Bohemian designer! *Chintz* was produced in three colourways and sold throughout 1932 and 1933. However,

BELOW: Berries *on an* Octagonal *plate,* Conical *sugar shifter,* Sabot *and a 369 vase*

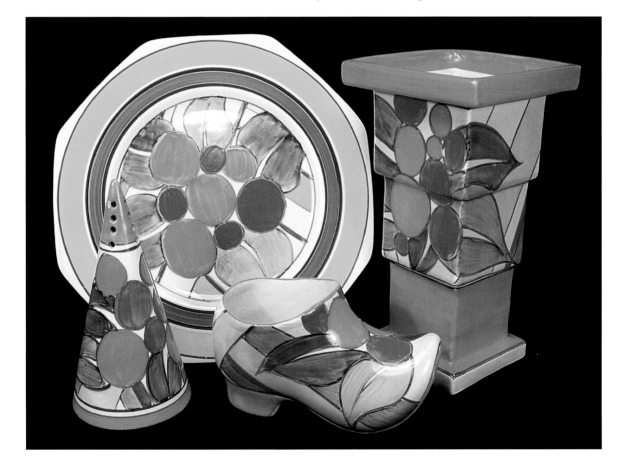

the equally colourful but more realistic *Nasturtium* was to prove a more commercial pattern. With coral, orange and yellow flowers against a brown *Café-au-lait* ground, it was so popular that a colour leaflet was produced just for this one pattern, showing some of the shapes it was available on.

Although new *Fantasque* scenes appeared in 1933 there were no major new abstracts issued. The *Fantasque* designs were issued until 1934 with the *Fantasque* backstamp, but later examples have a standard *Bizarre* mark. The

final *Fantasque* style designs used different painting techniques, reflecting the public's changing tastes from 1934. Designs such as *Bridgwater*, *Blue Firs*, *Coral Firs* and *Honolulu* featured finer lining and more busy detail. Eventually more natural colours were used on designs such as *Brookfields* and *Ferndale*. These designs used the much finer pen outlining. Typical was *Bridgwater* from late in 1933 which combined all the classic Clarice landscape elements in one image, a tree, a cottage, a river, a bridge, and even blue and purple reeds. This

ABOVE: Bridgwater *on a shape 279 vase, an* Octagonal *plate and a 495 vase in front of which is a* Bon Jour *tea-set*

design was more detailed than Clarice's earlier work but the bright colours and yellow banding overlaid with mustard lines, make it a major pattern. The *Bon Jour* set shows how skilled the paintresses were by this time at adapting the whole design to fit even onto small pieces. The shape 279 and 495 vases show the opposite sides of *Bridgwater*.

The *Fantasque* range finally disappeared when Clarice used the etching style of painting with the cottage and tree theme on *Trallee* which featured a thatched cottage in a garden; *Sandon* and *Fragrance*, were similar designs without the cottage. Etching was most successfully used on *Rhodanthe* and its various colourways.

Clarice Cliff's landscapes represent a very British style of art, though they are not true Art Deco. When she created them in the thirties, her intention was clearly commercial, but she was perhaps never fully aware of the long-term impact of the images. Today, they are one of the key reasons why her work has become so popular. In the last decade her 'cottage and tree' images have 'inspired' the production of millions of bone china mugs printed with pastiche versions of her designs. These are now found in homes in countries all around the globe. Along with her famous *Age of Jazz* figures, Clarice Cliff's multi-coloured landscapes, and cosy cottages have become a major icon of art from the thirties.

THE BIZOOKA AND THE STARS

She was impressed. This woman from the Midlands was very modest despite the outrageous shapes and colours of the ware that bore her name. She had been expecting someone rather louder, and perhaps a little bohemian, but although she was very fashionably dressed, she was down-to-earth, and very modest about her success. 'I think I have all the details I need about the ware displayed here, Miss Cliff, but I just wanted to ask you one more question. How on earth did you manage to get the colour ideas to create such a diverse range?'

Clarice paused, and then speaking firmly but quietly, said: 'Very tentatively at first I set to work, moulding new patterns, developing new and daring decorations. Ideas borrowed from meadow flowers, from gems, from bits of bright enamel as were produced by old Italian craftsmen… Everything with a touch of orange in it, I had noticed seemed to take people's fancy, while jade green was another "winning" colour.'

BELOW: Staffordshire architect Joseph Emberton meets Clarice Cliff and her Bizooka

The woman hastily finished her shorthand and thanked Clarice profusely. 'This will be in tomorrow's editions of the paper, along with some shots of the pottery horse, it should look splendid!' She glanced at the *Bizarre* creation which stood almost five feet tall. 'Oh. Is it meant to be a male or a female horse?'

'Well', said Clarice, 'originally I called her *Miss Bizarre*, but somehow it became known as the *Bizooka* amongst the men at the factory who helped me build it, and that sounds like a "he", so I'm not sure even I know!' She laughed, revelling in the interest the pottery horse had created.

'Thanks again', said the journalist, who shook Clarice's hand, before turning and heading for the lift with her notebook.

Clarice reached into her Liberty handbag for an enamelled cigarette case which Colley had bought her in Paris. She put a cigarette into the holder she always carried with her. Suddenly, Mr Colley was at her side with his lighter. 'That journalist was impressed, Clarice, I think you have really excelled yourself this time! I have never seen so much interest before. Now, what else do you still have to set-up?'

'I just have to arrange the *Autumn* ware on the table against the back wall, and Hilda and I will then go out and buy a mass of fresh flowers from that market just down the road. I think it should take no more than ninety minutes to finish.'

Colley smiled at her, 'Right, in that case I will be back here at noon to take you out for a special lunch!'

Clarice replied, 'That will be wonderful, Colley, I really would like a chance for a quiet chat.'

As he left he nodded politely towards her. She knew he would far sooner have given her an affectionate peck on the cheek but, always concerned with what was right and proper, he would not have dreamt of doing that in public! Colley entered the lift as Hilda Lovatt was coming out. 'Good morning, Mr Colley.'

'Good morning, Hilda.'

'Mr Colley seems in a good mood today, Miss Cliff', remarked Hilda.

'Yes, he is very pleased. And I need to thank you and the others for all your hard work both here and at the factory setting it up.'

Hilda could not wait any longer to ask. 'Is it true, Miss Cliff, that Sir Malcolm Campbell will be here this afternoon?'

'Yes, it was confirmed yesterday, and Mr Colley is most pleased.'

'I hope I will be able to get his autograph', said Hilda, 'and I'd better get a few for the girls back at the factory; they would never forgive me if I went back without them. I will get the magazine with him on the front cover in *Bluebird*. Do you think he will sign four?

'I'm sure he will', laughed Clarice, 'and to save any hurt feelings you'd better ask Mr Emberton for his autograph as well.' Hilda asked who he was. 'He is a very famous architect, and he was born in Audley, so he is *almost* a local man', said Clarice. 'Now, let's get the cask with the *Autumn* pieces unpacked, and then we can go and get those flowers…'

This partly fictional account of one of the many days Clarice and her team staged a large show is based on fact. When Colley Shorter arranged for Sir Malcolm Campbell to endorse *Bizarre* it was a major coup. Although every year Queen Mary or members of the royal family visited the British Industries Fair, this was primarily to stimulate sales so they were seen to 'buy' pottery from virtually every stand. Clarice recalled that the Queen, 'bought quite a lot of this pattern *[Crocus]* on traditional shapes every year, and she remembered the prices she had paid in previous years.' Colley Shorter realized that whereas many factories could utilize the royal patronage, he would attract even more interest from the public using Sir Malcolm Campbell, who was then a national hero. This style of endorsement was entirely new and one his competitors noted but failed to imitate. Clarice and Colley's promotional ideas were making buying tableware rather more appealing.

Promotions linking *Bizarre* pottery to stars and personalities of the day were spearheaded by the unmistakable image of the *Bizooka*. Just an imaginative drawing in a *Bizarre* advertisement in October 1928, by 1931 it was a ceramic and steel reality. In the original drawing Clarice showed the *Bizooka* constructed with vases, candlestick legs, a *Lotus* jug body and a teapot spout as the tail! Most of these items were decorated in *Original Bizarre* but the head was formed from a shape 358 vase decorated in *Broth* from the new *Fantasque* range, which was publicized for the first time in this advertisement.

ABOVE: Colley Shorter meets Sir Malcolm Campbell

It is hard to convey the impact that this image would have had in 1928. It was startlingly different from any advertising by other Staffordshire factories. Previously, there had been nothing resembling a horse made from vases and bowls! *Bizarre* ware had first been included in the company's advertising in the trade press in February 1928 as just a one-line mention. At that time the advert was headed with a drawing of ware from the John Butler range. However, underneath was a photograph of two kittens springing out of a tureen in the *Good Year* pattern. This photograph must have been Clarice's work as she took the publicity shots for the factory at this time, so even before the *Bizooka* appeared she was subtly changing the company's style.

In the advertisement in the March 1928 edition the mention of *Bizarre* was enlarged. The copy proclaimed '*Bizarre* ware is made in every variety of table and fancy goods. Get control for your town.' This was a reference to the fact that Colley had instructed his salesmen to let only one store in each town stock *Bizarre* in order to stimulate sales. Then, in October 1928, to save losing possible retailers, he launched *Fantasque* to enable other shops to stock the ware. However, as *Bizarre* was making a handsome profit by then, he soon marketed *Fantasque* as being the product of Wilkinson's to reduce the tax! With the launch of the *Bizooka* image in October 1928 Clarice's imagination had transformed the look of the company's advertising in under a year.

The *Bizooka* was used in *Pottery Gazette* until July 1929 and became an image strongly associated with Clarice. Even if she had not transformed it into a five-foot high pottery horse, its creation had the desired effect of making her products distinctive. It was such a unique idea in the late twenties that it was still a novelty when she decided in 1931 to create a real *Bizooka*! Clarice, Bill Rowley, the chief engineer at the factory and Jim Steele spent several weeks constructing it. Staff could not help but remember the strange sight of them creating the *Bizooka* in a garage under the works canteens. The *Bizooka* was built on a frame of steel rods which held pieces of *Bizarre* ware together which were pre-drilled with holes, and there were felt pads between each pot to prevent breakages. The head was made from two *Autumn* plaques with large black eyes added. Two bowls formed the mouth, and the neck consisted of a *Red Roofs* 342 vase and an *Isis* vase in *Bobbins*. The body was an umbrella stand in *Branch and Squares*. These designs were different from those in the *Bizooka* cartoon, but apart from that it looked very similar to Clarice's original drawing.

Making a real *Bizooka* was a piece of pure promotional genius! It was used as the focal point of the *Bizarre* display at the First Avenue Hotel, Holborn in London in September 1931. Not content with this attention-getting device, Colley also employed well-known personalities to visit the trade show to endorse *Bizarre*. They were in turn photographed with Clarice and the *Bizooka*. Many personalities attended, including Sir Malcolm Campbell. Having just set a world land-speed record in *Bluebird* in Florida a few months earlier, he was an international personality and had been knighted on his return. Other personalities included the band leader, Jack Hylton, and architect Joseph Emberton whose avant-garde work and Staffordshire background gave him a common bond with Clarice. Emberton had come to architecture through interior design and was responsible for pavilions for the British Empire Exhibition and the New Empire Hall at Olympia in London, where the British Industries Fair had moved to in 1929.

ABOVE: Clarice Cliff with the Bizooka *in 1931*

The press pictures taken of the *Bizooka* at the First Avenue Hotel attracted a great deal of publicity. Coverage even reached America where the *Pasadena Evening Post* commented, 'Miss Cliff has often been criticized for what they call low comedy, but she laughs at their well meant advice and reminds them that her business has increased steadily in the few years she has employed her talents for herself.' It was during this interview that she made her revealing comment: 'Having a little fun at my work does not make me any less of an artist, and people who appreciate truly beautiful and original creations in pottery are not frightened by innocent tomfoolery!'

It is easy to overlook the other promotional devices made of *Bizarre* ware that Clarice created at the same time, as the *Bizooka* is such a strong image.

A five-foot high *Bizarre* tree, cut out of board, was hung with colourful plates in *Umbrellas*, *Football*, *Circle Tree*, *Sunray* and *Swirls*. Clarice also constructed a small man with a *Lotus* jug body, a *Globe* vase head, and legs of candlesticks and *Sabots* and she called him the *Bizooka* jockey! However, the largest item was a cut-out of a bottle oven, hand-painted in bricks, with the *Bizarre* logo

ABOVE: The 1931 Crazy Day *parade with the* Bizooka *and the* Bizarre *'girl' jockeys*

on the side. In front of it Clarice's pottery was perched on stands made of lumps of coal! Sadly the only known photograph of this display is of very poor quality, but it was yet another example of an attention-catching promotional device loaned to *Bizarre* stockists.

The *Bizooka* was next used for the Newport Pottery float in the 1931 'Crazy Day' parade. The theme was 'Help your Hospital, Save the Race'. Clarice called a meeting and encouraged her 'girls' to dress up as jockeys. Outliner John Shaw was a talented sign-writer, and Clarice asked him to create the decorative boards used to cover the lorry. On these he painted horses and jockeys, as well as the slogan. On the day, Clarice arranged the float in such a way that it looked as though the *Bizooka* was actually rearing up at a 'jump' of real bushes and on the cab of the lorry was the 'jockey' who had been thrown over the hedge! It was another example of Clarice's sense of humour! The *Bizarre* 'jockeys' ran alongside the lorry shaking collecting-tins, while students from local colleges directed the traffic with sticks of rhubarb. A photograph taken at the end of the parade shows the 'girls' resting on the back of the float, tired after their long walk.

The *Bizooka* was instantly in demand by *Bizarre* stockists as a result, so Clarice had four more made and which became the centre of eye-catching displays. They were cleverly constructed so that they could be folded down to travel. The staff of Haven's in Westcliff-on-Sea, Essex even 'rustled' it from their window for a day to use on their float in a local parade. Inspired by the outfits they had seen Clarice's paintresses wearing when demonstrating in Haven's, all the female staff wore berets, bows, and carried artists' palettes covered in *Bizarre* colours!

At the start of 1932, a year in which she launched many new fancies, Clarice again stood at the British Industries Fair at Olympia. Colley was more and more aware by this time that whereas all the main Staffordshire manufacturers stood at this fair, his big advantage was in staging events exclusively promoting his factories' products. The majolica produced at Shorter & Sons, the hotel ware and tableware from Wilkinson's, plus Clarice's *Bizarre* enabled him to offer just about every type of ceramic object, apart from sanitary ware!

Clarice realized that the majority of female customers only went to big city stores a few times a year. The factory provided photographs and information to fuel large spreads in women's magazines which stimulated readers to send for the *Bizarre* leaflets they mentioned. Each featured the *Bizooka* in colour on the cover and promoted a different part of the *Bizarre* range: *Delecia*, *Latona*, *Fantasque*, *Crocus* and *Gayday*, *Inspiration* and *Appliqué*. Factory assistant Eric Grindley recalled that one girl was employed in the office for much of the thirties just posting these out. Customers receiving them would have been shocked when they visited their local store to be suddenly confronted with a real-life *Bizooka* five feet high!

After the success of the personality promotions in 1931, another show was staged at the First Avenue Hotel, in September 1932. Colley Shorter again hired personalities, and Marie Tempest, Marion Lorne, Adrienne Allen, Christopher Stone, Leslie Henson and Bobby Howes were amongst those appearing. They were photographed with Clarice and Colley, and presented with a set of their choice. Journalists were given exclusives with the stars and the stories appeared in magazines for months. Marion Lorne was appearing at the Whitehall Theatre, and *Modern Home* reported:

She takes a great interest in her home and loves to go out in search of pretty accessories to add to the charm of her rooms. She chose this lovely fruit set because it was so gay – not strikingly modern but just beautifully coloured. The set consists of six plates and a fruit bowl designed specifically for Miss Lorne by Clarice Cliff.

LEFT: Comedian Leslie Henson and friend appearing at the Clarice Cliff display at the First Avenue Hotel in 1932

ABOVE: Delecia Citrus on a Daffodil *shape coffee-set*

The ground is cream with a design of orange and yellow citrus fruit, and leaves of smoky blue and light and dark green, outlined in a soft shade of brown.

Christopher Stone, a broadcaster with the newly founded British Broadcasting Corporation, was photographed amidst an array of Clarice's fancies, holding a *Teddy Bear* bookend over a tank in which goldfish were swimming around an underwater forest of shape 437 cut-out *Trees*.

When Clarice returned to Newport Pottery she allowed herself a few minutes with the 'girls', showing them autographed photographs of the stars she had met, but it was one of the rare times she 'let her hair down'. In October 1932 she staged one of her most impressive shows, an exhibition in the top Kensington store, Barkers. Clarice created tableware displays coordinating a mass of shapes and designs, based on selling modern, functional tableware and fancies. The *London Evening Standard* reported on 24 October:

The whole department is a panorama of brilliantly coloured table settings, lights and decorations. Very futuristic is the dodecahedron table made of frosted glass, its twelve sides bound with green and illuminated beneath the glass. Part of the service on the table was serving plates decorated with gold fruit which are intended to remain on the table during the meal. Seeing this modern display of ware and table settings is to take a mental leap into the future.

The plates decorated with the fruit in gold were Clarice's *Delecia Citrus* pattern, and are now a rarity. Keen to maximize sales, Barkers produced extensive literature so that customers who did not buy on the day, or those who could not go in person, could purchase ware by mail order. *Delecia Citrus* was available on a *Bon Bon* set, a *Daffodil* tureen, a *Conical* candlestick shape 384 and a *Conical* bowl, listed as a 'striking modern shape complete with separate flower arranger'. This was a cone-shaped fitting with holes to support the blooms which is nearly always missing now. Some rarities on show at Barkers were a 460 *Stamford* vase in *Poplar*, and a 378 vase in *Orange Roof Cottage*.

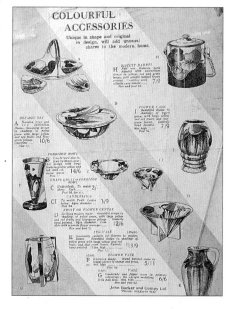

ABOVE: Part of the promotional leaflet produced by Barkers

A *Bizooka* was used once again for the Newport Pottery float in 1932. The theme was 'Kindle a Candle for the Kiddies Camp' as a children's home in North Wales was the beneficiary that year. The other *Bizookas* continued to be loaned to stores during 1932 and 1933 but as they became more dilapidated, and the patterns on them outdated, most of them gradually disappeared. One was sent to Australia, never to return, and another languished in a storeroom at Newport, where it was not discovered until the sixties…

As Clarice became well known in London she and Colley made many friends there. Charles England ran a popular café called the Wander Inn at Church End in Finchley. He was so impressed with *Bizarre* that he styled his café around it. Customers were served from *Bon Jour* ware, *Secrets* vases were used to display flowers, and the walls were decorated with Clarice's landscapes, including *Autumn*.

The First Avenue Hotel was again the venue used for the September 1934 show. Members of the then renowned 'Crazy Gang' attended, along with Lesley Henson, Bobby Howes and Noël Coward's closest friend, the actress Gertrude Lawrence. Much coverage followed in newspapers and women's magazines, which led to a further increase in home and export sales. Between 1930 and 1934 Clarice's pottery had been regularly featured in numerous magazines: *Modern Woman, My Home, Modern Home, The Lady, Miss Modern, Town & Country Homes, Ideal Home, Woman's Pictorial, Country Life, Woman's Journal, Home Notes, The Sphere, Woman's Life,* and *Woman's Film Fair.* Many of these were also sold throughout the Empire, which had created unprecedented interest. It also led to people copying Clarice's designs and incorporating them into crafts they did at home. Details of how to stitch the *Appliqué Lucerne* design onto table napkins and a teacosy, or how to make coasters and runners in *Crocus*, appeared in magazines such as *Stitchcraft* and were the start of what later turned into a major industry in its own right.

Bizarre ware became so well known, that it was used as a way of glamourizing magazine advertising and other printed material. Knitting patterns for teacosies were displayed with *Crocus* teaware, *Latona* vases adorned expensive furniture in Harrods advertising, and a *Shredded Wheat* magazine advert featured a *Biarritz* milk jug in *Secrets*!

ABOVE: A Biarritz *milk jug/sauce boat in a* Shredded Wheat *advertisement from 1935*

By the middle of the thirties Clarice was extremely well known. A regular series in the *Sunday Express*, 'Women Who Make Money', featured her on 24 November, 1935. It began, 'Every woman who has gone through a large china shop must have seen them – dinner sets, tea sets, vases, ashtrays, of modernistic design all signed with the name *Clarice Cliff*.' It described her training and meteoric rise through the pottery industry to the role of art director. Most interestingly, it showed that she had finally lost her natural reserve, but was still self-conscious about her age. 'What is she like? Small, dark, merry, happy as a lark. She makes friends with everybody, looks at everything because she says "every person and every scene tells me something". She is aged under thirty, is unmarried and lives in Burslem.' Clarice Cliff was thirty-six when she was interviewed!

Mixing with the stars of the West End stage, Clarice was inevitably invited to dinner parties and the theatre of which she had always been fond. To save any embarrassment to their families she and Colley always kept a low profile. But one night, in trying to avoid publicity, Clarice inadvertently made herself the focus of it. Charles England from the Wander Inn organized an event at the Finchley Town Hall to raise funds for the Finchley Memorial Hospital. The glittering event was featured in the London press which reported that there was dancing to the Harold Harrison band, and a floor show that included Bryan Sydney who 'caused amusement with his tap and contortionist dances'. Clarice and Colley were there, but when recognized she attempted to remain anonymous. Mistaking this for modesty the reporter wrote, 'Miss Clarice Cliff, the famous pottery artist, who created a *Bizarre* vogue in pottery ware, was present, but unfortunately she hid her light under a bushel and preferred to remain un-identified.' A well as demonstrating Clarice's celebrity status at the time, it also showed the strength of her brand name, as it was carried under the headline 'A "Bizarre" Affair'.

THE ART OF SHAPES

oday she intended to concentrate on water-colours of different colour-ways of several of her designs, and she also wanted to do some new floral patterns. She retrieved a key from a drawer by her desk and opened the tall bookcase which held her treasured volumes on art and some gardening books Mr Colley had given her, as well as *Mobilier et Decoration*, her favourite French design magazine. Pride of place though was reserved for the folios of pochoir prints by Edouard Benedictus. She had found one in a bookshop in Essex when returning from a promotional trip to Haven's and Colley had bought the other in Paris…

She was about to get *Nouvelle Variations* down when there was a knock at the door. She shouted, 'Come in', as she locked the bookcase. She had no intention of letting her beloved books get covered in factory dust and dirt! A very tall, handsome man entered, carrying a cardboard box, 'Good morning, Clarice.'

'Good morning', she replied, in a polite but cool way. Joe Woolliscroft was one of the few people who could still get away with calling her by her first name, as he was from the same generation as Colley Shorter. They respected each other but were not overly friendly.

Joe was the most skilled modeller in the factory, and was responsible for turning the very difficult shapes she sketched on paper into real objects. Clarice did not underestimate his skills, but sometimes his first reaction was to say, 'It can't be done' which had been his response when she had first explained the idea of flat-sided dancing figures to him the previous year. This annoyed her, as almost invariably he then managed to make the shapes *exactly* as she wanted them. For his part, Joe could not understand why Mr Colley kept on giving in to the strange ideas of a woman designer! However, mindful of the fact that she was keeping him extremely busy, and he had been given a wage increase, he played along for now…

Joe pulled a glazed but undecorated figurine out of the box. 'I managed to make it in one piece, but the firing caused the square base to warp slightly. There is no problem, as long as you don't mind them being ground down.'

Clarice took the figurine and inspected it. Joe had cleverly modelled it so that the woman's beach pyjamas were continuous from the base, forming the

RIGHT: A trio of Lido Lady *ashtrays including one with* Orange Chintz *on her beach pyjamas*

ABOVE: Joe Woolliscroft, Clarice's most skilful modeller

hollow body. There was little detail about the face, but she knew this was sufficient as her 'girls' would create the lips and eyes with a single-hair brush. She always admired the quality of his modelling and warmly said, 'Well done, Joe.' He thanked her politely, but only half-smiled. He knew that Clarice could do no wrong in Mr Colley's eyes but the whole factory seemed to have been taken over by the sixty 'girls' in her decorating shop. He was determined that at least one part would remain a male preserve!

The encounter between Clarice and Joe Woolliscroft is fictional but based on fact. Only Joe had the patience and practical skills to transform some of her more challenging shapes into tangible objects. But then again, without Clarice, Joe might not have had such a secure job. The many fancies that Clarice designed between 1927 and 1936 were a defiant commercial response to the severely depressed market as most parts of the world entered a strong recession from 1926 onwards. Fancies became important after the slump in tableware sales. When America succumbed spectacularly to the recession in October 1929 with the Wall Street Crash, trade embargoes removed it from the export market overnight. Fortunately Colley Shorter had spent years building a network of overseas representatives, and all his hard work paid off. When the recession hit other Stoke factories who mainly produced tableware, they had no alternative but to cut production and staff. Colley Shorter and his company were able to ride out the recession, thanks mainly to the diversity of the product range. Clarice Cliff's *Bizarre* ware captured the imagination and attention of the public, and those who could still afford to, treated themselves or their friends to something cheerful and unusual.

The word 'tomfoolery' that Clarice had used to describe her ware was a valid one, as the sense of humour in the twenties and thirties was very different from today. What was amusing then, is not necessarily what makes us smile now. People were intrigued by her comical figurines, teapots with flat sides, ingeniously fashioned vases, and other such novelties, which were quite unlike anything they had ever seen before. Clarice Cliff's ability at creating fancies that caught the public's imagination, sprang from her own mischievous sense of humour. She and Colley Shorter shared this and it may have been this which attracted them to each other initially. Clarice created what amused her; an egg-cup set with a duck as the handle, a baby's feeding dish with the rim modelled as a cat, an ashtray with a thirties bathing belle. Whilst these items were functional, they were also *fun*. Her competitors made egg cups, baby's dishes and ashtrays, but given the choice customers generally chose Clarice's zany pieces. The bright colours and imaginative shapes were a way of at least temporarily relieving the gloom of the recession.

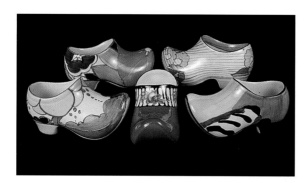

ABOVE: Sabots *in*
Gardenia *and* Capri
at the back,
Summerhouse, *a*
Wilkinson's *pre* Bizarre
*one with aerographed
and printed design, and*
Butterfly

*BELOW: An impressive
collection of* Muffineer
salt and pepper pots

When Clarice Cliff started her apprenticeship as a modeller, there were few fancies on the market. This type of ware was limited; many factories still only made the seaside novelties that harked back to Victorian days. The fancies she had inherited from Wilkinson's were mainly centrepieces for bowls, modelled as birds or animals. When she made the Louis Wain cat in a smaller size and covered it in colourful spots, she had captured the feel of her new style perfectly. She was to create a whole new market.

Clarice's fancies were initially based on the simple range that existed before she was the modeller for Wilkinson's. One shape that certainly pre-dates her is the *Sabot* which was designed to hold a single flower and had been a standard shape in the Potteries since the previous century. Clarice continued to make it for *Bizarre* ware throughout the thirties, so it is now found in many of her hand-painted designs. Previously, it was issued with one colour aerographed all over, and a simple printed design band around the rim.

The evocatively named *Muffineer* cruet set was another old shape favoured by Clarice, recalling the days of toasting muffins on a fork in a fire. The traditionally shaped salt, pepper and mustard were issued in a surprisingly large

number of designs and some collectors have concentrated on acquiring just this shape. The use of hand-painting meant that a customer could buy a tea-set, a coffee-set, vases, wall plaques and even a matching cruet. *Muffineer* cruet sets were sold in large quantities originally, but like all functional ware many became worn so mint examples now sell at a premium. Dating *Muffineer* pieces is difficult as they often have no backstamp, or only part of it because of the small base area. *Muffineers* were produced from 1927 to 1937 and can be found in almost all of Clarice's designs, except the prestigious *Latona*

ABOVE: A collection of Clarice Cliff jug shapes: a Perth *jug in* Sunray, *a* Crown *in* Red Tulip *and* Coronet *in* Moonlight. (*In front*) *an* Athens *in* Floreat, *a* Stamford *in* Sunburst *and a* Bon Jour *in* Lydiat

and *Inspiration* ranges. Other *Bizarre* cruets included her *Cock a Doodle Doo* cruet with salt and pepper chicks, a chick emerging from an egg as the mustard, and these stood on a tray, the handle of which was the mother hen!

Clarice created many jug shapes from the late twenties into the early thirties. The reason for this was mainly commercial; vessels with handles attracted less tax than vases, as they were classed as functional. This explains why some of her jugs are so colourful; they were sold as flower holders and not as kitchen items. These *Flower Jugs* as she called them had the advantage that the handle made them easier to carry when full of flowers. The traditional jug shapes produced before *Bizarre* ware, *Perth*, *Coronet* and *Athens*, were probably Clarice's work when she was a modeller. From 1929 she was free to add jugs in her *Bizarre* style: the tall *Conical* jug in 1929 was based on the coffee-pot, the *Stamford* jug in 1930 was a larger version of the teapot shape, and a stylish oval *Bon Jour* jug was based on the coffee-pot issued in 1933.

Clarice's incredible shape output is even larger than shown in the original factory shape sheets in the *Bizarre Index*. Research by Gordon and Irene Hopwood, in their book on *The Shorter Connection,* suggests that not only were some of her Newport Pottery shapes issued in Shorter's Aura glaze, but a series of modern vases from this period, including *Rhomboid*, *Thisbe* and *Pyramus*, were possibly her work. In the mid-thirties the modelling at the factory was the work of their own designer Mabel Leigh, but Clarice then seems to have been involved in creating the famous Gilbert and Sullivan figurines in 1940 which were mainly marketed after the war.

Clarice constantly returned to modelling figures throughout the thirties and in 1931 revived the style of her mid-twenties hand-made figures with the *Impressions* series. The press release that accompanied the picture of a group of these again reveals the influence of Colley Shorter. 'Clay Impressions *Bizarre* ware by Clarice Cliff constitute an endless variety of rough modelled clay impressions, full of humour and imagination, all done by hand without

BELOW: An Impressions *figure*

any mould whatsoever. Even the most humorous in many cases are beautiful, by reason of the range of colour glazes they are finished in. They rival many of the Chinese types and are fit for cabinet collection.' These now rare figures can be distinguished from the mid-twenties ones, as they are marked *Impressions Bizarre*.

One of the most popular pieces in Clarice's *Conical* range was issued in August 1931. The use of a pure cone shape as a sugar dredger did not occur until this time, even though the *Conical* concept had been introduced in April 1929. The *Conical* sugar dredger proved an ideal shape for her designs and became a popular addition to the thirties breakfast table, despite the pointed tip being rather susceptible to damage. The fact that so many examples have survived shows the vast quantities they were originally produced in. As they were not issued until two years after the original *Conical* series, dredgers are rarely found in earlier patterns, most are in 1931 to 1936 designs. Slightly earlier ones such as *Trees and House* are known from a few examples, and just two *Summerhouse Conical* dredgers are known. Most dredgers have banding

BELOW: A collection of Conical sugar dredgers in Chintz Green, Oranges, Xavier, Gibraltar, Alton Green, Coral Firs, Oranges and Lemons, Red Tulip and Poplar

at the top and the bottom, but occasionally the pattern covers the whole piece such as on the *Chintz* design, or on *Gibraltar* where the yellow clouds cover the pointed top. This shape was so popular that at one stage the factory supplied them in dozens just as '*Fantasque* assorted' which explains why the shape is found in many designs. All this has helped make the 489 *Conical* dredger one of the most collectable Clarice Cliff shapes.

In the second half of the nineties *Conical* sugar dredgers became one of Clarice's most collectable shapes, and in 1996 several broke the £2000 barrier at auction, an astounding price for something just five inches high designed to sprinkle sugar! *Conicals* also seem to break many of the 'price rules', as some designs, perceived as being less desirable on more common shapes, fetch higher prices when found on a dredger.

The colour advertising photograph taken by Clarice Cliff in 1931 gives an idea of the strength of her ranges both in their design and shapes. A selection of *Fantasque* and *Café-au-lait* in a stunning array of shapes must have been an unequalled sight at trade fairs! The photograph includes her space age *Stamford* bowl shape 441 in *Chintz Orange*, the extremely Cubist shape 461 vase in *Café-au-lait Autumn* and the matching bowl shape 515 in *Mango*. Such archive sources also show that there are still treasures to be discovered. The *Café* shape 460 vase at bottom right is a combination of design and shape *still* not known. These pieces are called 'Clarice Cliff time bombs' by collectors and the anticipation of their eventual appearance is yet another aspect which makes collecting Clarice Cliff so appealing.

By 1931 Clarice was devising her new shapes to be more functional, so that even her fancies would appeal to a larger market. In an interview in the *Bristol Times* in September she stated:

I know that women today like to strike an individual note in their homes. So it has been my aim to devise pottery that will help them to realize their ideal. At the same time I am aware that in these times of money scarcity articles that have a useful as well as a decorative purpose have a more general appeal.

Britain in the thirties was very different from twenty years earlier. After the war few people could still afford servants, and a new generation of women

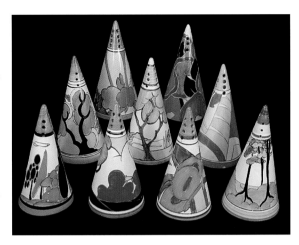

ABOVE: A collection of Conical *sugar dredgers in* Fruitburst, Chintz Orange, Green Erin, Gloria Tree, Xanthic, Trees and House Autumn, Bobbins *and* Blue Firs

BELOW: Clarice Cliff took her own advertising photographs in colour by 1931, such as this group of Fantasque *and* Café-au-lait *ware*

found themselves as 'housewives'. But, the middle and upper class customers Clarice sought to attract did not want to be tied to the kitchen, and Clarice reflected this by producing ware that was more functional. In doing this she was the first Staffordshire designer to issue streamlined shapes. Her close association with humorous fancies and Art Deco shapes has led to her innovation in this area almost being overlooked, but she knew precisely why functional ware was important as witnessed by her comments in a 1931 interview:

Labour-saving is another important factor I have taken into consideration. I am showing this year several things made in pottery for which this medium has never been used before, designed on lines that simplify its cleaning. There are no corners or flutings to harbour dust and grease. Many table accessories that have previously been made of metal I have designed to match the breakfast or dinner set with which they are used. Centre pieces for flowers, cruets, egg stands, and bon bon dishes are some of them. A novelty for the dinner table is a tray holding a box with a lid, for cigarettes, a match container and half a dozen ashtrays, piled one on the other. I am now introducing in vegetable dishes, a niche in which the serving spoon can rest without disturbing the lid.

It is impossible to chart each of Clarice's amazing fancies as between 1927 and 1939 over 100 novelty shapes appeared. However, the enthusiasm of collectors now means some seek just one Clarice Cliff shape. Inevitably this interest, even in smaller items, raises prices. One such piece is the very desirable *Beehive* honeypot, designed by Clarice in 1927 and found in most

RIGHT: A collection of Beehive *honey pots in two sizes. (Back row) in* Coral Firs, House and Bridge, Amberose, *(middle)* Fragrance, Delecia Pansies, Sungold, Nuage, *(front)* Tulip, Liberty *and* Chintz Blue

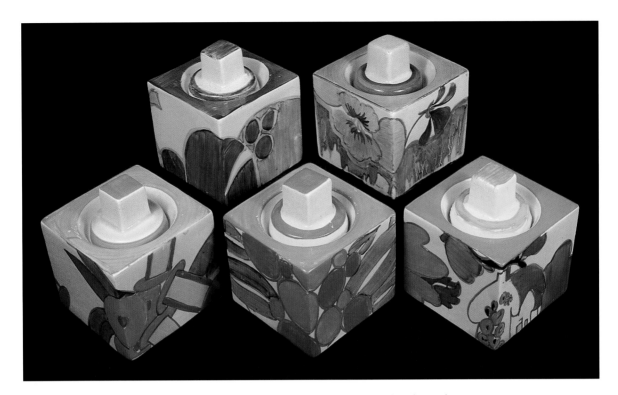

patterns from the following ten years. With a colourful bee as the knob, and a small 'door' on the side into the hive, it made a charming and functional gift. It provides further proof that by not taking her work too seriously Clarice produced very commercial ware!

The shape 458 *Inkwell* was another Cliff innovation. Introduced in 1931 this simple cube was immediately issued in many designs, but sadly the small neat lids are nearly always missing or damaged, so perfect examples are highly desirable. Even on these diminutive pieces Clarice's decorators skilfully painted large parts of the designs. The *Pastel Melon* on the back row has just a 'slice' of the design, but the *Red Roofs* is particularly clever as it has the whole design on just two sides. Amazingly the *Delecia Pansies* manages to combine the flowers complete with the 'runnings' within its two-inch height. The 458 *Inkwell* was developed into the equally stylish *Double Ink*, shape 462, which has two cubes of slightly different heights with a pen tray in front.

The cube-shaped inkwells inspired one of Clarice's most fantastic fancies. This consisted of a set of semi-circular flower troughs, square-section flower troughs, and cube-shaped candlesticks. The set comprised eight pieces which could be arranged in numerous ways as the centre-piece for a party

ABOVE: Shape 458 Inkwells *in* Pastel Melon *and* Delecia Pansies, *and in the front row* Bobbins, Berries *and* Red Roofs

BELOW: The original leaflet showing an arrangement of the As You Like It *set*

table. Using flowers and candles it was possible to create a different display for each occasion. A leaflet illustrating the set showed that Clarice's decorators had cleverly painted the *Blue Firs* landscape on to each piece, so that it formed a continuous landscape! The set was perhaps inspired by children's building bricks and was in a way a novel 'adult toy'. The concept is still utterly modern, yet Clarice thought of it in 1931. Her name for the set is further proof of her imaginative approach to ceramics; she called it an *As You Like It!*

Controlling both the shape and design output of Newport Pottery Clarice was able to mix and match any shape with any pattern she wished. This occasionally resulted in masks or figurines being covered in all-over patterns. The *Lido Lady* ashtray with *Chintz* patterned trousers is a modest example compared to what she did to the *Arab boy* candlesticks. These have been 'dressed' in several landscapes including *Secrets*! The tree covers his shoulders, the cottages decorate the baggy trousers, and he is standing in the estuary! This rare fancy has also been seen decorated in *Rhodanthe*, *Moonlight* and *Honolulu*.

By 1932, reorganization at Newport Pottery meant the glost warehouse was centralized at Wilkinson's so Clarice's shapes awaiting decoration were stored alongside those from Wilkinson's. They had already started using Clarice's shapes for patterns not designed by her, which enabled them to sell modern ware in a cheaper price range than *Bizarre*. The pieces only bore Wilkinson's backstamps but nowadays some dealers try to convince collectors that they are 'unmarked Clarice Cliff'!

It is impossible to illustrate all the shapes issued between 1927 and 1936 but the original shape sheets reproduced in the *Bizarre Index* give an idea of how vast Clarice's range was. The appeal also lay in the fact that theoretically *any* shape could be offered in any design. This resulted in pieces such as the shape 420 *Cigarette and Ashtray* in *Nuage Bouquet*, a pedestal dish from an *Almond* set in *Propeller* and a *Daffodil* shape jampot in *Alton*. The square shape 556 napkin ring was generally sold boxed in sets of four but if you wanted something more amusing there was always *Bubbles the Elephant Napkin Ring*! Amazingly, a five-bar toast rack had the *Chalet* design painted *between* the bars! The shape 463 *Cigarette and Match Holder* consisted of two semi-circular containers back to back which Clarice based on a shape made in metal and glass in 1905 by Josef Hoffmann for the *Wiener Werkstätte*. It is remarkable that she was aware of such work in 1931, but it demonstrates her extensive knowledge of design. The shape 463 was just one of many smokers' accoutrements, which was a large market at the time.

Clarice took great care modelling even her smallest items, and simple cruet sets became works of art. In the mid-twenties she had produced a peg doll shape, which was initially just covered in bright banding, but these were revived for the Joan Shorter ware. Her *Shell* cruet sets from 1931 were designed so that each place-setting at a dinner party had its own cruet. The *Conical* cruet evolved from the *Conical* sugar dredger in 1932 and the *Bon Jour* cruet utilized the round and oval shapes of *Bon Jour* ware. Even on the smallest items the design was painted in miniature, showing the lengths to which Clarice went to customize such pieces. Later cruets were modelled as comic fish and cartoon-style rabbits. These generally have just a Wilkinson mark but were still probably Clarice's work, or produced under her supervision.

During the *Bizarre* years many striking new styles appeared in quick succession. The 1929 *Conical* included dozens of shapes based on the theme,

BELOW: A selection of cruet shapes: Peg doll, Shell, Conical *and* Bon Jour

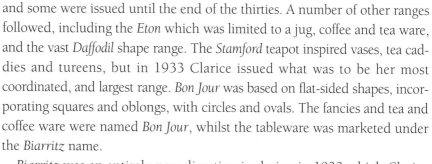

ABOVE: The Biarritz *backstamp is found both with and without Clarice Cliff markings, as Wilkinson's also produced designs for this shape range*

BELOW: Honolulu *on a* Biarritz *plate and an* Arab boy *candlestick*

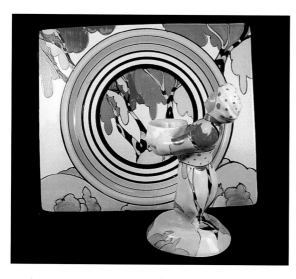

and some were issued until the end of the thirties. A number of other ranges followed, including the *Eton* which was limited to a jug, coffee and tea ware, and the vast *Daffodil* shape range. The *Stamford* teapot inspired vases, tea caddies and tureens, but in 1933 Clarice issued what was to be her most coordinated, and largest range. *Bon Jour* was based on flat-sided shapes, incorporating squares and oblongs, with circles and ovals. The fancies and tea and coffee ware were named *Bon Jour*, whilst the tableware was marketed under the *Biarritz* name.

Biarritz was an entirely new direction in design in 1933 which Clarice pioneered spontaneously from the geometric shapes. Her design skills were finely honed by this time, and these flat-sided shapes, while still presenting casting and firing problems, could be produced in bulk. *Bon Jour* and *Biarritz* instantly became her best-selling shapes, and the *Biarritz* plate helped re-establish the factory in the North American market which was recovering in the mid-thirties. To spread the tax load, Colley Shorter registered *Biarritz* as a Wilkinson's *Royal Staffordshire* product, and every piece had this added underglaze. Pieces lacking the on-glaze *Bizarre* backstamp, are probably decorated with Wilkinson's patterns as the shape was so popular that Wilkinson's also used it for less expensive tableware. At one stage retailers ordered *Biarritz* ware undecorated just to ensure deliveries arrived in time for busy selling seasons.

The *Biarritz* plates were primarily functional tableware, but Clarice also used them as fancies, covered in her bright, all-over patterns. In this oblong format, the plate was literally a 'ceramic canvas', upon which her decorators were the artists. This was hand-painted ware in its nearest form to art. Fully decorated *Biarritz* plates are most commonly found in *Coral Firs*, *Honolulu*, *Moonlight*, *Rhodanthe* and their alternate colourways, but theoretically any post-1933 design might be found, and matchings in the 1931 *Autumn* design are known.

The *Biarritz Honolulu* plate shows how cleverly Clarice's banders and liners adapted the new shape by creating jazzy banding sequences in the shallow circular well, with the design featured either side. The *Arab boy* candlestick demonstrates how Clarice coordinated her newest shapes and some of her older ones into a cohesive range in 1933. One can only fantasize how striking a table full of *Bizarre* and *Bon Jour* ware in *Honolulu* might look!

The success of *Bon Jour* ware encouraged Clarice to create some exciting new shapes to enlarge the range. A variety of round and oval vases were made,

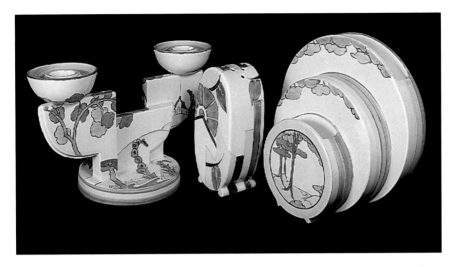

LEFT: *A* Bon Jour *double candlestick in* Bridgwater Green, *a* Bon Jour *sugar dredger in* Moonflower Blue *and a shape 647–3* Triple Bon Jour *in* Coral Firs

including the *Triple Bon Jour*, shape 647–3, shown in *Coral Firs*. This was made by joining together the single vase *Bon Jour* vase, shape 647–1, and the double, shape 647–2. Sadly, these wonderful shapes were technically demanding so were expensive originally and are now hard to find. The *Bon Jour* candlestick was a technical masterpiece as it was cast as a one-piece mould, apart from the sconces which were attached at the green clay state. Clarice's paintresses adapted the design to flow up the sides, so the quality of their work was taken to new levels. It is easy to forget that Clarice intended her pottery to be functional, and in use many of these had their sconces broken off and simply stuck back on, so collectors should not be too fussy about such rarities being perfect!

The sugar dredger from the *Bon Jour* range 'escaped' and became popular as a single piece, and thousands were bought as presents. It initially sold alongside the *Conical* dredger from 1933 and was then produced until 1939. The shape actually displays the patterns more fully than the *Conical* but despite this has proved more affordable.

The quantity and diversity of designs *Bon Jour* dredgers are found in is clear from the groups shown, which date mainly from 1933 or 1934. Some of Clarice's earlier patterns were produced on the shape such as the 1932 *Citrus Delecia* example on the back row of the first group. Abstract designs were few by 1934 so the example in *Xavier* in the front row is a rarity. The latest pattern shown in the group is the central one in *Brookfields*, a full rural landscape in natural colours. This design is covered with fine concentric lines and to produce these the bander had to lay the piece flat on their wheel, centralize it, and then carefully apply

BELOW: Bon Jour *sugar dredgers in* Delecia Citrus, Spring Crocus, Solitude, Brookfields, Coral Firs, Bridgwater, Xavier, Windbells *and* Honolulu

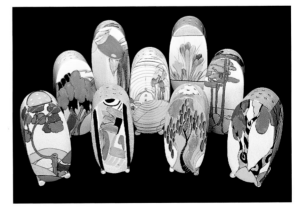

ABOVE: Bon Jour *sugar dredgers in* Viscaria, Fragrance, Blue Crocus, Forest Glen, Idyll, Delecia Pansies, Moonlight, Canterbury Bells *and* Green Erin

BELOW: An extensive range of Bizarre *ware from 1934*

the brush in ever-larger circles – an ultimate test of the bander's skill!

The second group of *Bon Jour* dredgers includes the central example in *Idyll*, a design first issued as part of the *Appliqué* range but then moved to *Fantasque* so this is a very early pattern to find on the shape. The *Blue Crocus* example is from late 1935 and is a rarity. The *Forest Glen* dates from the same period and is one of the last really outrageous patterns Clarice made. It was produced over the period when the *Bizarre* tradename was dropped, as recounted in the *Goodbye Bizarre* chapter.

The amazing diversity in the techniques used to produce *Bizarre* ware is demonstrated in the advertising photograph taken in 1934 (below left), which includes ware covering a range of bodies and finishes. The standard hand-painted ware is represented by the *Appliqué Idyll* plates. The *Lynton* shape ware is in the mottled *Goldstone* body, designed to offer a more rustic look of hand-thrown pottery, in the style of village crafts. In sophisticated contrast, the later *Conical* bowls and vases, and the *Daffodil* ware, is aerographed with single colours against a plain edge. The fancies include the *Arab boy* candlesticks, still popular seven years after their launch, a highly modelled *Peg Doll* baby dish, and a *Flora* wallmask in *Goldstone* with bright enamelling. The cosy, brightly coloured, *My Garden* oblong wall plaque, contrasts sharply with the very plain *Milano* ware vase in stark black and yellow, which Clarice probably based on the plain grooved earthenware shapes Keith Murray had designed for Wedgwood in 1933. The smallest items include the *Elephant* and square shape 556 serviette rings, small decorative bird figures and even a *United Services* cruet set. The photograph demonstrates beyond doubt that Clarice was *the* most prolific designer of shapes in the Potteries in the mid-thirties!

Clarice's gift for creating unrivalled shapes was perhaps best expressed in the 464 *Flower Tube* vase. Today, we are used to seeing glass tubes designed to hold a single stem, but Clarice was very advanced when she created this impressive shape in 1931. The 'S' shape fins support the tube and her decorators spread the design lavishly over them. The *Solitude* 464 has the mysterious coral red 'bridge' beautifully

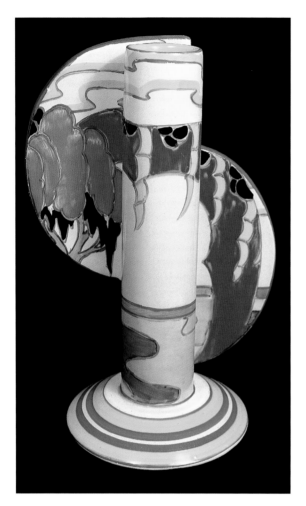
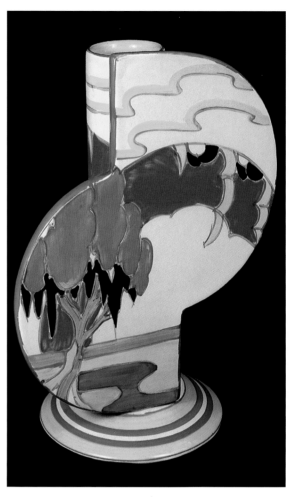

following the curve of the flat-sided fins. The vase is just as imaginatively painted on the reverse. Never one to be content with her own creativity, Clarice used lateral thinking to create the shape 465 vase which had a tube *both* sides!

Clarice Cliff was so productive that it is just not possible to detail her full output of shapes, but a selection of other shapes is shown in the *Bizarre Index*. She did not have a serious competitor, as her teapots, sugar dredgers, inkwells, flower jugs and even cruet sets, were all distinguished by the ingenuity of their design. The catalogues of other Staffordshire factories confirm that none of them created such individual ware. There are three prime reasons why she was to dominate the market from 1927 to 1936: she dared to be different, she had a unique and diverse product range and Colley Shorter's promotional skills. It is easy to see how together they led the market.

ABOVE LEFT: *The front of a* Flower Tube *shape 464 vase in* Solitude

ABOVE RIGHT: *The back of the* Solitude *vase*

CLIFF FACES

BELOW: Grotesque facemasks in bright enamel colours, the central one is in a Clouvre glaze finish

ashions in clothing, music and entertainment had all changed dramatically after the First World War. The advent of the motor car, talking pictures and the wireless had made Britain a very different place to live. Despite the strikes of 1926 and the recession of 1929, which almost crippled the country, life had undergone a revolution in many ways. *Bizarre* ware, with its gaudy colours, novel shapes and humorous ideas, was a reflection of that revolution in ceramics.

One of Clarice Cliff's most singular achievements was her ability to sell decorative fancies in the middle of the Depression. At a time when one might have expected the market for these to have been very small, she was producing ever more fanciful objects. Most notable was her series of stylish wall masks issued from 1929, and wall pockets from the mid-thirties. The wall masks were purely decorative, so the fact that she issued over twenty in all shows how intensely she cultivated the market for ceramics. Other Stoke factories issued these as the fashion for them reached a peak in the thirties but, whereas Clarice's were mainly of stylish women, the main subject matter of her competitors was of animals or birds.

ABOVE: The Chahar *mask*

Her earliest mask, *Chahar*, dates from 1929. It was initially marketed along-side the *Archaic* ware as described in the *Birth of Bizarre* chapter. The *Chahar* image was based on part of a column decoration in the Owen Jones book *Grammar of Ornament* and was skilfully modelled in bold relief, being an impressive eleven inches high. Whereas *Archaic* ware was produced for less than a year, *Chahar* was issued until at least 1933. Although many of Clarice's fancies were offered in a variety of colourways, *Chahar* is reasonably consistent, most examples having dominant coral, jade and yellow.

Grotesque was the next mask issued by Clarice's factory. This magnificent piece seems to have been inspired more by Italian than Egyptian art. It resembles the stone gargoyles used to decorate medieval gardens in certain parts of Italy. Although it was marketed as Clarice Cliff ware, it was designed by a young apprentice at the factory, Ron Birks, under Clarice's supervision. Born in 1906, Ron was the son of Lawrence Birks, who had worked at Minton with Louis Marc Solon on *pâte-sur-pâte* ware, and then established Birks & Co in 1895. Ron worked briefly at his father's factory and then joined Wilkinson's as an apprentice, studying modelling and hand-painting under Clarice. He produced two hand-painted designs featuring images of art and industry but these were exercise pieces never commercially sold. Ron left to re-join Birks Rawlins but when it was absorbed by the makers of Carlton ware he returned to the export department at Newport and strangely was never to design again.

BELOW: Ron Birks with his wife in 1935

The *Grotesque* mask appeared at the same time as the *Inspiration* range in 1929 and it was first issued in the vibrant blue *Inspiration* glazes. Many examples were then produced with just two or three bold enamel colours emphasizing the Cubist features. The most outrageous early version known featured an actual *Fantasque* pattern, *Broth*, covering the whole mask. Clarice

RIGHT: The Marlene *mask*

paid royalties on the shape to Ron, and the early batches also included his initials impressed on the edge.

The next mask Clarice issued was perhaps the most successful. *Marlene* appeared in 1931, clearly inspired by Marlene Dietrich whose 1930 film *The Blue Angel* had made her an international star. *Marlene* wears an elaborate Art Deco style head-dress and large pendent ear rings and these were painted in many different ways, early examples being brightly coloured but by 1934 in more subdued pastel shades. *Marlene* was very popular and remained in production in the late thirties.

Marilyn, a rare facemask from the early thirties, was made under Clarice's supervision by Esme Bailey, the daughter of a major *Bizarre* ware stockist. Sydney Bailey ran Hardware Bristol supplying stores in the south-west of England. Esme was a student at the West of England Academy in Bristol and was just eighteen when her father took her to Newport and was rather surprised by the condition of the works.

Colley Shorter showed us the bottle ovens, and the kilns, and then we were taken into the studio of the designer Clarice Cliff and introduced; Clarice was small and vivacious, very friendly. We then went into the decorating shop, where the girl artists sat in a big room. Clarice gave me a lump of clay, sat me at a bench, and said that since I was a student I could make something! My father went off with Clarice and Colley for a business lunch, and I sat there and decided that since masks were very fashionable I would model some.

Esme spent several days in Stoke and divided her time between the *Bizarre* shop and seeing the annual display of lights along the sea front in Blackpool. When she left she had completed a mask of 'a flapper with Marlene Dietrich eyebrows, kiss curls, and big earrings, and pouty lips'. Her mask resembled *Marlene*, which she had presumably seen in her father's shop or the factory showroom. Just a few months later a package arrived at the family's home of four masks, with 'designed by Esme M. Bailey' printed by the *Bizarre* backstamp. *Marilyn* was sold alongside *Marlene* and *Chahar* but produced in smaller quantities and phased out by 1937. Esme did not pursue a career as a designer but kept in touch with Clarice and Colley, and when she married in 1936 their wedding present to her was a complete, monogrammed, *Biarritz* dinner service.

ABOVE: Esme Bailey and fellow students aboard a Viking boat in a charity parade on the river

The fact that Clarice credited Esme Bailey and Ron Birks on the pieces they designed illustrates that as early as 1931 she realized that her role as art director was to cultivate the skills of her workers. This obviously contradicts later claims by academics that she plagiarized other people's work.

Clarice's next facemask was inspired by her love of flowers. *Flora* featured a young woman's face wreathed in a floral headdress of densely modelled daisies, asters and bell-shaped flowers. *Flora* was issued in a wide choice of colourings, so customers could select bright or pastel shades. Two sizes were made, the smaller was seven inches high and cost just three shillings and sixpence, but the fourteen-inch size was fifteen shillings, the price of a basic *Early Morning* set! *Flora* proved as popular as *Marlene* had done.

BELOW: The Marilyn *mask*

Clarice continued to issue new masks every year and the next, *Pan*, featured a youthful face with pointed ears, and the hair garlanded with flowers. As well as a wall mask, a wall pocket version was made which could be used to display dried flowers or filled with water to hold fresh flowers. This represented a trend towards more functional pieces and Clarice capitalized on it by then issuing *Marlene* and *Flora* as wall pockets.

In 1933 Clarice designed a pair of facemasks of chubby-faced cherubs called *Jack* and *Jill*, but these only sold in limited quantities. The most distinctive facemasks that year were some extraordinary examples of the *Grotesque* mask painted in *Fantasque* landscapes! The pattern *Secrets Orange* was boldly painted right across the whole mask. The smoke from the chimney crossed the eye-holes, and the rest of the landscape covered the angular features. This, and an example in *Honolulu* were exported to a South African stockist. They were probably too *Bizarre* even for Clarice to seriously think that they would sell in any quantity. In all probability she combined the amazing shape with her vivid landscapes as an eye catching way to draw attention to her more functional ware.

As fashions changed during the thirties Clarice responded to the market by introducing some smaller masks which had holes in the top so that they could also be used as ceramic pendants. The range was quite large and as well as honeyglaze were available in new tinted glazes, a pale copper glaze, and also a matt mushroom glaze. At least eight different faces were made and being of a similar size they form a collectable group.

BELOW: A Grotesque *mask in* Secrets Orange *from 1933*

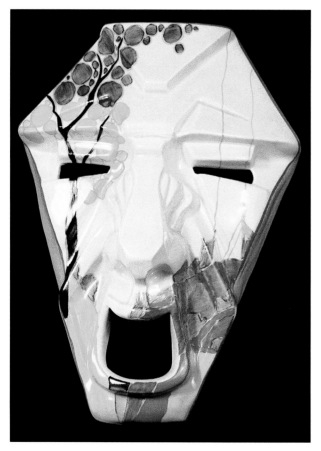

Bizarre 'girl' Doris Johnson recalled that Clarice used paintress Ivy Tunicliff as her subject for a mask which featured a woman with a flower in her long hair and a hand next to her face. The names Clarice gave these masks are not known, so as Ivy modelled for this one we have named it after her, and to help classification the later masks have now been given the names of *Bizarre* 'girls'. The other masks in the range are similar and feature a variety of heads from various angles with ribbons, scarves or hats as their only decoration. As several masks have the same shape number, 787, they may have been sold in small sets.

The next masks were modelled under Clarice's supervision by a student that she had discovered at the local Burslem School of Art. Peggy Davies joined Newport on a three year apprenticeship in the middle of 1936 and worked alongside the *Bizarre* 'girls' as a trainee modeller. She learned her trade from Clarice in the same way that Clarice had worked under John Butler ten years earlier. Peggy was initially involved in modelling the flowers on the later examples of *My Garden* ware. In 1938 Clarice

asked Peggy to devise a range of masks representing different nationalities. The *Heads of Nations* series featured a Japanese beauty with a pagoda-shaped hat, a Dutch girl, Cleopatra, an Indian squaw and an Eastern maiden with an elaborate head-dress. These were only produced briefly and are now quite rare. However, they are of particular interest, as after her three year apprenticeship with Clarice, Peggy Davies eventually joined Doulton, where she trained under the famous Charles Nokes. After the war she became one of their premier modellers, with over 250 figurines to her credit. As fashions changed in the late thirties, the items issued by Newport Pottery were more traditional and included the *Bluebird* wall pocket, the very plain *Shell* wall-pocket and *Lady Anne*, an eighteenth-century woman amidst trees.

Clarice Cliff's facemasks represent a significant part of her output and none of her competitors issued them in any quantity or with the same style. They were her innovative response to the market for Moderne fancies, and trying to collect all of them presents a real challenge to collectors who appreciate ceramics in a true British thirties style!

ABOVE: A beauty pageant of Clarice's facemasks: (top) Sadie, Cleopatra, Ellen, Vera, Dutch Girl, *(bottom)* Peggy, Clara, *and* Ivy

TAKING TEA AND COFFEE

In the book *Taking Tea with Clarice Cliff* we showed that Clarice Cliff was the first woman to design teapot shapes. She was amazingly prolific as between 1927 and 1939 over twenty shapes appeared! When you include her surprisingly different coffee-pot shapes from the same period you appreciate how talented she was.

The full impact of her original shapes is not apparent until we review the traditional shapes she inherited. Newport and Wilkinson's had just two teapot shapes before 1928, the *Globe*, a traditional Staffordshire teapot, and the *Athens*, a faceted six-sided shape with elaborate handle and spout, based on old silver teapots. Amazingly, the early *Bizarre* designs were rather incongruously first issued on these, but because the designs are so stunning we notice the pattern more than the shape. The *Athens* teapot pictured is in *Sunburst*, a 1929 pattern which developed the simple triangles of *Original Bizarre*. It shows how quickly the designs evolved, and the harmonizing colours are a great deal more sophisticated. The *Athens* and *Globe* teapots continued in production for most of the thirties as many customers preferred *Bizarre* patterns on more traditional shapes. Today, the contradictory amalgamation of shape and design is yet another curiously appealing aspect of Clarice Cliff's output.

BELOW: An Athens *teapot and a plate in* Sunburst

The *Conical* teapot was designed by Clarice shortly after she created her innovative *Conical* bowl. She realized that a market keen to buy modern shapes in bowls and vases would certainly be stimulated by a new teapot shape. When it appeared in July 1929 the solid triangular handle, pyramid-shaped spout, and square flat knob, created a mass of interest. Within months it was a fashionable wedding or anniversary present amongst the 'bright young things'. Clarice was the first designer to issue such an original shape in Britain with the result that features about the new style began to appear in women's magazines, and

sales increased dramatically. A few *Conical* tea-sets were issued in simple partial designs but almost immediately, in what was to become the true spirit of *Bizarre*, she covered them with lashings of colour! Many of the *Fantasque* designs were put on *Conical* teaware, and an unusual colourway of *Umbrellas* is shown. At the same time Clarice was equally happy to put *Fantasque Pebbles* on the *Globe* shape teapot.

Copying shapes from other factories was rife in the Potteries and inevitably similar products soon appeared. In 1930 Eric Slater at Shelley Potteries used the *Conical* concept for his *Mode* and *Vogue* tea and coffee ware which featured solid triangular handles and a similar teapot. Concerned, Colley Shorter quickly registered the *Conical* teapot to stop further copies. In later years Clarice herself recalled: 'We were copied by so many that we eventually had to patent many shapes. Even the Japanese copied some!'

As the principal market in Britain and its empire was for teaware Clarice only inherited one coffee-pot shape when she launched *Bizarre*. The *Tankard* was a tall cylindrical coffee-pot with a long spout and functional but ungainly handle, sold with small coffee cans with loop handles. In 1929 Clarice designed a *Conical* coffee-pot to replace the *Tankard*, but the solid handle was

ABOVE: A selection of teapot shapes: (back) Conical *in* Umbrellas, Globe *in* Pebbles, Conical *in* Delecia Citrus, *(front)* Stamford *in* Circle Tree, *the large size* Stamford *in* Gloria Trees *and a* Stamford *in* House and Bridge

totally impractical to hold when the pot was full of hot coffee so it was withdrawn and in March 1930 a version with an open triangular handle appeared. This was initially sold with the small milk and sugar from the *Conical* teaware, teamed with the traditional coffee cans but the *Conical* coffee cans, with solid triangular handles, soon appeared. The set looked particularly striking when combined with the very modern patterns. *Conical* coffee-pots were made in two sizes, and the sets were issued until around 1936. Clarice always found innovative ways to market ware and the coffee-pot was also sold with two cups as a cocoa set!

An early *Conical* coffee set, with solid triangular handles on the cans, is illustrated in *Umbrellas*. This pattern was unusual as it was outlined in green, and the stark black, red and blue gives a very Art Deco effect. Clarice lightened the intense pattern by using her vivid egg yellow in the banding. The plate was not part of the set but customers could buy any extra items they wished to make a fuller set.

In 1930, just a year after her *Conical* teapot, Clarice introduced the flat sided, 'D' shaped *Stamford* teapot. Few Staffordshire factories would have attempted to produce a teapot with so many square edges and flat sides, and

ABOVE: A Tankard shape coffee, milk and sugar in Apples

RIGHT: A Conical *coffee-set and plate in* Umbrellas Coral

even Clarice's skilled technical staff found it hard to make at first. The set was completed with a matching milk and sugar, and *Conical* cups and saucers. Clarice based the *Stamford* closely on a silver Art Deco teapot designed by Tétard Frères of Paris, and this fact has attracted criticism from some academics who have implied from this example that she had few original ideas. On the contrary, the vast majority of her shapes were original and she was certainly not guilty of plagiarism as there had been a long tradition in the Potteries of basing ceramic shapes on pieces originally made in silver. In the previous century this had led to the 'Queen Anne' style teapots, and ceramic copies of silver tureens and candlesticks. Clarice was simply following in the footsteps of this strong tradition.

The *Stamford* set was an instant success when launched alongside the *Age of Jazz* figures in September 1930. The full *Early Morning* set shown in the *Poplar* design dates from the following year and is a rarity. *Poplar* was one of the few landscapes issued under the *Bizarre* backstamp.

It is hard to assess which was Clarice's best-selling teaware shape at this time, as because of their solid handles many of the *Conical* teapots were dropped when full of tea, so more *Stamford* teapots have survived. The other indication of relative popularity is that the *Conical* was issued in three sizes, for two, four and six cups, whilst the *Stamford* was just issued in two and six cup sizes.

ABOVE: A 1931 Bizarre ware advertisement with a Stamford *teapot,* Angel Fish *flower holder and* Bignou *teaware*

BELOW: A complete Stamford Early Morning *set in* Poplar

RIGHT: An Eton *teapot in* Solitude *and an Eton coffee-pot in* Circle Tree

The key to Clarice's success was not just the innovative shapes but her understanding of the market. All factories produced six-person tea sets, but in the 'new world' of the thirties young couples did not need full sets. They also wanted something a little cheerier than the chintzy china their parents treasured. Clarice spearheaded what became a trend for smaller sets with just two cups and saucers. These *Early Morning* sets were for a couple to have tea in bed before starting the day, and later they were promoted as 'afternoon sets' for housewives to serve tea when a friend called.

The *Stamford* teapot was clearly a remarkable piece and attracted publicity in all the countries to which it was exported. In Western Australia Caris Brothers stocked the *Stamford* teaware in Clarice's matt glaze *Gloria* ware. Their advertisement prophetically said:

There is nothing more typical of this age of simplicity in design than Clarice Cliff's work, and it is safe to say that early twentieth century design will be inseparably associated in the minds of collectors of the future with the name of Clarice Cliff

Although the demand for the *Conical* and *Stamford* ranges was strong, Clarice designed yet another innovative teapot in 1930, the *Eton*. The cylindrical body had an angular handle, diamond-shaped in cross-section, which perfectly balanced the spout, and was capped with a square lid inspired by a mortar board, hence the name. Just three shapes were made, a teapot, a coffee-pot and a jug, and sets were completed with *Conical* ware pieces. The actual shape was well ahead of its time as the tall *Eton* coffee-pot is a forerunner of today's typical electric kettle shape. Clarice's customers already

had a choice of *Stamford* or *Conical* ware so few sets were produced. An *Eton* coffee-pot is shown decorated in the *Circle Tree* design. The combination of pattern with shape makes it a perfect example of functional everyday art, as this 1929 design is reminiscent of paintings by Sonia and Robert Delaunay which Clarice would almost certainly have been aware. A detail which makes this piece even more collectable is that whereas most examples have just colour on the lid, this is decorated with the full pattern!

ABOVE: Conical *coffee ware in* Circle Tree

Eton shape ware was issued until as late as 1937 but only in small quantities.

The representative parts of a *Conical* coffee-set in *Circle Tree* show that it is impossible to separate shape from pattern completely. The design looks very different when executed on other shapes. The *Conical* coffee-pot has a narrow area of design with broad yellow banding, so even though it might have been painted by the same decorators the shape dictates the use of the pattern. The milk jug in this set is the second version which replaced the original, rather impractical footed milk jug in both the tea- and coffee-sets. The *Conical* coffee-pot was also marketed with two beakers and a tray as a 'milk or hot lemonade set'.

Clarice's paintresses needed a great deal of patience to decorate these sets. Outliner Rene Dale recalled that each shape required the pattern to be adjusted to fit in a different way.

When we did tea sets, we had to reduce the pattern to squeeze it on the cups. You did so many teapots, so many sugars, and then the creams. You did a day on teapots, and a day on cups, although it depended on the order. Sometimes you were a week or two on one pattern, or one order! We had a board to put outlined ware onto, then passed it to the enamellers who would fill-in.

During 1931 and 1932 the *Conical* and *Stamford* remained the most popular teaware shapes, and were issued in a vast number of Clarice's patterns.

RIGHT: Conical teaware in Summerhouse

Summerhouse was a popular new landscape in 1931 and is found on most of Clarice's tea and coffee shapes from this time. A selection of pieces from a *Conical Early Morning* set are shown which surprisingly were sold in 1931 with the rather impractical 1929 milk jug. The yellow and orange banding is non-standard as early sets normally had coral, or orange and jade banding, but Clarice still seems to have allowed her banders freedom in the choice of colours used.

ABOVE: Daffodil *shape coffee ware in* Delecia Pansies

Clarice issued a graceful, innovative shape range in 1931, the *Daffodil*. This was a vast range with vases, bowls, fancies, and both tea and coffee ware and every part of each set was custom designed including the milk and sugar. The distinguishing features were the waisted shape, and handles ribbed to resemble the corrugation of daffodil petals. On the teaware the cups had open handles, but the smaller coffee cans had solid handles. In June 1931, Colley Shorter was interviewed about the *Damask Rose* pattern, and commented:

Pottery is reflecting a phase of curves and curls, in the feminine fashions of dress and home decoration. There is a definite breaking away from the hard severe lines which have been the vogue in pottery as well as in everything else. The autumn designs are all on soft and beautiful lines.

Although initially issued in a pink body called *Damask Rose*, and decorated with simple motifs, this ware was soon sold in all-over patterns on a

LEFT: Daffodil *shape coffee ware in* Orange Roof Cottage

standard honeyglaze body. *Daffodil* coffeeware in the 1932 *Pansies* design has the mix of freehand flowers and *Delecia* style runnings executed even on the small cans. Occasionally the shape was produced in landscapes such as *Orange Roof Cottage*. This required the decorators to blend the Art Nouveau inspired shapes with typical Clarice landscapes in zany colours, thus making truly *Bizarre* creations. Such elaborately decorated sets were marketed as gifts for special occasions and were not really meant for everyday use.

One of Clarice's few failures was issued in 1932. *Le Bon Dieu* was a series of ware modelled as tree boles which was unlike anything else she had made. Interestingly, we have a few clues from Clarice on the creation of this strange ware, as she said:

The idea of my latest design came by chancing to find a tree bole of curious formation which, however, I thought might serve as a model. The result was a nobbled pixie-like form and with the additional gnarled handle made a dumpy jug. From these I proceeded to use smaller boles, one inverted on top of the other for teapots. The pottery is painted in soft shades of green and brown with colours running into one and other, suggesting moss peat pools and other dreamy notions which are the basis of fairy lore.

Many collectors dislike this ware, as did the public in 1932 when it sold poorly. However, her ability to design in a wide range of styles shows the breadth of Clarice's personal tastes, and this was the quality which made her successful as an industrial designer.

BELOW: Bon Jour teaware in Honolulu

In 1933 Clarice issued the *Bon Jour* tea and coffee ware which was teamed with the fully coordinated *Biarritz* tableware, and was to be her best-seller for the rest of the thirties. The *Bon Jour* teapot shape followed on from the *Stamford* in that it was flat-sided, but this time comprised a circle, resting on two thin tubular feet. The milk jug was a similar shape but with a flat base and, as the *Stamford* sugar bowl followed the same form, Clarice did not need to design a custom sugar, and *Conical* cups and saucers were used. Sales were so strong that there was little need to issue it in the older *Bizarre* and *Fantasque* patterns so *Bon Jour* shapes are mainly found in 1933 to 1940 patterns. The full *Early*

Morning set in *Honolulu* is a typical example and the distinctive overlaid band-ing used for the design has even been adeptly painted on the saucers!

Bon Jour Early Morning sets proved as popular for presents as the *Conical* had done in 1929. Designs custom-created for the shape included Clarice's brilliant *Eight O Clock* which simply had a clock face painted on the side of the teapot! Some designs were so popular that she reverted to her trick of issuing them in different colourways. Gorringes in London offered the highly decorative *Cowslip* in four colourways. The teaset was fourteen shillings and sixpence, several days' wages for a *Bizarre* 'girl' at the time!

Occasionally *Bon Jour* sets were sold with two plates, as customers could order any combination of ware they wished. The set in *Secrets Orange* shown was exported to Australia and the customer ordered a large size *Bon Jour* jug to hold hot water to top up the pot. The impressed date marks on this set show it was issued in the middle of 1933 so the rare orange colourway of *Secrets* may have been the original with the more muted *Secrets* in dominant green following shortly afterwards. A change was made to the *Conical* cups in 1933 when the solid triangular handles were given a slight indentation to make them easier to hold.

ABOVE: A complete Bon Jour Early Morning *set with a* Stamford *hot water jug, in* Secrets Orange

RIGHT: Later Clarice Cliff teapots: Nautilus, Cockerel *and* Raffia

Because *Bon Jour* tea and coffeeware was sold alongside *Biarritz* tableware, the sets were made in several configurations. Some have oblong *Biarritz* saucers, and some cups have a *Bon Jour* shape handle. These are found in patterns such as *Coral Firs* as whole dinner services were produced with this design as a shoulder pattern. The cup and saucer with the pastille shaped handles were based on an original by Margarete Heymann-Loëbenstein and only produced briefly. A milk jug with the same handle is known, but no coffee or teapot has been found so perhaps the pieces were trials not put into full production. This design device was also used on later *Conical* ware as detailed in *Goodbye Bizarre*.

Trieste was the last teaware in the true *Bizarre* tradition. The name refers to the three-sided, triangular form of the teapot, milk and sugar which were extremely well modelled and cast, with finer bodies than the earlier shapes. The teapot handle and spout echoed the triangular concept, and Clarice created three-sided plates and saucers, and cups with special *Trieste* shape handles, so it was a cohesive design. Unfortunately it seems that by 1935 the market for the *Early Morning* sets was shrinking so sets are often found with the later *Conical* cups with an open handle. The set shown to the right is in *Newlyn*, the blue colourway of *Forest Glen*, one of Clarice's last great patterns before the *Bizarre* name was withdrawn. The set incorporates some of the most skilled modelling and finest painting from Newport Pottery.

BELOW: Trieste shape teaware in Newlyn

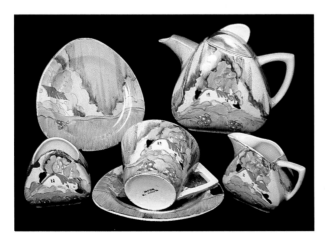

In the later thirties a more conservative approach to design, and more reserved ceramics in printed designs such as those by Susie Cooper became fashionable. Undaunted, Clarice did what any good industrial designer would do and issued a shape the market wanted. Her *Windsor* tea and coffee ware was clearly named after the royal family, and the pear-shaped bodies were a traditional form that was functional and easy to decorate. She persisted in issuing these pieces mainly in hand-painted designs as by this time her paintresses were so skilled that small motif patterns which could have been printed were still mainly hand-painted. A more inventive shape was the *Nautilus*, a range based on the shell, which only seems to have got to prototype stage. A full tea-set was produced in *Raffia* ware, which featured detailed surface modelling with etched colouring. The new direction Clarice's fancies were to take in the later thirties was typified by the outrageous *Cockerel* teapot. Today we are used to novelty teapots, but then this really was an outlandish piece – not a serious teapot! Although such pieces are not in the spirit of *Bizarre*, and so less sought by collectors, they were ahead of their time as they pre-date the fashion over the last few decades for novelty teapots in fantastic shapes.

Clarice 'broke all the rules' when she designed her tea and coffee shapes, and by 1940 had created over twenty teapots, and ten coffee-pots. In the thirties Clarice Cliff teapots sat on the parlour table full of best Empire tea; today they are displayed in locked cabinets in the lounge. Somehow, Clarice succeeded in turning teapots into art!

ABOVE: Rare Biarritz *and* Bon Jour *shape cups*

BIZARRE MEETS BLOOMSBURY

In 1932, the same year that Clarice and Colley enjoyed their very successful promotion at Barkers of Kensington and the events with stage and screen stars at the First Avenue Hotel, they became involved in an interesting but ultimately fruitless project. It was instigated by a speech made by the Prince of Wales to encourage a closer liaison between the pottery industry and artists. The aim was to improve the standards of commercial products by employing top artists of the day to design them. It was partly masterminded by Thomas Acland Fennemore, art director of E. Brain, the manufacturers of the Foley China. Together with the designer, Milner Gray, and painter Graham Sutherland, Fennemore selected 'suitable' artists. They invited Vanessa Bell, Duncan Grant, John Armstrong, Angelica Bell, Barbara Hepworth, Paul Nash, Ben Nicholson, Dod Proctor and her husband Ernest, and Albert Rutherston to contribute.

The brief to the artists was to create designs for dinner sets and tea-sets which would be issued in limited editions of twelve, each marked 'First Edition'. It is not known whether the artists compared what they intended to submit, but several of the designs seem to have been influenced by the freeform, foliate work of Vanessa Bell and Duncan Grant, of which all of them would have undoubtedly been aware. Bell and Grant were married by this time and living a very Bohemian life (though not together) at Charleston in Sussex.

The pieces were produced in bone china by Brains under Fennemore's supervision, and Colley Shorter arranged that the earthenware examples would be made at Wilkinson's under Clarice's direct supervision. This was quite a coup on his part, because as early as 1932 her success had increased

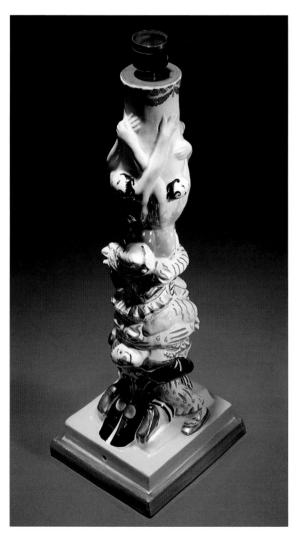

rivalry between the Staffordshire factories and it gave Clarice even more cred- ibility. However, she was not enthusiastic about the project, and the *Bizarre* 'girls' recall that it led to disagreements between her and Colley.

Fennemore's motives in promoting the project were probably to encour- age sales at what was a slack time at Foley China. Colley Shorter's factories were busy so his ultimate goal was just to link his star designer with this pres- tigious project. He certainly achieved this as when issued the ware had the artist's name next to an elaborate backstamp, *Produced in Bizarre by Clarice Cliff Ltd England*.

By this time Gordon Forsyth was involved and he wrote to Acland Fennemore, 'I do hope Colley will not use such a distinguished bunch of artists to advertise Clarice Cliff! No one could object to Newport Pottery by Frank Brangwyn R.A. but he should not use Clarice Cliff's name, except for pottery designed by her.' Forsyth, with his academic background was no match for the more worldly Shorter, and indeed every piece of the ware cred- ited Clarice. But, as the story unfolded, it became clear that more than anyone she deserved credit.

Of the thirteen artists only Vanessa Bell and Duncan Grant are believed to have visited Stoke, the rest just sent water-colour drawings or ink sketches which Clarice was left to adapt onto tableware. To decorate the ware she had

ABOVE: The Field Flowers *design by Eva Crofts on* Bon Jour *tea and coffee ware shapes*

to take some of her best decorators off *Bizarre* so Ellen Browne and Fred Ridgway were involved for many months. At the same time Fennemore developed the patterns for production on china at Foley. From the beginning there was an artistic divergence in how Cliff and Fennemore interpreted the patterns: Fennemore seems to have made the Vanessa Bell design on Foley China overly fussy, with cross-hatching, swirls, foliate shapes and an in-filled colour background. In contrast Cliff's production of Bell's design featured similar motifs but on a much larger scale, mainly limited to underglaze blue covered with a grey glaze.

The pieces were first seen at the exhibition British Industrial Art in Relation to the Home at Dorland Hall in London, opened on 20 June 1933 by H.R.H. Prince George. They solicited an unfavourable reaction from both the press and public. The project had to continue, and luckily Colley had more control at this stage. In an unusual move, he co-operated with Gordon Forsyth as they both realized it needed fresh ideas as many of the designs were not suited to tableware. They compiled a further list of artists which included Freda Beardmore, Eva Crofts, John Everitt, Dame Laura Knight, Ann Riach, W. P. Robins, Billie Waters, Allan Walton and Michael Wellmer. Also on the new list were Forsyth and his daughter Moira.

Fennemore did not have any modern shapes at Foley China so was limited to their mundane traditional shapes. However, Clarice had the advantage of modern shapes she could use to make even the indifferent designs more interesting. For example, Eva Croft's designs, which were basically just busy,

BELOW: Dame Laura Knight on a visit to Newport Pottery

rambling cartoons unrelated to any shape, were condensed on to Clarice's *Bon Jour* shape tea and coffee sets which made the designs look a great deal more proficient.

Ironically, Clarice found herself in charge of producing Gordon Forsyth's work on her earthenware. The man who had overseen all the schools of art when she was just a student had submitted designs which owed much to the Bloomsbury style. One was a simple scrolling foliate design, and another had pink flowers and blue leaves spiralling around the ware. Clarice executed these with a matt, pale lavender glaze on her *Biarritz* plates and tureens.

Laura Knight's designs were to prove the most successful. Clarice had met Dame Laura on a train in 1933 and as they became friends Laura took a personal interest in the project. Clarice excelled herself as, rather than just transferring designs onto plates, she developed a complete, modelled tableware set. Reverting to her first love of modelling she used Laura Knight's sketches to develop shapes with circus characters as embellishments. Two chubby clowns leant against a candlestick, a teapot had a trapeze artist as the handle with the heads of clowns as the finials. Most impressive was a massive centrepiece featuring all the circus acts precariously balancing on top of each other to form a lamp base. It took months of work by Clarice and Joe Woolliscroft to evolve the shapes. Each plate had a different circus scene in the centre, with the audience pictured around the rim and needed detailed painting to add the enamels to the printed pink outline. Unfortunately, the hours of work needed to decorate them gave *Circus* ware an artistic price tag!

The complete series of designs was unveiled in October 1934 when all the ware was displayed at Harrods. The exhibition, Modern Art for the Table, was opened by Sir William Rothenstein, President of the Royal Academy of Fine Arts. Twenty-seven artists had contributed over the two years and some had three designs. A set of tableware of each design was displayed by the original framed artwork, literally linking art and ceramics. Two of Clarice's own designs were included, a new one called *Hello*, and her 1929 *Ravel*

LEFT: *Sir William Rothenstein inspects the* Circus *ware display at Harrods*

pattern now on a range of modern shapes. It was later recalled as a 'glittering party', and artists, journalists and titled celebrities all mingled.

Naturally, the *Journal of the Royal Society* gave a glowing review to the exhibition, singling out Vanessa Bell and Duncan Grant's pieces, but their verdict was not typical. The influential *Studio* publication commented, 'It must be regretfully noted that some of the designs were quite unsuited to the purpose for which they were intended.' Frank Pick, a campaigner for industrial design, instantly delivered his opinion to Fennemore in a letter sent before the exhibition officially opened. He had seen it with various other members of the Council for Art and Industry, and said it was a 'brave venture', but qualified this, 'I cannot approve of all that you have done. In several instances the designs did not seem to me altogether suited for the treatment which it receives in connection with the pottery.' He ended his letter 'I hope your venture has proved commercially successful', but it was rather premature to look to income.

Apart from the art establishment's journals, little praise was handed out in the popular press. However, the *Circus* ware distinguished itself amongst the displays and reports noted that Gracie Fields, the most popular entertainer in Britain at the time, had paid £70 for a complete *Circus* set. Milner Gray, one of the originators of the project, came in for severe criticism in *Pottery Gazette* over his *Whoopee* design. 'There are no doubt people who are attracted by it and who may even like to possess it but if there are we simply cannot share their taste. Perhaps it has been incorrectly described as a "morning set" and is intended for the nursery? Much more acceptable to us is a pattern christened *Hello*, one of the designs of Miss Clarice Cliff. This is a decoration which is modern without being so trying to our patience.'

Clarice's versions of the artists' designs on earthenware were only intended as a more affordable alternative to the bone china which was meant to be the 'star of the show' and Thomas Acland Fennemore's interpretations of the artist's designs dominated the display. He had been encouraged by Gordon Forsyth, who wrote to him in July 1934, 'I bet you all I possess that it will be a great success in every way and Mr Brain will be quite happy about the results. When the bouquets are being presented you *must* get the biggest one because you not only had a big idea but you courageously stuck to it.' Forsyth continued, 'we will look back on this with great joy.'

Forsyth had been a key figure in establishing the North Staffordshire branch of the Society of Industrial Artists. He was a fervent believer in his own opinions on linking art and industrial design and had taken part in many academic debates to further his cause. As the events that followed showed, his encouragement to Fennemore was premature, as with no positive consensus of opinion the art establishment had to brush the project 'under the carpet'.

The final hope of turning the project into a commercial success was when the exhibition toured the country. However, the negative response in London was echoed early in 1935 when the ware went to large stores in Derby, Birmingham and other big cities. It was announced with a local fanfare but sales were poor. Colley Shorter later sent the Wilkinson's earthenware examples to Australia where they were received with interest, and eventually sold. He had lost quite a lot of money on the project, but for Thomas Acland Fennemore it was to be even worse. The china was even more expensive than the earthenware, and many of the limited editions were never completed. Gordon Forsyth had encouraged Fennemore to expect acclaim, but the failure was to affect the rest of his career.

Contrary to Gordon Forsyth's assertion that Colley Shorter should 'not use such a distinguished bunch of artists to advertise Clarice Cliff', in putting their artwork on her startling, modern *Biarritz* and *Bon Jour* shapes, she enhanced many of the less suitable designs. Most significantly, Clarice had produced the only modelled ware for the project. The *Circus* ceramics are completely in harmony with Laura Knight's famous paintings of Carmo's Circus, so Clarice really did manage to bond contemporary art with industrial design.

Ironically, although few members of the public 'ate off the art', some of the artists did, as they received sets of their ware! Duncan Grant's floral tableware produced under Clarice's supervision was used on a daily basis by him and Vanessa Bell for several decades at Charleston, where it is now on permanent display. But time has not been kind to the *Artist in Industry* pieces as they are now called. Clarice Cliff finally commented on the project in 1951: 'I remember what headaches we had over the reproduction, but sad to relate, from a commercial point of view, sales to the public, it was so disappointing that it was the closest thing to a flop that I am glad to say, I have ever been associated with.' The final judgements came from the artists; Graham Sutherland told the authors of the L'Odeon book that he did not want to be further associated with his ware, and would prefer them not to illustrate it. Milner Gray, one of the three who had instigated the project, emphatically stated in 1973, 'it was a complete flop!'

Despite the efforts of twenty-seven artists, time has shown that the best combination of art and ceramics produced in 1933 and 1934, and the most collectable, were made by one artist. With classic designs such as *Blue Firs*, *Solitude*, *May Avenue*, *Bridgwater*, and *Windbells* produced on shapes of her own devising, Clarice Cliff combined art with industrial design. Even the long hours working on the project did not cloud her perspective of what her ceramic art was really about.

GOODBYE BIZARRE

Throughout the thirties, despite her hectic career and the social whirl that went with it, Clarice still managed to find time to see her mother and assorted nephews and nieces. She had tried to explain the ideas behind her work to her mother, but Ann Cliff never really understood. However, Clarice still remained close to her mother and every year took her and her niece Nancy to see the shows staged by the Stoke Amateur Operatic Society. Clarice's older brother Frank was in the chorus and Nancy remembered that, 'We were treated to him practising the songs at home when we weren't supposed to be listening. He had a lovely tenor voice and we saw him performing in "The Mikado", "The Pirates of Penzance", "Merry England" and many others.'

BELOW: Forest Glen *on an eighteen-inch* charger *with a* Globe *teapot, a rare vase, a* Bon Jour *jam pot and a* Coronet *jug*

Clarice's career still dominated her life though, and finally free of the *Artist in Industry* project she could return to her own creations. She had a huge range at this time, as many of the shapes from 1929 onwards were still available, so customers could order *Stamford* or *Eton* teaware, *Teddy Bear* bookends, or even a *Subway Sadie* comport, although by 1935 these were issued in very pastel colours. She issued new landscapes, but from 1935 onwards the outlining techniques used on *Taormina* were gradually replaced with free-hand painting, such as on *Dryday*, and the new style lacked the impact of her earlier work.

The key to Clarice's success in the second half of the decade was some-thing very different from the *Fantasque* landscapes. In July 1934 she had launched *My Garden* ware at the *Daily Mail* Ideal Home exhibition. The concept for *My Garden* stemmed from her 1931 *Marguerite* ware, which featured a few simple modelled daisies as the handle or base. Clarice developed the idea by modelling vases and jugs with detailed leaves and flowers on the handle and base. The flow-ers were then picked out in bright enamels and the body was in soft amber *Delecia* runnings. The massive Ideal Home exhibition was an ideal location to launch *My Garden* and it caught the public's imagination. Clarice soon had to pro-duce new variations to fill the demand for exclusive pieces.

During 1934 Clarice had introduced a new painting technique called 'etching' for some of her ware. Until this time most of her patterns were outlined and then filled in with enamel colours, but with etching the decorators applied the enamels freehand. The colours were over-lapped and woven together with broader brushstrokes, using harmonious colours. For

BELOW: A Subway Sadie *comport*

the first major design, *Rhodanthe*, orange blended with yellow, which blended with brown to form tall marigold-type flowers on sinuous brown stems.

The Silver Jubilee celebrations of George V made 1935 one of the busiest years for Clarice as she was involved in several commemorative projects. It was also the year when the last of her major patterns appeared. *Forest Glen* featured a cottage in a forest under a blood-red *Delecia* sky. The design con-trasted violently with the more pastel shades that now predominated on her ware, and it was the swansong of the true *Bizarre* years.

Clarice's business trips enabled her to spend more time with Colley and the factory staff inevitably noticed. He tried to be discreet and went to great lengths to save Clarice any embarrassment, but all the Shorter family were aware of their liaison. His daughter, Margaret, later recalled, 'Mother would not have that woman's name mentioned in the house.' Annie Shorter had known about the affair for many years, but by this time was infirm, and was tended to by their servants. Daughter Joan had a private tutor so lived at home, and was aware of her mother's unhappiness. Clarice never spoke about Colley to her family, with the possible exception of her closest confidante, her sister Ethel.

Colley made regular trips to Australia during the thirties as the Shorter family had strong business links there, and during an interview in the *Sydney Morning Herald* in June 1935 he let slip the fact that Clarice had visited Europe. Speaking of her success as a female art director, he added that it 'began in a small way and has resulted in one of the biggest jobs of its kind in Great Britain. She travels frequently to Europe, visiting the art centres of Paris, Prague, Vienna, Brussels and Berlin.' It seems unlikely that he was exaggerating Clarice's travels as Prague was the venue of an annual trade fair. Details about the trips remain fragmentary as Clarice and Colley obviously discussed them with few people.

BELOW: A vast display of Bizarre ware at Scott's Hotel in Melbourne in 1936

Another Australian magazine article suggests that Clarice and Colley had visited Italy. A major Sydney stockist, Anthony Horden, staged a display which included many pieces of *My Garden* decorated in the *Azure* colourway. The *Sydney Sun and Guardian* reported, 'Clarice Cliff culled her ideas on a

continental tour which lasted several weeks and on returning home the fruits of her experience abroad were presented in the form of new ideas in designing.' The designs later named after Italian locations seem significant, and include *Taormina* and *Capri* from 1935, and *Napoli* from 1937.

The *My Garden* range was selling so well by 1935 that Clarice created a variety of new shapes and colourways for the company's annual tradeshow at the First Avenue Hotel in September. It would have been evident to any buyer that, compared to the previous year, there were fewer fancies and many new tableware sets. A new traditional shape called *Margot* was issued, and a typical design was *Stroud* which featured a cottage and tree motif set amidst fine edge banding. The *Biarritz* tableware range was now large, with plates in various sizes so sets to suit every dining occasion could be bought. The *Biarritz* shoulder patterns of stylish motifs had sophisticated names such as *Kensington* and *Grille*, and pattern 6450 was particularly popular; it comprised the customer's monogram, hand-painted on a corner, with gilt or silver banding.

The rash of shapes and designs that had appeared since *Bizarre* was launched in 1927 make it easy to forget that in the following years the *Crocus* shop beneath the *Bizarre* shop was constantly busy. Fifteen to twenty paintresses decorated *Crocus* to meet demand, and late in 1935 Clarice produced a new colourway, the very unusual *Blue Crocus*. This demonstrates how she was able to diversify even her 'signature' pattern. Demand for the

ABOVE: A Trieste Early Morning *set in* Capri

MODERN TABLEWARE

The "Stroud" pattern in modern Staffordshire shows a broken circle in brown and amber lines with decorative foliage in greens and browns on a warm honey-glaze. This is the "Margot" shape.

ABOVE: An impressive Blue Crocus *collection including a* Cauldron, *a* Lynton *shape coffee-pot, a* Lotus *jug, a* Conical *dredger, an* Athens *shape jug. A* Bon Jour Early Morning *set is spread around the group, including its original ceramic tray*

original *Crocus* remained strong, however, and *Blue Crocus* seems to have only been produced in limited quantities.

Clarice was able to enjoy the fruits of her labours, as her ware was bringing in profits from all around the world. She was generous with birthday and Christmas presents to her mother, her sisters and her nieces and nephews. Clarice remained close to Nellie's daughter, Nancy, and despite her hectic schedule found time to take her on weekend trips. In return Nancy would run errands and get Clarice's library books as she found fiction a perfect foil to her busy professional life. Every Tuesday Nancy had dinner with Clarice, which was served on *Biarritz* ware with a 'CC' monogram, and fruit was then served in a *Honeydew* set. After dinner Nancy spent many hours chatting with her now famous aunt, who rarely mentioned the cavalcade of places she had visited, or the famous people she had met. Nancy recalled that when Clarice had to replace her adored but worn out 'Jinny', she treated herself to an Austin Seven Pearl Cabriolet, but promptly named it 'Jenny' which was 'less Staffordshire'. Eric Grindley handled its purchase and, as Clarice specified custom, ruby-coloured leather seats and chic grey paintwork, it cost £197! The first time Clarice drove BVT 980 into the works it caused a sensation, as most of her staff did not even own a bicycle, and the works manager only had a three-wheeler car.

In just nine years Clarice had revolutionized ceramic design in Staffordshire. Her ware offered extremes of style to suit all customers, from the thoroughly modern *Bon Jour* shapes in sophisticated designs, to the cosy, charming, highly coloured *My Garden*. However, the sheer breadth of her work must have prompted the question, 'What next?' In November 1935 she reached the high point of her career, but a very low point in her personal life. The events of that month seem to have been the catalyst that led to a change in the direction of both.

November saw the climax of weeks of planning for a prestigious charity ball at the Dorchester Hotel in London. It was to celebrate King George V's Silver Jubilee, and raise funds for the Paddington Green Children's Hospital. Clarice and Colley were on the organizing committee where their lack of any title was very apparent, as they were with Lord Strathcona, Lady George Cholmondeley, Lady Seton-Karr and Sir Hugh Smiley. In return for helping to organize the event and donating prizes of Clarice Cliff teaware, there was a prominent double page feature in the impressive, round programme. It did not mention *Bizarre*, but *Clarice Cliff Ware by the Royal Staffordshire Pottery*. Colley was keen to stress the 'Royal' connection, as the guests of honour were the Duke and Duchess of York. No one could have anticipated that just a year later they would be the King and Queen. Clarice tastefully displayed the Laura Knight *Circus* ware and interestingly was still using her 1930 *Age of Jazz* figures as table decorations. Colley Shorter had shrewdly arranged for the following accolade about the 'decorated tables' to appear in the centre of the programme:

The ware used on the tables is the conception of the brilliant Lady Artist, Clarice Cliff, art director of the A. J. Wilkinson group. Miss Clarice Cliff was the first designer associated with any pottery manufacturer in Great Britain to visualize the possibilities of modern design applied to Ceramics. The world-wide demand for what was at first a tentative launching of a new idea has exceeded all expectations, and Miss Cliff's productions, which all bear her signature on the ware are always interesting, always varied, and definitely new.

A lavish formal meal, accompanied with glasses of G. H. Mumm champagne, and then dancing to Ambrose's Band, must have brought back memories of their secret evening at the Café de Paris just five years earlier. The difference now was that as the managing director and art director of a company their dancing together was perfectly acceptable. The impressive tableware displays and Clarice's prominence in the programme, meant all the dignitaries knew exactly who Miss Clarice Cliff was. Mixing in such company may have prompted her to re-evaluate her work, as the *Bizarre* tradename was noticeably absent from the programme. Perhaps Colley had already decided that Clarice's name alone was sufficient now. Certainly, they were able to

ABOVE: A post-1936 Clarice Cliff backstamp

BELOW: Clarice Cliff advertised her Blackbird Pie Funnels *peeking out of a pie*

appreciate all that their combined talents had brought them, as they danced the last waltz of the evening, 'Bitter Sweet Selection'.

Just three weeks after that magical evening in London, Clarice found herself at the Haywood Hospital in Burslem on 30 November. Her younger sister Dolly was having routine surgery but suffered a heart attack and died. Clarice had been waiting to see her after the operation and was extremely shocked. Dolly had always been so energetic and devoted herself to her dancing. Clarice had to arrange the funeral as her other sisters were married, and her mother was unwell. It was attended by the *Bizarre* 'girls', many of whom had enjoyed watching Dolly giving dancing demonstrations, or appearing in stage shows at the Hippodrome in Stoke.

Clarice's thirty-seventh birthday was on 20 January 1936. King George V died the same day and the whole of Britain went into mourning. The Newport Pottery advertisement in January's *Pottery Gazette* had the full *Bizarre* logo, but in February the slogan in their copy for the British Industries Fair read, 'Everyone knows Clarice Cliff designs, but her latest creations even surpass her renowned *Bizarre*.' The *Bizarre* backstamp was replaced with a simple new mark, bearing the *Clarice Cliff* signature above either *Wilkinsons* or *Newport Pottery*. The loss of the so significant *Bizarre* trademark was not noted at the time by the 'girls', who were soon busy gossiping about 'Edward and Mrs Simpson'. It did, however, mark a move to a new range of ware, a mix of modelled fancies and simple elegant tableware. The tableware was produced in simple patterns with just banding or small motifs, in the range 6500 to 7300. There was a large choice of tableware shapes, as *Odilon*, *Stamford* and *Daffodil* were still marketed and new mid-thirties shapes included the more traditional *Lynton*, *Bristol* and *Delph*. Clarice still led her competitors a merry dance with the huge *Biarritz* range which remained unique to her factory as she had wisely registered the shapes.

In contrast to the sophisticated *Biarritz* ware, one of Clarice's most humble pieces was the *Blackbird Pie Funnel*. Although these were later produced by many companies she had the original idea and had registered it as 809138 late in 1935. Teams of the younger paintresses applied the underglaze yellow and black on the *Blackbirds* which were sold to retailers in boxes of 144. Wilkinsons renewed the registration for as long as was possible, so it was only in 1951 that copies appeared.

The loss of the *Bizarre* name coincided with Clarice taking on many new modellers. As detailed in the *Cliff Faces* chapter, Peggy Davies modelled masks for Clarice, and also large vases with comic fish, and a lamp base as three fish. Peggy recalled how Clarice often went away for long periods just leaving details of work she wanted doing. Clarice also recruited Nancy Greatrex and Betty Silvester from the Burslem School of Art. Betty Sylvester modelled the *Student* and *Showgirl* bookends that were issued in 1937 and designed the innovative *Wigwam* teapot which was not actually produced until 1947 when it was sold in Canada as a tourist item. In 1937 Clarice recruited Aubrey Dunn from Paladin China and he worked alongside the 'girls' and modelled the *Fruit and Basket* ware.

Clarice still found time to model, and her sense of humour was evident in a number of amusing, novel shapes. Animal ashtrays included a *Hippopotamus* with a gaping mouth to hold the cigarette. Her *Book* vase was modelled as a bound volume with the top open for flowers, and was sold with a choice of 'titles and authors' on the 'spine'. In October 1938 twelve *Horoscope signs* were issued, with the corresponding dates for each sign stylishly written in calligraphic script. Clarice even produced an impressive modelled car, designed as a table centrepiece, which she based on Colley's Jaguar SS sports car. These last few fancies were shown at very quiet tradeshows, so exports became the mainstay of the company.

Colley Shorter entertained the hope that his daughter Joan might eventually run his factories, and to this end had encouraged her to work in the offices at Wilkinson's. She was interested in the factory but working in close proximity with Clarice Cliff inevitably caused problems, and when they came into contact several of the 'girls' overheard them arguing.

Clarice celebrated her fortieth birthday on 20 January 1939. She received a special present from her sister Ethel whose husband Arthur Steele was the

LEFT: A Harvest *teapot and flower jug*

RIGHT: A Winston Churchill toby jug, the plaque by Betty Silvester, and Clarice's traditional toby which was also issued by Shorter & Sons

ABOVE: Paintress Edna Cheetham joins the WAAF

BELOW: Modeller Aubrey Dunn who served in Burma during the war, and then returned to Wilkinson's as decorating shop manager

clay manager at Wedgwood in Etruria. Ethel decided to get Clarice a piece of their prestigious black basalt ware and as Clarice's niece Nancy worked in the office asked her to help them choose from three large plaques. Nancy chose one by Victor Skellern which had a scene of galloping wild horses. One Saturday sometime later when she went to Snow Hill, she saw the plaque in the lounge and Clarice told her, 'Mr Colley is doing his best to get it off me, he mentions it every time he visits!' At the end of the *Bizarre* years, Clarice could have had no idea that exactly fifty years later, her work and name would be part of the Wedgwood company, who would stage the exhibition to celebrate her centenary…

One of the last ranges to appear before the war was *Harvest*, intricately modelled with sheaves of corn and floral handles. It was exported overseas where it was soon to be patriotically renamed *England*. Just a few months later, on Sunday 3 September, the Second World War started. At the Newport factory the watchman ran around the factory telling the skeleton staff that war had been declared. Massive staff changes soon started to take place, but hand-painted ware continued to be produced for export. *Crocus, Rhodanthe, Harvest* and other lines were decorated by an ever-decreasing number of paintresses as the decorators left to work in munitions factories or join the Forces. Paintress Edna Cheetham enlisted in the WAAF and modeller Aubrey Dunn in the army.

Clarice responded to the war effort by modelling some items that could be exported. At Colley's suggestion she created a magnificent Winston Churchill toby jug in the style of a series designed for Wilkinson's twenty years earlier by Carruthers Gould. She had already produced a set of toby jugs for Shorters, and after the war these were issued with her backstamp. Betty Silvester also modelled a plaque showing Winston Churchill and these were mainly exported so are rarely found in Britain. These pieces were painted by less than ten paintresses, who, to back the war effort, knitted for the troops and practised first-aid during their lunch breaks.

The most significant event for Clarice and Colley in the first few months of the war was the death of Colley's wife after a long illness. Annie Shorter was just fifty-one when she died at Chetwynd House on 2 November, 1939. Clarice and Colley soon became inseparable, but he found it difficult to reconcile his wife's death with the fact that he wanted to marry Clarice. However, he was persuaded that he should do exactly that by his closest drinking friends at The Leopard. When Edward Wenger of Wenger's Colours advised him, 'It's about time you married that girl!' he took his advice. They were married on 21 December 1940 but just a few family members were told, and the marriage was kept secret for nearly a year. Salesman Ewart Oakes was one of the first to know when Clarice wrote to him nearly a year later on 10 December 1941. 'I have been trying to sneak ten minutes to write to you for the last several days, and this is my first chance. I have a bit of news for you which may not come as much of a surprise – Colley and I are married. This at the moment is not generally known, but I know that you can be discreet.' Clarice wrote from the Castle Hotel in Ruthin, North Wales where Colley had taken her to meet his aged mother. A note in the margin of the letter said, 'If you write, don't forget it is "Shorter", not "Cliff", or we might get turned out, what a joke.'

Clarice personally told her remaining paintresses and Marjory Higginson asked, 'Do we call you Mrs Shorter now?' Clarice replied, 'No, no. Miss Cliff will do nicely.' They were not surprised to hear of the marriage and were happy for Clarice. However, the Shorter family were not pleased, and never really accepted her or her family.

When Newport Pottery was finally closed in 1942, the remaining workers moved to Wilkinson's and Clarice and Colley were not really needed at the works. They now found that, unlike the thirties, they had abundant time to spend together, and Chetwynd House became their private haven during the war years. Clarice turned her attention from designing ceramics to learning about gardening, an art she was most certainly to use on Chetwynd's four and a half acre garden in the following decade.

MRS CLARICE CLIFF-SHORTER

Throughout the thirties Clarice Cliff had devoted herself to her career, her *Bizarre* 'girls' and 'Mr Colley'. Her life changed dramatically when she suddenly became Mrs Clarice Cliff-Shorter. The delight of being his wife, and moving in to his glorious Art and Crafts house, was obviously tempered by the fact that Colley was now fifty-eight years old. However with Britain at war Clarice was content just to spend time with him in their spacious home. She found that many of the daily duties were filled by the servants Bessy and Alice, so had time to enjoy her new life.

Colley continued working at Wilkinson's long after the introduction of wartime restrictions, though he was not really needed there. He enrolled in the Home Guard, but the authorities objected when he reported for duty in a full military uniform! Colley also 'acquired' the title of 'Lieutenant-Colonel Shorter' during the war. Clarice was content to enjoy her time in the vast gar-

BELOW: Clarice in Bermuda in 1953, admiring bananas, which were an exotic fruit in Britain until rationing ended the previous year

den at Chetwynd, or devote time and attention to her sister's children, all of whom were fond of their much-loved 'Auntie Clarice'. They initially visited on days when Colley was away, but soon he became part of the extended family and seemed to enjoy being 'Uncle Colley'. Chetwynd took on an even greater importance for Clarice and Colley as they faced the war years together.

In the elated post-war atmosphere Clarice and Colley planned their future. The house was a shared priority, and they altered the internal courtyard, which the designers Barry Parker and Raymond Unwin had thought an integral feature. It was transformed by installing a glass roof, making it a high, light room, which soon became Clarice and Colley's favourite part of

Chetwynd. Colley's priority was Wilkinsons, where he master-minded a massive modernization scheme. To make way for new gas-fired continuous ovens, the dirty, out-moded bottle ovens were demolished. Nostalgically, he photographed them, and captioned the slide, 'the last four bottle ovens at AJW'.

Clarice's biggest challenge was trying to relate to Colley's two daughters. Margaret was head-strong like her father and inevitably went her own separate way. Colley was extremely fond of Joan, but it took Clarice many years to get to know her, as Joan could not accept the woman who had come between her parents. Colley's hopes that Joan might manage the factory had been dashed when she asserted herself by joining the WAAF during the war, which had led to her meeting a Canadian airforceman. Colley was delighted when they married in 1948 but dismayed when they decided to live in Canada. This caused him to focus his overseas marketing on North America, which enabled him to visit Joan in Toronto several times each year.

Colley's other pride and joy was his 1938 Rolls-Royce. He had it extensively customized at great expense, and it was a stunning combination of turquoise and chrome. He had forsaken having a chauffeur as he now preferred to drive himself everywhere, although his friends and family were often alarmed by his autocratic driving style.

Clarice had no ambition to be the sole designer at Wilkinson's, and appointed Aubrey Dunn as decorating manager to re-establish a hand-painting shop. Hilda Lovatt re-assembled a team of paintresses, and Rene Dale, Winnie Pound, Florrie Winkle and Clara Thomas returned to a brand new *Bizarre* shop with a clean, modern, working environment. Everyone in the factory continued to call them the *Bizarre* 'girls'! A new backstamp was evolved for Clarice's ware which appeared in many guises, but which linked her name with *Royal Staffordshire Ceramics*. The 'girls' were again sent on hand-painting demonstrations and as early 1949 appeared at Welwyn Garden City. However, restrictions on the home market meant that the bulk of Wilkinson's output had to be printed ware for export, until 1952.

ABOVE: A photograph Colley nostalgically captioned 'the last four Bottle Ovens at AJW, 1954'

BELOW: Colley Shorter's other 'pride and joy' was his 1938 Rolls-Royce

ABOVE: The post war backstamp found in various configurations on ware produced between 1946 and 1964

Norman Smith, a young man who had joined Wilkinson's in 1940, was soon being trained by Colley to fill many of the roles he had previously embraced, as he recognized that he needed a successor. Norman was keen to learn, and soon was held in such high esteem by Clarice and Colley that they treated him as though he were a family member rather than an employee. He recalled Clarice as being a very kind person, but by this time she centred her whole life around Colley's tastes, his art objects, and the many friends they entertained from around the world.

Colley persuaded Clarice to go with him on some of his overseas trips, and for Christmas 1949 organized an extensive tour of North American cities. This culminated with a visit to Joan and her husband Raymond, as Colley was now a grandfather. Colley stayed with Joan when he went by himself, but when Clarice was with him they stayed at an hotel as Joan still did not fully accept her.

The sales of traditional ware overseas were so strong that from 1952 there was little need for Clarice to design new patterns. The factory produced mainly printed patterns such as *Tonquin*, *Lorna Doone*, *Chelsea Basket* and *Georgian Spray* which were major sellers in North America, New Zealand and Australia. By 1953 a range of bold, printed and enamelled floral patterns were

RIGHT: Joan Shorter with her son Roger, baby Chris, and Colley, at the family home in Canada in 1955

issued, designed by Clarice and Eric Elliot whom she had recruited from the Burslem School of Art. Clarice's treasured hand-painting shop was used to add details to all this ware, and *Crocus* was still selling well.

Clarice went through a period of ill health in 1952 and relaxed by venturing out into the garden. This became a mutual passion for her and Colley and as well as their weekend trips to local nurseries, they employed up to five gardeners to ensure the four and a half acres were perfect. Each summer it was vibrant with colour: a mass of roses, rhododendrons and hydrangeas, and the rockeries teemed with aubretia and gentians. In high summer they would spend whole days sitting or working in the garden. As Norman Smith recalled, occasionally Colley was so engrossed that he forgot to go into the factory, but as Norman realized, he *was* now over seventy! Colley was inveterately fond of his Russell lupins, and when they self-seeded over the deserted tennis court he persuaded Clarice to sit right in the middle! His interest in photography, stimulated in his youth by his father, was shared by Clarice. Their photographs provide a charming insight into the special relationship they shared.

Clarice's much-loved paintresses were left in the care of Hilda Lovatt when she and Colley went away, and she even managed to find them work when they were having their children. Rene Dale recalled that, 'In 1952 I was allowed to paint ware at home when I had just had my daughter. Aubrey Dunn came round to see if I would work from home and then delivered ware for decorating.' Despite it not being the most economical way to produce ware, Clarice seemed determined to use as many of her original paintresses as possible. Recalling the summer trips and 'Crazy Day' parades in the thirties, Clarice organized an outing to Blackpool for virtually the whole factory. They travelled by train, and were treated to a meal at Hills department store, the local Wilkinson stockist.

Between 1953 and 1957 Clarice and Colley went on numerous overseas tours, often leaving the factory for up to a month, but confident that their

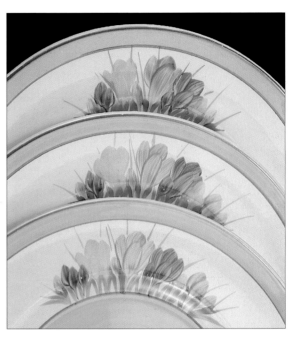

ABOVE: Spring Crocus

BELOW: 'As you sow so shall you reap, Russell Lupins self-sown, old ash tennis court home', Colley's caption for his *photograph of Clarice amidst his Lupins*

RIGHT: Clarice enjoying café con cognac at the Hotel Miramar in Napoli in 1953

ABOVE: Clarice, Colonel Keane and Vic Dancer in Venice

carefully picked staff would keep the business running. They toured Italy in the Rolls, visiting many locations and staying at the best hotels. In Napoli, at the Hotel Miramar, Colley captured Clarice on the balcony in a photograph he captioned 'Café con Cognac'. They toured Sorrento and Capri and could not resist taking a photograph of the home of Gracie Fields who over twenty years earlier had bought a complete Dame Laura Knight *Circus* set!

Colley Shorter always ensured that his trips were claimed against tax, which is perhaps why they spent part of the Italian trip with two buyers from Eatons in Canada, Colonel Keane and Vic Dancer. In Venice they were so busy sightseeing, that one day lunch consisted of a sandwich eaten by the side of the Grand Canal. In Florence, Clarice and Colley went to see Michaelangelo's famous *David*, and they also spent many days visiting the wonderful Italianate gardens and palaces. They visited Rome where Colley took Clarice on a romantic ride around the city in a horse-drawn carriage.

They found it hard to go past pottery factories and visited a number of specialist ceramic galleries and showrooms. In Salerno, Clarice inspected oblong plaques which perhaps reminded her of the *Biarritz* shape. They were decorated with bold, hand-painted, floral motifs which may have inspired a range called *Sunkissed* which the factory issued shortly afterwards

Inevitably, their long trips away meant that they had to delegate more work, and by the mid-fifties Wilkinson's was still successful but began losing key staff to other factories. Colley Shorter had never been an easy person to work for, and was to lose workers who had been with him for fifteen or twenty years. Eric Grindley, who had joined in 1932, tried to leave on several occasions, but as Colley was a freemason his influence over other employers made it difficult. Eventually Eric changed jobs and his new employer, who was not a freemason, told him, 'If you can work for Colley Shorter you can work for anybody!' Norman Smith took on more responsibility as other staff left and his reward was to accompany Clarice and Colley on their 'business' trips. In Montreal they took the local representative to a restaurant where it was traditional at the end of the meal to give the diners a piglet to feed!

In-between Clarice and Colley's oversees trips Chetwynd House was frequently over-run with nephews and nieces from both families. A regular visitor was Colley's nephew John Brereton-Shorter, who had taken on a major role at the Shorter factory. With his wife Charlotte, and their children, they spent many happy hours sitting in the garden chatting, while the children sneaked off to the pond to see if they could spot the carp amongst the waterlilies. Nancy occasionally still visited, and recalled, 'When I visited after Clarice and Colley married, they would laugh and talk with each other, and say things only they understood. It was not easy for her to make the change, but she did not let it show – she became a lady.' One year, when Colley went on a trip alone, Clarice's niece Rita stayed for a while and helped her hand-paint a design in Indian inks on one of the original pieces of Parker and Unwin furniture!

Clarice and Colley's longest overseas trip was in 1955. They travelled by plane and ocean liner, and started in New York where Clarice photographed the top of the classic Chrysler Building from the Empire State Building. They then went to

ABOVE: Clarice visiting the Ernestine pottery at Salerno in 1953

BELOW: Colley Shorter, Norman Smith and a Canadian client, meet an unexpected dinner guest!

RIGHT: *Clarice enjoying a weekend visit with the family of John B. Shorter at Chetwynd House*

ABOVE: *Clarice with Joan Shorter and Joyce Dafforn, at Eastbourne in 1957*

Washington, Alberta, the Grand Canyon, New Mexico and New Orleans. These visits were always blended with a short sales trip and the friends they made overseas were then invited to stay at Chetwynd when they came to Britain. A regular visitor was Phil Sherman their North American representative, while Alan Topham, from Robert Raine of New Zealand stayed in 1957.

Clarice and Colley were visited by Joan and her three children in 1957, and they toured the Staffordshire countryside together. Joan's youngest son Chris later recalled that Clarice very much liked children, and was, 'lots of fun when she took us out for the day'. He also recalled that she was 'very creative, doing wonderful drawings', and showed them how to paint and draw. They also visited Eastbourne on the south coast where Joan had spent a year at finishing school, so Joan could renew her friendship with an old school chum, Joyce Dafforn. Keen to please her father, by this time she and Clarice got on, but they were never to be close.

LEFT: Still enjoying a little 'tomfoolery', Clarice at the Surf Club in Bermuda in 1953

As late as 1958 Clarice still occasionally got directly involved with designing, and when a Canadian company asked for a set of character beer mugs she showed she still had her ability to combine shape and design. The mugs had a handle shaped like an arm, and were decorated with playing card symbols of Kings, Queens, Knaves. However, such whimsical pieces were not the style that consumers sought in the fifties.

Colley's photographs of one of their last overseas trips together captured a couple who clearly knew how to have a good time. They visited Bermuda where Arthur Cooper, a very old friend of Colley's, was the local Wilkinson and Wedgwood dealer. During the day they toured the tropical island or went out fishing on his boat. Coming across a banana plantation, Colley could not resist taking Clarice's picture with them, as they had been unavailable in Britain during the war. The evenings were spent at the Surf Club where they drank and dined next to the ocean, and they obviously had a lively time as Colley's photograph shows!

With Colley nearing his eightieth birthday, in the following years they began to live more quietly. Summers were spent in England, motoring in the

ABOVE: The Christmas tree in the courtyard at Chetwynd House

BELOW: Colley Shorter at Chetwynd House, photographed by Clarice in 1958

Rolls to old towns and villages in Wiltshire, Somerset and as far south as Devon. Wherever they were, Clarice always insisted that they did not miss her favourite radio programme, *The Archers*, although she disliked television. On winter evenings Clarice and Colley often retreated together to the cosy inglenook at Chetwynd. Christmas was celebrated in a very traditional way, and Clarice was lavish with presents for her great nephews and nieces, who always looked forward to the individual rhymes she wrote in their cards. A splendid Christmas tree was always erected in the courtyard, and the colourful bulbs were left on through the night.

In 1961, when Colley announced he was retiring as overseas salesman for Wilkinson's, he had filled the role for an amazing fifty-four years, and this naturally attracted coverage in the press. However, Colley was an irrepressible traveller, and in 1962 he and Clarice undertook a tour of North America to celebrate his eightieth birthday. After the usual sojourn seeing the grandchildren in Toronto, they visited friends in America. Clarice had arranged for a birthday bouquet to be sent from Hilda Lovatt and the last seven *Bizarre* 'girls'. As they were away for some considerable time, Colley wrote a thank you note whilst they were staying at the Palmer House Hotel in Chicago.

My dear eight young friends,

You really did quite embarrass me with your very nice thought on my attaining the status of an octogenarian (I can hardy spell it). The bouquet was just lovely, it added so much to the enjoyment of my birthday with so very many cables, telegrams, letters, cards, from all over the world, that eight nice girls, who had probably known me longer as a group then any, to most of whom, at one time or another I have been, not too polite, with my grumbles or complaints, should have jointly sent me a trophy, a beauty, with such a nice message, made me wonder if perhaps, hoping of course, there might be something about the 'Old Man' a little nicer than his own opinion.

I felt too, very honoured, to be for the second time asked to partake of a cake of Hilda's, this time again with you all. If I'm with you in another 10 years, I shall look forward to another slice.

Now I wish you all; may you be as happy as I am, when you arrive at my age, may you have enjoyed the long years behind you as I have, and you know I've had plenty of troubles too, but when overcome, one only remembers the pleasure of having beaten said troubles.

Miss Cliff, who now thoroughly spoils me at home, joins me in sending all of you a very considerable amount of affection, and thanks for many years of very loyal work, and good work too.

At my age I think I may safely finish with, My Love
Very Sincerely

Colley A. Shorter

Colley died on 13 December 1963 and four days later the service was held at St John's Methodist Church in Wolstanton. Quite a few of the 'girls' paid their respects, and as Clarice put roses on the coffin, Rosa Rigby noticed that they still had the morning dew on them.

Without Colley, Clarice had no desire to work again at the factory, and by December 1964 had decided what she was going to do and called her workers together. Paintress Cissy Rhodes, who had been in the *Bizarre* shop since 1927, recalled, 'She told us she was finishing, and had sold the business to Midwinters on condition that they took us all on. We did not have a party when Miss Cliff left as of the original girls there was only myself, Rosa Rigby, Ethel Barrow and Florrie Winkle.' Clarice Cliff and Norman Smith ceased to be directors of Wilkinson's on 8 December 1964, when Roy Midwinter and Harry Rogers assumed these roles.

Clarice retreated to Chetwynd, where every room must have constantly reminded her of Colley. She found it hard to come to terms with his death, and soon became a recluse. She spent her time cleaning and sorting Colley's much-loved collection of antiques and arranged for many items to be donated to the museum in nearby Newcastle-under-Lyme. Her family continued to visit, but apart from a nightly conversation with her sister Ethel, she avoided phone calls.

Hilda Lovatt had retired to North Wales, and Clarice's letters to her are one of the few insights into her thoughts. In August 1965 she wrote of her efforts to use a lawn mower to tackle the acres of grass in Chetwynd's garden, but also revealed how she really felt.

I escape from the house every moment I can, I get so depressed washing and cleaning things we have loved, I am wrapping them in cellophane and putting the different kinds together so the house is always somewhat upset. It looks as though it will be another twelve months before I am through with it all. Sometimes I think I cannot carry on from early morning till late at night. Then I get a fresh burst of energy. I hear things about the works occasionally and start to worry, and then I think like your husband, it is best to try and forget. My dream is to have a bungalow in some nice restful spot, and that keeps me going, although in some ways I am glad I have got a lot to do, it stops me thinking, especially when I am outside.

By January 1966 she had clearly taken the idea further as she wrote to Hilda:

I am negotiating for a small house, part of Madely Manor. It should be settled by the end of February. I saw it advertised by chance and went the next day. A marvellous open view at the front, no hedges, just enough garden to play about with but a very large patch of lawn with Cedar of Lebanon. One very big room twenty by nineteen foot, nice small hall, little kitchen (after mine) & pantry & coals, three beds with basins. I am dying to go looking so that I can make up my mind what I want done. I have not told anyone except my sister and the solicitor. There are such a lot of decisions to make regarding everything; it frightens me sometimes. However, I have got to do it now.

It seems that Clarice must have discussed selling Chetwynd with her sister Ethel, and eventually decided not to, despite the onerous responsibility it

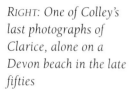

RIGHT: One of Colley's last photographs of Clarice, alone on a Devon beach in the late fifties

presented, and her concerns for its security. She bought a shotgun which her family were amused to find she kept under her bed, but the valuable antique collection was either on display or in drawers and cabinets all over the house. The only thing in the safe was Colley's ashes.

Clarice undertook redecorating the house, and drew swirling patterns with her fingertips in the wet plaster on the walls, sometimes aided by her niece Rita. She covered the whole of the kitchen ceiling with a collage of colourful flowers cut from magazines, and the upstairs bathroom was covered in Alphonse Mucha prints. She also repainted some of the woodwork in a combination of vivid yellow and blue. Perhaps asserting herself by decorating the house, in a way Mr Colley would not have approved of was her way of being able to remain there.

Clarice always found out what her old workers were doing, and when a couple who had worked for her for many years both became ill, she arranged with *Bizarre* 'girl' Mary Brown that they would have a holiday on the North Wales coast. She stated emphatically, 'I will be responsible for all the cost for a fortnight.'

Clarice's major passion in the late sixties was to be Chetwynd's vast garden, and to help her tackle this her former clay maker Reg Lamb was recruited as a gardener. She wrote to Hilda that, 'In between hedge cutting we are trying to make the work less. This year we have taken away the grass borders from the rose garden and replaced them with paving, it has been a big job but it will save two days work cutting and trimming hedges.' Many letters record her love of gardening: 'It has been a good year for hydrangeas I think that the warm weather ripened the wood. There are still flowers on the holly, we had to trim quite a few green berries off it had got very straggly.' Like Mr Colley she was concerned that the suburbs were now encroaching nearer and nearer to Chetwynd and wrote nostalgically, 'We used to smile when my mother used to tell us that she could remember that where we lived used to be all green fields when she was a girl, and Father picked honeysuckle and put it round her hat.'

Clarice never again travelled to Canada or saw Joan and her family, but they did keep in touch as in 1970 she wrote to Hilda, 'Had a card from Joan with coloured snaps of her three – two boys and a girl. Well! Roger the eldest is twenty-two so I suppose they are among the grown ups now. How the years slip by!! I am keeping well – count my blessings – and do not feel much different until I see myself reflected in a shop window, and then I say to myself – for goodness sake, is that me?'

Clarice was vaguely aware of the growing interest in the *Bizarre* years, as she found herself receiving letters or telephone calls. She invariably ignored these, or refused to help, insisting that all the records of her work were lost.

However, Martin Battersby who was organizing the Brighton Museum exhibition put an appeal in *The Times*, and her attention was drawn to it by Guy Shorter. She donated most of the remaining examples of her work to the museum, a *Conical* tea-set, a *Biarritz Honolulu* plate, and four of the *Impressions* figurines, a 'banjo player', a 'kilted Scotsman', a 'bear and a polar bear'. She begrudgingly wrote notes for the catalogue, but these showed that she had forgotten the vast majority of her achievements in the thirties. She refused to go to the opening but was quietly pleased when sent a record of the exhibits, and showed this to a few close friends. The only pieces of her work that remained at Chetwynd were a *Stage coach* cigarette box, which had Colley's initials on the side in gold, and the 1924 *Tibetan* ginger jar she had worked on with John Butler.

The Brighton exhibition created an immense amount of interest and Clarice found herself receiving more telephone calls and letters, but avoided any further involvement. However, one of the enthusiasts took his courage in both hands and dialled Stoke-on-Trent 57991. His name was Peter Wentworth-Sheilds and he was writing a book on Clarice Cliff with his American girlfriend Kay Johnson. Peter had the foresight to record the conversation. Clarice was gently spoken, and apologized for not being able to help, but was interested as Wentworth-Sheilds was a well-known family in the Potteries. As Peter was already being helped by Ethel Cliff, he decided to try to contact Clarice again at a later date.

Clarice Cliff died on 23 October 1972, but many of her old workers did not realize as in the local paper she was listed as 'Clarice Shorter'. The mourners at her funeral included her sisters, some of her *Bizarre* 'girls', Reg her gardener and Dick Wenger, the executor of her estate, whose father had made the timely comment to Colley back in 1940.

The *Tibetan* ginger jar Clarice had decorated back in 1924 was sold along with hundreds of other valuables at an auction held a few months later...

BELOW: Clarice's Tibetan ginger jar, and the shape 445 Stage coach cigarette box with Colley Shorter's initials on the side

CLARICE CLIFF: MYTH AND FACT

Dr Phil Woodward

Since her death in 1972 Clarice Cliff has become both the most celebrated and most controversial figure in British twentieth-century ceramics. She has been celebrated by thousands of collectors, but confusion and controversy has come from academics and the media. Clarifying the facts is essential as some recent speculative writing has done an injustice to her work and achievements. Contemporary publications fully explain how and when she achieved the position as the first woman art director in the Staffordshire Potteries. They also prove that she created such a vast number of shapes and designs that she needed the skills of over sixty decorators and several hundred other staff to satisfy demand, and she was clearly the pre-eminent ceramic designer in Britain between 1927 and 1939.

The key fact concerning Clarice's emergence from being just a gilder, enameller and lithographer was that in 1922 she was given a second apprenticeship as a modeller. Working directly under Wilkinson's art director John Butler, she gained a comprehensive education on the technical side of producing ceramics whilst still under the influence of Butler's very conservative design ideas. Her formal training was initially limited to periods of study at the Staffordshire Art Schools in Tunstall and Burslem, where Gordon Forsyth ensured the classical concept of art dominated the curriculum.

In 1927 she took short courses at the Royal College of Art in Kensington and the Central School of Art in Bloomsbury, and she finally had the chance to break free of the artistic constraints of the Potteries establishment. A clandestine visit to Paris further widened her artistic outlook. As this volume illustrates, the unique quality she was to bring to ceramics was not only inspired by her academic and technical experiences, but by her love of the contemporary art of the day, which was not considered as a design source in the Staffordshire potbanks.

When *Bizarre Artware* was test marketed in October 1927 it could not have been launched at a worse time. The devastating effect on the economy of the General Strike of 1926 meant many factories cancelled their stands at the British Industries Fair. Unemployment in the Potteries had risen to twenty-four per cent of the total workforce in January 1927, yet despite the economic conditions, *Bizarre* was an immediate success. The first-hand

RIGHT: An impressive selection of shape 14 vases in Picasso Flower, Secrets Orange, Branch and Squares, *(middle)* Limberlost *and* Chintz Blue, *(front)* Gibraltar, Orange House *and* Summerhouse

testimony of the paintresses Clarice employed *en masse* to meet the demand is indisputable. The amazing promotional innovations Clarice then pioneered is evidenced by the memories of the paintresses who visited major department stores to demonstrate hand-painting from 1928 onwards, and throughout the thirties.

Between 1927 and 1931 Clarice Cliff was responsible for the production of new ware covering a vast range of styles and functions. These shapes are recorded on the contemporary sheets used by the factories' salesmen and run in a sequence from 341 to 581. Over 100 other shapes were not given numbers, such as her *Conical*, *Stamford*, *Daffodil* and *Eton* tea and coffee ware, so in total she issued over 350 shapes in just five years.

Clarice's involvement with twenty-seven of the most important artists of the day in the *Artists in Industry* project is well documented. Her skills made a reality of the simple water-colour designs of Vanessa Bell, Duncan Grant, Graham Sutherland and a host of others. Her modelling skills were responsible for the only original shapes made for the project, and resulted in its most memorable and collectable pieces, the *Circus* ware of Dame Laura Knight.

Given the short but factual précis of her career, one would expect Clarice Cliff to be highly celebrated today – and amongst collectors she is. However, some writers have expressed the opinion that she was *not* the leading ceramic designer of her day. Others have suggested that she was not an innovator but a copyist, who merely followed in the path of another designer.

Tracing how this academic perception arose we can go back to 1948 when the Council of Industrial Design published a document, sent to every school and college in Britain, which illustrated a *Conical* lemonade set decorated in *Ravel*. The caption read, 'Now fortunately outmoded but still to be seen, and avoided. The unfunctionable handle and the decoration provide a useful cautionary study.' Yet, the *Conical* jug and beakers were pure, uncluttered shapes, with a simple motif in three colours of the type heralded as 'elegant' when found on Susie Cooper's wares. The systematic denigration of Cliff's work had begun.

In 1978, in the *Phaidon Dictionary of Art*, Iain Bennett stated, 'The *Bizarre* designs of Clarice Cliff have unfortunately come to be considered a major British contribution to Art Deco; they were not at the time held in much esteem, nor should we afford them much today.'

In 1979 the major *Thirties* exhibition at the Hayward Gallery included just one piece of Clarice Cliff's work. It was a 1929 *Inspiration* vase vaguely dated as being 'about 1935'. Yet there were four examples of the work of Eric Slater. These included his *Vogue* teaware, the solid triangular handles and shapes of which were copied from Clarice's *Conical* shape, and his *Harmony* ware, copied from Cliff's *Delecia*. Susie Cooper was represented by two pieces. Five of Keith Murray's Wedgwood ceramics were shown. Even Vera Huggins merited having three of her Doulton stoneware vases included. In the catalogue Jennifer Hawkins ignored Clarice Cliff's ceramics, praised Eric Slater, and spoke of 'the singular, even unique achievements of Susie Cooper'.

Despite the lead offered by Jennifer Hawkins, it was not Slater, Murray, Huggins or Cooper who emerged as the leading designer of British ceramics in the thirties. In the wake of the exhibition the verdict of collectors made it a 'one horse race'. However, readers and students studying the thirties were offered information on the relative importance of the designers based on academic rhetoric rather that the contemporary evidence. The proponents of 'Fitness for Purpose' were entrenched in the teaching system and allowed no alternative view to be expressed. Cliff's work, which had caused a sensation when it appeared, was retrospectively ignored or dismissed by the design establishment. When, in the early eighties, television and the press began to rediscover Clarice Cliff and her work, some design historians compared Cliff with Cooper in an attempt to detract attention to their chosen protégé.

In 1987 Ann Eatwell of the Victoria and Albert Museum wrote that Susie Cooper was 'the most important and influential ceramic designer of her generation to emerge from Staffordshire'. In 1990 Cheryl Buckley wrote in *Potters and Paintresses* that 'Only one other designer achieved anything like the same sort of prominence as Susie Cooper, this was Clarice Cliff.' Taking their lead from these academics, several authors on Cooper tried to consolidate these opinions. They had perhaps been influenced by Cooper herself who in 1985 stated on *Pottery Ladies*, a television programme, that 'Cliff was a pupil of mine'. Any student undertaking a thesis on the subject could have been forgiven for following the frequently stated establishment opinion that Susie Cooper was pre-eminent.

However, it simply is not possible to substantiate the claims made either on Cooper's behalf, or by her. The facts are that between 1928 and 1936, over 360 articles about Cliff and her work were published in the trade press, women's magazines, national and local newspapers. This excludes the coverage of the *Artists in Industry* project. In the same period, 1928 to 1936, Cooper received fewer than twenty reviews, all bar one in the trade press.

What did this coverage say of Cliff and her work? The major trade journals both reviewed *Bizarre Ware* in March 1928: the *Staffordshire Pottery and Glass Record* reporter wrote that Newport Pottery 'were showing their very conspicuously coloured ware rightly described as *Bizarre*'. The *Gazette* reported 'the aspect and aim are right, and one cannot help but admire the spirit of adventure which is revealed in the new *Bizarre Ware*.'

In 1929 the national *Daily Sketch* reviewed the Chesham House exhibition and said, 'The most successful of the very modern designers is Miss Clarice Cliff… whose wares have gone all over the world and whose exhibit is the brightest in the show.' In 1930 Cliff's wares were described as 'a brilliant show of extra ordinarily original designs', and she was stated to be 'Art Director' of Newport Pottery. The mentions continued unabated. The press of the day was aware of the unique talents of Clarice Cliff. Can the same be said of Cooper?

Susie Cooper's name was not seen in print until 1929 when a trade journal mentioned that she had presented a tea-set to a royal visitor at Gray's factory. It was decorated with silver lustre and green with a grapevine design. There was absolutely no mention of the Art Deco patterns Cooper did in late 1928 and early 1929. These totalled just four in number, but are now used as evidence of her having designed in this style before Clarice Cliff. However, a review of Gray's pieces from the 1929 British Industries Fair stated 'a special feature was the bizarre patterned coffee services etc., somewhat Cubist in type with blobs of colour and streaks…' The reviewer used Clarice's trade name as it was clearly the easiest way to convey to the reader the style of Cooper's pieces. Whilst Susie Cooper had clearly been influenced by Cliff's style when she was at Gray's, the evidence of the small quantity of these pieces found now suggests that they were only produced briefly and so not successful. If Cooper had started this style before Cliff why was press coverage of it limited exclusively to Cliff? The facts were that when Cliff was employing dozens of new paintresses to fill large orders for *Bizarre* ware, Cooper anonymously left Gray's in October 1929, and did not have a job to go to.

Several books and catalogues have claimed that Cooper's 'Liner' mark, including her name, had been used by Gray's from 1923 onwards. However, if it was in use from 1923 why was there not a *single* press mention of this in six years? If Cooper was a significant designer at Gray's, why did this attract no press coverage? There is also a dearth of pieces bearing the Susie Cooper 'Liner' mark between 1923 and 1927. The catalogue of the 1987 Victoria and Albert Museum Susie Cooper exhibition gave two examples. One piece from 1923, a 'soup tureen and cover in pattern 2866', did *not* have a Susie Cooper backstamp, only a Gray's one. The other was listed as plate 13 and dated 'about 1926.' The backstamp was listed as '4d', the liner mark, but turn to page 94 and the reader will find that the mark 4d is the liner mark without 'designed by Susie Cooper'. Of thirty-four items credited as her work between 1923 and 1929 only sixteen had her mark. All but two of the sixteen pieces were in the 7000 or 8000 series pattern number range, which the catalogue acknowledged dated to 'about 1928 or 1929'. There is no example given of a piece with a Susie Cooper backstamp from 1924, 1925, 1926 or 1927 let alone 1923.

ABOVE: Sliced Circle *on a shape 14 vase and a* Pastel Comets *plate*

Gray's ceramics, in lavish all-over floral and abstract designs, are used as evidence that Cooper's designs pre-dated similar pieces from Cliff. Yet the only authoritative documentation on this period, a catalogue of the Gray's Pottery exhibition held at Stoke in 1980, stated 'Susie Cooper's designs use simple floral groups in stylized form but leaving a lot of plain ground, conversely Dorothy Tomes produced all-over decorations with great emphasis on black and green with floral shapes of almost abstract form.' Many pieces attributed as being by Cooper could actually be the work of Dorothy Tomes from 1930 onwards, but Tomes has been conveniently overlooked by subsequent writers. Today, the pieces with all-over floral decoration, bearing just a Gray's backstamp, are sometimes offered for sale as 'unmarked Susie Cooper'.

Susie Cooper stated many years later that she left Gray's in 1929 to start her own factory. Her departure coincided with the biggest slump in orders ever seen in the Staffordshire Potteries, with forty-eight per cent of the workers on short-time working. Why should she choose to leave at such a time? The fact is that she did not leave to run a new business, as it took her two months to even find premises. She then achieved just one firing of ware before this business closed. The pieces were blanks from other manufacturers, hand-painted by just six paintresses, whereas in 1930 Clarice Cliff had over 200 original shapes, and needed over sixty decorators to fill orders. There was a gap of a further five months before Cooper established her next venture, which again was temporary and just painted blanks. In September 1931 she rented space from one of the dynastic firms, Wood & Sons, at their Crown Works in Burslem. This would have brought her into contact with John Butler, who had been Cliff's former mentor, as he was then the art director for Woods.

The trade press first reviewed Cooper and her ware in April 1930, two years after Cliff's initial review. The majority of the text detailed her training under Gordon Forsyth and the search for factory premises. It did not mention that she had been a designer for Gray's, and neither did any of the other articles. The next report, in 1931, concentrated again on the person rather than on her products. In 1932 Cooper was reported as being 'a newcomer to the British Industries Fair'. The wares exhibited were not Art Deco but included, 'pretty nursery ware decorated with grey or black dogs… a conventional tulip in black on a matt surface… a more ordinary, but very pretty decoration was the Briar Rose'.

In 1985 Susie Cooper claimed on the *Pottery Ladies* television programme, 'Cliff was a pupil of mine'. Asked about Clarice Cliff as a competitor, she stated that she knew she 'wasn't the only pebble on the beach'. And yet on 13 September 1973 Susie Cooper had written to a researcher 'I do not think I can be of a great help to you in your research on "Clarice Cliff pottery". Although the late Mrs Shorter and myself are somewhat of the same vintage, so to speak, I never actually met her or have any recollection of her as a student at the Burslem School of Art.'

The argument by writers such as Cheryl Buckley that 'only Cliff achieved anything like Cooper's prominence,' is negated by the volumes of their respective sales. The extant *Bizarre* order books show that in 1932 there were around 600 stockists. Between 5 March and 30 April 1932 a total of 202 of them ordered by mail. Further, the list of overseas stockists is recorded in advertisements carried every month from March 1928 in *Pottery Gazette*. In contrast, prior to 1932 Cooper was nomadic and produced very little ware.

Her first advertisement was placed in 1932, her first overseas agents, in Australia and South Africa, were finally appointed in 1936 and 1939 respectively. Cheryl Buckley also argued that technically Cliff's production was 'quite a small part of Wilkinson's total manufacturing output,' but compared to Cooper's it was massive. Newport Pottery office worker Eric Grindley saw the order books on a daily basis and stated that Cliff was producing 1500 dozen (18000) pieces of *Bizarre* ware each week, which produced an income of £2000. In contrast, prior to 1932 Cooper produced very little ware. Her first order from a department store was not placed until 1932.

The imbalance in their relative importance is evidenced by the fact that in 1933 when Cooper and her business partner sold the Susie Cooper Pottery Company, to Woods on 7 April, the price paid for the business and goodwill was £500 (Companies House File no 171246). Thereafter Cooper was just one of eight directors of the Crown Works and held ten per cent of the issued shares. It was only after John Butler's untimely death that she became art director in 1935, five years after Cliff had led the way. In sharp contrast, if Colley Shorter had wanted to sell Cliff and her goodwill, a figure of £100,000 would only have represented one year's turnover, which would have been a very attractive buy to most businessmen. In the *Bizarre* years of 1927 to 1936, Cliff was infinitely more productive than Cooper.

Even when the major facts about Clarice Cliff's work had become clear, some writers still made erroneous claims. As late as 1990 Cheryl Buckley stated that in 1936 'Cliff was designing wall masks and jazz-age figures such as dancing couples, pianists, banjo players, drummers and trumpeters, which were modelled by Peggy Davies.' The *Age of Jazz* figures were designed by Clarice Cliff back in September 1930 when Peggy Davies was only ten years of age and still at school!

So what are the full facts about Susie Cooper's career? We will probably never know. However, her first employer, Gray's, was just a small potbank. Gray's used blanks from other factories, it did not manufacture shapes as Wilkinson's did. In 1924–25 Cooper decorated a lot of very traditional *Gloria Lustre* ware in designs by her mentor Gordon Forsyth and produced a few patterns of her own in this lustre style, but there is no endorsement in the press about her being their designer. The only facts concerning this period came retrospectively from one source – Susie Cooper. In contrast, the contemporary reports, of which there are many, illustrate that from 1927 onwards Cliff was the most influential designer of ceramics in Britain.

From 1935 onwards Susie Cooper did begin to achieve recognition, but this was nearly all for conservative printed, spotted, or banded tableware. She was a favourite of the Queen Mother, who regularly purchased ware from her exhibitions, so it is not surprising she was awarded an OBE in 1979; it was a fitting reward for a very long career. Susie Cooper lived into her nineties, for the last fifteen years of her life as a 'living legend', so was understandably revered by design historians. But collectors do not look at a piece of pottery and gauge its importance by how long the designer worked. Clarice Cliff's *Bizarre* spell of ten years captivates a great many more collectors. However, Cooper's contradictory statements about Clarice Cliff, and her dating of her own early work, were partly responsible for some of the misconceptions now being perpetuated, and this is the right place to correct these. Perhaps buoyed up by the interest in her work, she later, unwisely, tried to recall events she had forgotten?

My personal belief is that the magic surrounding Clarice Cliff's name today is simply an echo of the situation in the thirties. Her ware was colourful, challenging, exciting, and young, and being just an ordinary woman she was identified as a working-class hero. In contrast Susie Cooper was born into a much more fortunate life, and this was reflected in her output which was elegant and well painted but lacking in charisma, as it primarily consisted of tableware. Susie Cooper also lacks the on-going intrigue of Clarice Cliff, as her output was more orderly, whereas virtually every week, even now, new Clarice Cliff shapes or designs are discovered.

We have finally discovered the answer to the question 'Why *Bizarre*?' We now know that when she was studying in London in 1927 Clarice heard of a set of prints which Campbell Dodgson had just donated to the British Museum. These extraordinary images by Giovanni Batista Bracelli, created between 1624 and 1649, which he named *Bizarrie*, gave Clarice the theme for her ideas in 1927, and demonstrate her extreme interest in art. Cliff was inspired by them, and her use of the word *Bizarre* can be seen as both an acknowledgement and homage to Bracelli.

There can be no doubt that Clarice Cliff was the 'Doyenne of Hand Painting' between 1927 and 1937. The numbers of shapes and designs, allied to the massive scale of production, make Cliff unique. Every taste was catered for, from the avant-garde, with ultra modernistic designs influenced by the Parisian School, to vivid floral designs to brighten up the homes of less adventurous buyers. Children were designed for, as well as the day tripper who wanted a keepsake of a day out. Cliff was truly gifted in her ability to appeal to every segment of the market. But that should not deflect our attention from the fact that all of her production was, and still is, artware of the very highest calibre. There is art history in every hand-painted brush stroke. Cliff's work recognized the art tradition of the past and added something to it, to become the tradition of the future.

THE CLARICE CLIFF PHENOMENON

A window at Chetwynd House has a signature scratched into the glass. The inscription, 'Clarice Shorter', is cut with a diamond. It must date from after Colley's death, when we know she contemplated leaving Chetwynd. Clarice stayed, but her way of accepting life there alone, was to make her mark on the house, and having done that, for the last time, she signed her work.

Clarice filled her final years redecorating the house, in her own rather unorthodox manner. She painted woodwork in vibrant blue and yellow, and made swirling patterns with her fingers in wet plaster on the walls, hard work for an elderly lady. The bathroom and kitchen cabinets, were covered with a collage of colourful cuttings and Art Nouveau prints. One can picture her, in

her sixties, on a ladder, sticking cut-out paper flowers onto the scullery ceiling. It echoes the day forty years earlier when Nancy watched her young aunt as she decorated the bedroom ceiling in Tunstall with squares of gold paper, or the early thirties when Clarice took shiny yellow and black paper from the factory to decorate her bathroom ceiling at Snow Hill. Little had really changed since she had made papier mâché maps as a child.

Clarice Cliff was an artist who liked to get her fingers wet and dirty. Her artistically intense encounter with *Bizarre* from 1927 to 1936 was a creative rush that embraced lots of hands-on work for her and her team. Having spent years modelling vases, bowls, figurines and fancies from clay, her skills came into sharp focus from 1927. Hundreds of shapes, the likes of which had not been seen before, poured from her studio. She combined these with the rainbow splashes of *Delecia*, or the thick blobby enamel brushstrokes of her *Autumn* trees. One of her paintresses recalled that she was 'slap-dash' when . painting ware, applying the enamels hurriedly, eager to move on to her next project. This was the life-blood of *Bizarre*.

After the *Bizarre* years, Clarice never really put down her brushes, palette knives, or sculpting tools. She kept returning to colour and form. During the war, and the later years when she devoted herself to Colley, she still found time for creative pursuits, but her passion was the multi-coloured flowers, and shaped beds and hedges, of their wonderful garden. Then, with Colley suddenly gone, she was alone and rather lost in the large house. She transcended her solitude by decorating the house. Her preoccupation with it meant she was never to fully understand what she had achieved with *Bizarre*, as she did not visit the 1972 Brighton exhibition. Without Colley, there was probably little point, and she died the same year.

But what has been Clarice Cliff's impact since her death? Her unique talents were first recognized by a bohemian section of society. The early collector Martin Battersby had worked for years with Cecil Beaton, and then reinvented himself as a trompe l'oeil artist. His exhibition at Brighton partly inspired Kay and Peter to write the first book, which they had spent years researching as they busily worked on films such as *Clockwork Orange* and *2001*. Meanwhile, theatre producers, movie stars and fascinating devotees bought Clarice Cliff pottery as soon as it arrived in London from the provinces. Demand always outstripped supply. Then, when the L'Odeon exhibition started, it made Clarice Cliff into an instant icon.

The sun was bursting out of its blue socket the day the Clarice Cliff exhibition opened at L'Odeon last week. The high priestess of the hand-painted pottery sunburst is being publicly celebrated for the second major time.

Sunday Telegraph, 25 April 1976

A review of the book and exhibition in *Honey* magazine, was headlined, 'Outrageously expensive Bizarre' which was ironic as they noted that some dealers were charging £5 for a single plate! Begrudgingly at first, London auction houses included a few pieces of Cliff pottery in their Decorative Arts sales. The interest and results surprised them, and soon it had become a regular if incongruous presence alongside glass by Lalique, Daum and Gallé.

The fervent response to the L'Odeon exhibition meant that reproductions of her ware were contemplated as early as 1976. Roy Midwinter, who had bought Wilkinson's, was now working as the Group Design Coordinator at Wedgwood, and wrote to Peter Wentworth-Sheilds, 'I'm still very keen on the idea of producing a limited-edition Clarice Cliff plate.' The vision was a little premature, but reflected the intense interest her work was already stimulating.

Prices soared in the wake of the exhibition. The L'Odeon book was re-released in 1981, and attracted yet further collectors. When Kay and Peter moved to America, and L'Odeon later closed, it all became part of the Cliff legend. The book, immediately scarce, was soon selling for over £100. Thirsty for new information on the intriguing woman whose wares they sought, collectors eagerly joined the newly launched *Clarice Cliff Collectors' Club*.

In 1983, Christie's did the unthinkable and held an auction of just Clarice Cliff pottery. A stunning *Appliqué Lucerne* plaque shone on the cover, and collectors who confidently arrived that evening with £300 to £500 to spend were dismayed to find that at least double that was needed to buy. When an *Age of Jazz* figure sold for an unheard of £1,750, gasps and applause mingled incredulously in the air. Clarice had certainly arrived!

BELOW: The Appliqué Lucerne *plaque featured on the 1983 Christie's catalogue cover*

The need to satiate circulation and viewing figures meant that much of the coverage of Clarice's work in the eighties was sensationalized. The press concentrated on 'amazement' at the growing cost of the ware, never quite realizing that intense competition would inevitably keep prices spiralling. Television did Clarice a disservice when the *Pottery Ladies* programme introduced this term to describe the three Staffordshire designers it featured. There was very little in common between Clarice, Charlotte Rhead and Susie Cooper. However, as Clarice's star rose, Susie Cooper's reputation also grew, and the fact that Miss Cooper was still alive to enjoy the adulation, helped draw attention to this 'living legend'. As Phil Woodward has shown, had the researchers gone back to the original material,

it would have been clear that history was just repeat-
ing itself, as Cooper had also followed Cliff the first
time around. Astute collectors recognized that the
meagre supply of Cooper's Art Deco work made it
more than clear who had been the dominant commercial force.

From 1989 Christie's held all Clarice Cliff auc-
tions, and they were soon twice-yearly events.
Devotees flew in from around the world, and were

glad to pay thousands of pounds for ceramics that had been priced in the
low hundreds a few years before. Clarice's pottery invariably caught the attention of the press, and a typical headline was, 'Vases that cost a few pence at
Woolie's are sold for £4000.' That story in the *Daily Mail* about two damaged *Yo Yo* vases reiterated the myth that her ware had been sold at
Woolworth's stores. Luckily, at the same time BBC Radio 4 *Woman's Hour*
interviewed several of the original *Bizarre* 'girls'. Now hale and hearty octo-
genarians, Alice Andrews, Elsie Nixon, Rene Dale and Marjory Higginson
reminisced about working for 'Miss Cliff', and their good fortune to be
employed throughout the Depression. Their Staffordshire origins and impetu-
ous humour soon burst through and Alice quipped, 'We may not have the
looks, or the husbands, but we're there, we're right at the top, the Clarice
Cliff girls!' Clarice would certainly have chuckled. In sad counterpoint, the
Bizarre shop by the canal was being demolished to make way for a housing
estate. Just a few miles away, and two years later, a new decorating shop was
established by Wedgwood to paint Clarice Cliff reproductions. It was in her
home town of Tunstall.

*ABOVE: The demolition
in 1996 of the building
which housed the
Bizarre shop and the
Crocus shop at Newport
Pottery*

*LEFT: Clarice's 1935
Austin was a surprise at
the Bizarre girls 1995
reunion. From the left;
Alice Andrews, May
Booth, Jessie Mackenzie,
Doris Johnson; inside the
car, Elsie Nixon and
Ethel Barrow; then
Annie Beresford, Phyllis
Tharme, Winnie Pound,
Nora Dabbs and
Marjory Higginson*

RIGHT: *Just one example of surprising prices for Clarice Cliff ware, a* Bon Jour May Avenue *tea-set which sold for £13,800 in 1998*

RIGHT: *Just one example of surprising prices for Clarice Cliff ware, a* Bon Jour May Avenue *tea-set which sold for £13,800 in 1998*

Even the collectors eventually became the focus of attention, as Christie's were deluged with them. Their Clarice Cliff sales attracted more people than any other held at South Kensington. A magazine noted, 'the Cliffie's themselves can spot a 1934 *Bizarre Nasturtium* vase at fifty paces in dark glasses and have its value down to the nearest decimal point before you can say buyer's premium'.

The value of Clarice's pottery continues to totally fascinate people, but disbelief is at last giving way to understanding. Collectors know that whatever the prices are today, within a few years their 'expensive' buys will start to look quite reasonable. Books that valued the patterns and shapes were outdated soon after publication, so I make no apology for the fact that this volume does not enter this price minefield. A current Christie's auction catalogue, or a visit to an Art Deco fair (which are held virtually every weekend in Britain), are the most accurate ways of gauging the market. I believe that if you *really* want a piece of Clarice Cliff because you love it, the price you decide to pay is its value.

Ironically, Clarice's biggest error was that she was over-productive, and some of her best work was originally overlooked. As we try to date the sequence it appeared in, it is clear that she must have been moving from department to department, delegating work to suit the skills of her team. The

Bizarre Index gives an insight into her major patterns and shapes, but a further book would be needed to portray the whole output. In the month I completed this book, three new designs and one new shape were recorded, and I believe there is still much to be discovered. One recent surprise was the shape 469 *Liner* vase painted in its original style. I was amazed at her ingenuity in cleverly creating an ultimate Art Deco image as a functional vase.

Clarice's last years, spent keeping her garden colourful and tidy, or covering ceilings in cut-out flowers, reminds one of Matisse directing an assistant to paste coloured paper onto board to make his final art, or Monet relishing his garden at Giverny. She was just as much an artist, although her canvas was earthenware, and she lacked the romantic surroundings. For many years Clarice's Staffordshire background remained a hurdle her reputation could not surmount. It is easy to visualize an artist working in the fresh air, building light into pictures, but a working-class girl from the Potteries suddenly taking colour to Britain and much of the world is a harder concept to absorb. Had Clarice designed in a Chelsea studio, she might have been accepted by the establishment more easily. But Clarice was a true Staffordshire artist who reflected the heritage of this unique part of England in a way only she could, and in a way only she knew how. From her cosy *Crocus* to the outrageous *Tennis* she simultaneously embraced art in its most traditional and avant-garde forms.

The towns of the Potteries are associated strongly with Josiah Wedgwood, Arnold Bennett and Reginald Mitchell, but Clarice Cliff was the first woman from the area to distinguish herself on a world-wide basis. However, she did this by freeing herself from its historical constraints, which might otherwise have tainted her achievements. She is now accepted as a thoroughly modern artist and designer, whose colours and shapes are as fresh today as they were when her young paintresses executed them in the *Bizarre* shop by the canal. And yet amazingly, it has taken until her centenary year for Clarice to be celebrated in her home town.

Though sheer gritty determination, creative ability, and strong belief in herself, Clarice was able to transcend the artistic boundaries of conservative and traditional teaching to create *Bizarre*. The repercussions of her turning the design world upside-down are still being felt, and when they hit the twenty-first century, Clarice Cliff will stand alone, as the one person who had the vision to unite colour and form in the thirties. Her ware was not just *Bizarre*, it was magnificent. She conquered the world, and now she is returning home for good.

ABOVE AND RIGHT: A Clarice Cliff 'time-bomb', a rare shape 469 Liner vase in its original colourway

BIZARRE INDEX

—

A TO Z OF CLARICE CLIFF HAND PAINTED DESIGNS

This listing mainly covers Clarice Cliff's hand-painted design output between 1927 and 1936. In addition, major patterns that featured a printed outline which was then enamelled, such as *Solomon's Seal* and *Nemesia*, are included, but listed as 'printed'. Some post-1936 patterns are included, but not later tableware, printed or lithographed designs.

DESIGNS: These are listed alphabetically followed by a brief pattern description. If they are part of a range they are marked with a *. For example, you will find *Spring Crocus* and all other colourways under *Crocus*, but as colourings varied greatly on designs these are not detailed.

DESIGN NOMENCLATURE: *Original* design names and *attributed* names are not distinguished. Where original design names were not known, attributed names were given in *Bizarre Affair* and the *Reviews* of the Clarice Cliff Collectors' Club. These have since gone into general use. Where an original name has since been discovered the attributed name is given in brackets.

DATES: The year of introduction is given in brackets. Most designs were produced for less than a year. Some were created late in the year for the British Industries Fair the following spring. Matchings were theoretically available of all designs until 1939 but these are decorated noticeably differently.

COLOURWAYS: Many designs had several colourways and in most instances the design is included under its name with the colour afterwards, except where this does not make sense, i.e. *Blue Firs*, *Red Roofs*. The 'red' colour on Clarice's ware was called Coral in the factory, so this is used except where an original design, such as *Autumn Red*, is already established.

BACKSTAMPS AND MARKINGS: These designs nearly always have a printed backstamp with a *Clarice Cliff Hand Painted Bizarre* mark, under a *Fantasque, Crocus, Appliqué, Latona* or other range name which is either printed or

hand-painted. Pieces with just *Clarice Cliff* probably date from after 1936. The only exception are very small pieces which may be unmarked or have part of a backstamp due to small base area

The main backstamps and hand-painted range names showing the range a design was from, are given in brackets after the design name: (A) *Appliqué* (B) *Bizarre* (C) *Clarice Cliff* (F) *Fantasque* (I) *Inspiration* (S) Sample (U) A custom mark, or a partly hand-painted mark above a printed mark.

ACORN (B) Red acorns and oak leaves, with yellow and tan *Delecia* runnings (1934)

AGAVE (C) A tall, flowering cactus by an expansive bay, on a turquoise glaze (1937)

ALTON (B) A tower amidst bushes, flowers and pendant leaves. Colourways *Alton Green* and *Alton Orange* which has blue bushes. Named after Alton Towers in Derbyshire (1933)

AMBEROSE (B) A yellow and pink rose with smaller roses and leaves on brown branches amidst circular bands (1933)

ANEMONE (C) Detailed flowers sometimes with runnings, in full or edge pattern (1937)

APPLES (F) Apples and grapes with pink, yellow and orange leaves, and black oblongs (1931)

APPLIQUÉ* A range produced with more and brighter colours than *Bizarre* or *Fantasque*, mainly featuring landscapes. *Lucerne*, a mountain scene with a castle (1930); *Lugano*, a mountain scene with a water-wheel (1930); *Avignon*, a bridge and lake scene (1930); *Caravan*, a gypsy caravan under an orange tree (1930); *Etna*, a pink and grey volcano with sea in the foreground (1931); *Monsoon*, a windswept tree in an oriental landscape (1931); *Palermo*, red sailed yachts on the bay with a climbing plant in the foreground (1930); *Red Tree*, a very stylized tree scene with grey sky (1930); *Windmill*, a blue windmill with orange sky (1930); *Bird of Paradise*, a yellow and red bird on a branch with black berries (1930); *Blossom*, clematis and lilac against a trellis (1930); *Eden*, a brown flower surrounded by orange flowers, a blue and green landscape (1931); *Garden*, a tree with a black trunk with heavy foliage in orange or blue colourways (1931); *Appliqué Idyll*, a crinoline lady standing under a tree in a garden, later issued in the *Fantasque* range with pastel banding (1931)

ARABESQUE (B) An Isnic-influenced design in red, blue, yellow and green (1929)

AUREA (B & C) see *Rhodanthe*

AUTUMN (F) Sinuous trees, bushes and a small cottage. Numerous colourways named after dominant foliage includes blue, red, orange, yellow, green, pastel (1930 to 1934, matchings until 1940)

AVON (C) A bridge over a river and two fisherman (1937)

BAMBOO (B or C) A bamboo tree with etched flowers and leaves, sometimes with an oriental hut (1935)

BAZIQUE (I) A river scene with an Arab dhow and tall stylized trees (1930)

BEACH BALL (B) Black and orange balls between outlined blocks in green and orange (1932)

BERMUDA (C) A tree with blue and yellow foliage, on a green, brown ground (1937)

BERRIES (F) Red and orange berries, with leaves and yellow and green blocks (1930)

BIGNOU (B) A sunburst in green, orange and yellow, a shoulder pattern on tableware (1930)

*BIZARRE** Clarice's first range from 1927 of designs of randomly coloured diamonds or triangles, called *Original Bizarre* in factory literature from 1930 onwards. In 1928 *Bizarre* became the umbrella title for all Clarice Cliff ware until it was dropped in 1936

BLACK FLOWER (F) A stencilled black flower on a striped ground (1929)

BLUE DAISY (B) A freehand blue, pink, and orange daisy with curling lines (1930)

BLUE-EYED MARIGOLDS (B) Orange flowers with blue centres and clear leaves, on a black ground (1930)

BLUE FIRS (F) A green landscape with blue fir trees, also coral and green colourways (1933)

BLUE RIBBON (B) Freehand orange flowers with purple centres, with ribbons (1932)

BLUE 'W' (B) The 'W' motif surrounded by geometric forms in orange, green and purple (1929)

BOBBINS (B) Red and yellow 'bobbins' with blue and green leaves (1931)

BOWLING (B) Horizontal banding with freehand bulls-eye motifs (1929)

BRAIDWOOD (B) Turquoise cornflowers on a green glaze with border hatching (1935)

BRANCH AND SQUARES (B) Overlapping oblongs, some with a branch motif (1930)

BRIDGWATER (B) A river scene with a question-mark shape tree, a bridge and cottage. Colourways: orange, green, blue (1934)

BROOKFIELDS (B & C) A rural scene with a cottage, bridge and ploughed field, covered in fine lining which is omitted on some shapes (1936)

BROTH (F) A busy mass of circles and lines, named after the circles of fat on top of broth. Clarice adapted this from a John Butler design. Originally *Fantasque* pattern 105. Colourways: orange and red (1928)

BRUNELLA (B) Blue and rust stylized flowers as an edge motif, similar to *Ravel* (1929)

BUTTERFLY (F) Freehand butterflies on a striped ground, based on a Benedictus pochoir print (1929)

CABBAGE FLOWER (B) Green and brown flowers on brown crescents (1934)

CAFÉ (B) Freehand grey, red and black squares above a black band with dots. Colourways: orange and coral (1931)

*CAFÉ-AU-LAIT** (B or U) Ware completely or partially stippled with one colour with a design then painted over this. Numerous examples including *Autumn*, *Bobbins*, *Gardenia*, *Red Roofs*, *Red Tulip* (1931–33)

CANTERBURY BELLS (B) Bell-shaped and daisy flowers, green leaves with brown *Café-au-lait* above, yellow below (1932)

CAPRI (B) A simple outlined garden with large flowers beneath trees, covered with radial banding. Colourways: orange, green, and blue (1935)

CAPRICE (I & B) A landscape with fantastic stylized trees and an elaborate bridge. Originally hand-painted on a grey glaze then simplified for the *Inspiration* range (1929)

CARIBBEAN COTTAGE (B) A cottage and trees scene in pastel colours (1933)

CARPET (B) Curvilinear shapes and dots. Colourways: coral or orange (1930–31)

CASTELLATED CIRCLE (B) Circles and castellated shapes,

some with solid colour, sometimes with triangles behind. Numerous colourings (1929)

CHALET (C) A chalet in a garden with *Café-au-lait* sky and ground (1936)

CHERRY (F) Blue fruit with purple leaves, outlined in jade (1928)

CHERRY BLOSSOM (C) A simple tree with finger-dabbed flowers over *Delecia* runnings (1936)

CHINTZ (F) Brashly painted waterlily buds, and leaves. Colourways: blue, orange, and green (1932)

CHLORIS (U) A colour lithograph of stylised flowers with hand-painted banding. Issued mainly with a Wilkinson's backstamp it is also found with a *Bizarre* backstamp.

CIRCLE TREE (F) A freehand spiky black tree with foliage of multi-coloured circles (1929)

CIRCLES AND SQUARE (F) A band of overlapping geometric forms in green, yellow orange and blue, called 'Allsorts' in Australia (1929)

CLOUVRE* (I) Freehand on-glaze floral designs on a light or dark blue *Inspiration* ground. Variations include *Tulip*, *Water Lily* and *Bluebell*, which was based on a pochoir print by Benedictus (1930)

CLOVELLY (C) Red-roofed houses by the sea, and a small, distant island (1937)

COASTAL OAK (B) A stylized tree with a few large red and brown leaves by a stylized coast (1934)

COMETS (B) Interwoven comet shapes with small floral motifs (1929)

CORAL FIRS (F) A full landscape with fir trees by a plain, sometimes with a black-roofed cottage and cliffs. Also a *Biarritz* tableware pattern (1933–39)

COWSLIP (B) Stylized flowers and leaves with fine details and *Café-au-lait* shading. Colourways: blue, yellow, green and brown (1933–34)

CRAYON SCENES* (B) Freehand scenes of England in natural colours executed on biscuit ware with ceramic crayons, then glazed over. Variations included *Beech*, *Brookside*, *Kenilworth* and *Peel* (1934)

CRÊPE-DE-CHINE (U) An all-over black printed floral pattern, enamelled in several colourways (1933)

CREST (B) Blue, red and black flowers with red spotted centre, and a green crescent surround (1933)

CROCUS* (U) Freehand painted flowers issued in numerous colourways between 1928 and 1964. Original *Crocus* (sometimes called *Autumn Crocus*) had orange, blue and purple flowers (1928–64); *Awakening*, a tableware motif

of crocus flowers above a wavy line (1932); *Blue Crocus*, the flowers with yellow and blue banding (1935); *Gloria Crocus*, the flowers underglazed in pastel colours (1931); *Peter Pan Crocus*, the flowers by a *printed* tree, in silhouette (1930–32); *Purple Crocus*, the rarest colourway (1933); *Spring Crocus*, pink, yellow and blue flowers (1933–64); *Summer Crocus*, the flowers on a green glaze (1934); *Sungleam Crocus*, orange and yellow flowers (1931–33)

CUBIST (B) Overlapping cubes and oblongs in orange, yellow, green and blue (1929)

DAMASK ROSE (U) Not a design but a body produced by mixing slip with a pink colourant. Once cast and fired the biscuit ware pieces were then given a clear glaze. The pink body was decorated with freehand fruit or floral motifs (1931)

DELECIA* (D & B) A decoration made of randomly coloured runnings created by mixing colour with turpentine, originally as an all over decoration in 1929 and 1930. Then used with various motifs including: *Delecia Daisy*, blue and pink flowers with blue and green runnings; *Delecia Pansies*, with the *Nasturtium* design in pastel shades; *Delecia Poppy* (all 1932)

DIAMONDS (B) A geometric design of two panels in yellow, orange and blue, one with diamond-shaped motif, the other an abstract (1929)

DORÉ (U) A *printed* flower and leaf pattern within a cartouche, produced for Harrods (1930)

DOUBLE 'V' (B) Black and yellow 'V's dividing panels of abstract shapes (1929)

DRYDAY (C) A tree with white enamel detail, by small egg-shaped flowers (1937)

EATING APPLES (C) Yellow and red apples with green and grey pears and leaves (1937)

ELIZABETHAN COTTAGE (C) A red-roofed cottage with leaded windows half-hidden amongst trees (1937)

ERIN (B) Cloud-shaped bushes with egg-shaped devices floating above. Colourways: orange and green (1933)

FANTASQUE* An umbrella title for a range of designs introduced to make Clarice's hand-painted designs available to more stockists as *Bizarre* was originally offered on an exclusive basis in each town. Many patterns were issued in the *Fantasque* range between 1928 and 1934 but the majority were Clarice's distinctive cottage and tree designs. They are distinguished here (F) but some only had a *Bizarre* backstamp

FARMHOUSE (F) A cottage with a tall chimney, amidst trees and bushes (1931)

FEATHERS AND LEAVES (B) A stylized feather shape on a background of geometric forms and black leaves (1929)

FERNDALE (C) A tree with etched foliage, and a distant red and yellow cottage (1937)

FLORA (B) A printed outline of buds painted in blue and orange (1930). *Flora* was also the name of a wall mask

FLOREAT (B) An orange flower with green and plain leaves, and black detail (1930)

FLOWER MUSIC (B) Flowers painted as notes on sheet music (1933)

FLOWER WAVE (B) Blue, yellow and green flowers with angular stems on a blue wavy ground (1934)

FLOWERS AND SQUARES (B) Overlapping oblongs with a daisy motif in some (1930)

FOOTBALL (B) A complex geometric design with a blue net (1929)

FOREST GLEN (B & C) A country cottage on an etched hill side under a blood red *Delecia* sky. Was also pattern number 6614 (1935)

FRAGRANCE (F) A country garden with an etched tree and tall delphiniums with small pink and blue flowers. Alternate colourway is *Sandon* (1935)

FRUIT (F) Geometric fruit in red, yellow and orange against diagonal purple hatching (1929)

FRUITBURST (B) A motif of stylized fruit with radiating orange blocks (1930)

GARDENIA (F) A bold orange or coral red flower with green and black leaves, with smaller purple and blue flowers (1931)

GARLAND (F) A bold rim or shoulder pattern of freehand flowers on a black ground (1929)

GAYDAY (B) Orange, red and purple asters with green leaves, banded in brown, yellow and green. See also *Sungay* (1930)

GEOMETRIC FLOWERS (F) Cubist yellow, red, orange, blue and purple flowers with diamond-shaped leaves (1929)

GEOMETRIC GARDEN (F) Cubist flowers on Cubist stems with square flowers in the distance (1929)

GIBRALTAR (F) The Rock of Gibraltar in pastel shades with yachts in the foreground (1931)

*GLORIA** (B) Underglaze decoration in pale water-colours covered with a *Latona*-type glaze, featuring versions of other patterns, e.g. *Crocus*, *Tulip* and *Bridge* (1930)

GOLDEN ORANGES (S) Oranges with gold leaves and grey and black diagonal blocks. Known only from a water-colour in the sample books (1929)

GREEN HOUSE (F) A wind-blown tree in coral, green and yellow tree over a green house (1930)

HELLO (Full Circle) (B) a partly printed tableware design of fine concentric black bands with random green or yellow 'bubbles' (1934)

HOLLYHOCKS (B & C) Pink and lilac flowers with pale blue, yellow and brown banding (1936)

HOLLYROSE (B) Pink and yellow flowerheads and yellow leaves with blue contour lines (1932)

HONEYDEW (B & C) Green and yellow flowers in *Rhodanthe* style. See also *Sundew* (1936)

HONITON (B) Finger-dabbed flowers with delicate shaded banding. Originated by Bizarre 'girl' Marjory Higginson (1936)

HONOLULU (B) Trees with variegated trunks and pendulous red orange and yellow foliage. See also *Rudyard* (1933)

HOUSE AND BRIDGE (F) A red-roofed cottage by a winding road, a bridge, and a tree with pendulous orange, red and brown foliage (1931)

HUBERTO (U) Printed and enamelled children's ware featuring cartoons telling the story of a wandering hippopotamus, made for the South African market (1931)

HYDRANGEA (B) Delicate flowers with fine bands, colourways orange and green (1934)

IDYLL (A & F) A crinoline lady near a tree in a garden. Issued as *Appliqué* with banding in black, red, black (1931) then *Fantasque* with pastel banding (1932)

*INSPIRATION** High-fired art pottery using metallic oxide glaze colours painted on biscuit ware. Designs include: *Caprice*, a landscape with trees, and a decorative bridge (1929); *Inspiration Embossed*, old Newport Pottery shapes covered in *Inspiration* glaze (1929); *Delphinium* (1930); *Lily* (1929); *Garden* (1930); *Nasturtium*, a blue, purple and pink version of the hand-painted *Nasturtium* pattern (1930); *Rose*, (1930); *Inspiration Knight Errant*, a knight on horseback by a castle wall. See also *Latona Knight Errant*. The design was done by John Butler in 1926 (1930–31)

JAPAN (B) A delicate tree, a lake and an oriental summerhouse with *Café-au-lait* sky and ground. Colourways: blue and green (1933)

JONQUIL (B) Green flowers, with smaller green and yellow flowers and leaves above *Delecia* runnings. See also *Lydiat* (1933)

KANDINA (F) A stylized tree with amoebic shape lobes, with pendant 'V' shapes (1928)

KELVERNE (B) Grey leaves, orange and red berries and vertical lines (1936)

KENSINGTON (B) Tulips, printed in outline with geometric hatching through them, issued on *Biarritz* tableware (1936)

KEW (F) A red pagoda between wedge and bubble shape trees, produced as both a full design, and tableware cartouche (1932)

KEYHOLE (B) A geometric design in yellow and orange, sometimes with green (1929)

KILLARNEY (B) Green and brown triangular wedges with shaded banding. See also *Sungold* (1934)

LATONA* (U) A milky-coloured glaze on which a large range of sophisticated floral designs were produced. These include: *Blossom* (1929); *Bouquet* (1929); *Cartoon Flowers* (1930); *Dahlia* (1930); *Daisy* (1929–30); *Flowerheads* (1929–30); *Garden* (1930); *Gentian* (1930); *Grape* (1929); *Inca* (1930); *Movie Flowers* (1930); *Orchid* (1929); *Red Roses* (1929); *Shell Flowers* (1930). Other *Latona* designs include *Tree* (1929) and *Aztec* (1930). *Geometric* was the earliest design, fine triangles in purple and orange as an edge band (1929); *Knight Errant*, the same design issued as *Inspiration* ware but with details in coral and silver (1930); *Mushroom* (1929); *Stained Glass* (1929); *Latona Brown* was a pale brown version of the glaze only produced briefly in 1929

LEAF TREE (B) Stylized flowers under a tree with giant orange leaves. Clarice based this on a similar design by John Butler in his *Tahiti* series (1933)

LIBERTY (B) Ware covered in bands of random thickness and colour, produced to bulk-up orders (1927 onwards)

LIGHTNING (B) A geometric design of discs with lightning flashes (1929)

LILY (F) Brashly drawn lilies and leaves. Colourways: orange, brown and white (1928)

LIMBERLOST (B) A tree with tan foliage, and white flowers, with a green plain background (1932)

LINE JAZZ (B) An abstract geometric with Cubist shapes in black, orange, brown and yellow (1930)

LISBON (B) Overlapping squares with floral motifs (1931)

LODORE (U) A printed shoulder pattern with flowers in green and yellow with black hatching (1929)

LONDON (B) An abstract design of crescents and geometric blocks (1930)

LORNA (C) A landscape with a cottage, a bridge and a river flowing into the foreground (1936)

LUPIN (B) Lupin flowers with *Crocus* banding (1928)

LUXOR (B) Pyramids and stylized trees. Colourways: orange, blue, black (1929)

LYDIAT (B) Pink-edged orange flowers with small yellow flowers and black leaves, above *Delecia* runnings. See also *Jonquil* colourway (1933)

MANGO (B) Orange and red fruit with a double outline, and black leaves (1931)

MARIGOLD (B) Orange and yellow marigolds etched on-glaze, on an *Inspiration* ground (1931)

MAY AVENUE (F) An avenue with spade-shaped trees and red-roofed houses and a *Café-au-lait* tree (1933)

MAY BLOSSOM (U) Finger-dabbed flowers on a branch with a colour wash background. Colourways: green, pink and yellow (1935)

MELON (F) A band of geometric fruit, with 'contour-line' effect between. Colourways orange, red, green, blue and pastel (1930)

MILANO (B) A range of partly ribbed shapes with simple broad bands of black and a colour (1935)

MODERNE* (U) Tableware with a cartouche featuring a printed design, including *Casa Mia*, a simple cottage; *Jewel*, stylized flowers; *Norge*, two fir trees; *Odette*, fruit and flowers; *Paysanne*, stylized flowers (1929)

MONDRIAN (B) Overlapping geometric forms in orange, green, blue and yellow (1929)

MOONFLOWER (B) Green flowers amongst blocks of green, grey and yellow. Colourways: green and blue (1933)

MOONLIGHT (B) A pendulous blue tree, over pink, yellow and turquoise flowers. Other colourways: *Cornwall*, in dominant green, *Devon*, in dominant orange (1933)

MORNING (B) A variation on *Rhodanthe* with flowers covered in fine pastel lines (1935)

MOROCCO (B) A simple abstract, similar to Arabian arches. Colourways: orange and blue (1928)

MOSELLE (B) A large yellow and orange flower with a bull's-eye centre, on a broad red band (1934)

MOUNTAIN (F) A stylized tree and cottage with a mountain rising behind. Colourways: orange and pastel (1931)

MOWCOP (C) A tower amongst trees on a hill, named after a Staffordshire Victorian folly (1937)

NAPOLI (C) A garden with a water fountain under gold stars, on a mushroom glaze (1937)

NASTURTIUM (U) Red, orange and yellow flowers by a brown *Café-au-lait* ground. Also known with a *Delecia* ground (1932)

NEMESIA (B) A printed outline of small orange, yellow and green flowers, applied to handles or edges of ware (1930)

NEW FLAG (B) A variation of *Original Bizarre* given a separate name (1929)

NEWLYN (B & C) A country cottage on an etched hillside, under a blue sky of *Delecia* runnings. See also *Forest Glen* (1935)

NEWPORT (B) Geometric lines and forms and small flowers in pastel shades. Colourways: coral and blue (1934)

*NUAGE** (U) Similar to *Café-au-lait*, but with thickened paint to give a more textured surface. Designs, painted as if stencilled, include *Bouquet* and *Flowers* (1932)

OASIS (B) A landscape with a blue cloud-shaped tree and yellow grass (1933)

*OPALESQUE** (B) A range name for ware in a thin *Inspiration*-style glaze, produced briefly in 1934. Variations include several numbered florals, *Stencil Deer* and a tree design called *Bruna*

ORANGE AND BLUE SQUARES (F) Heavy black outlining with blocks in orange, blue and yellow (1929)

ORANGE BATTLE (B) Orange circles with vertical stripes and flying droplets (1929)

ORANGE HOUSE (F) A cottage with orange walls and black roof under a red, green and yellow blowing tree (1930)

ORANGE ROOF COTTAGE (F) A cottage in a garden by a bridge. See also *Pink Roof Cottage* (1932)

ORANGES (B) Orange fruit with leaves in mauve, blue and green (1931)

ORANGES AND LEMONS (B) Red, orange and yellow fruit with black leaves (1931)

ORANGE 'V' (B) Geometric forms in orange, yellow and red, with 'V' shapes (1930)

*ORIGINAL BIZARRE** The first designs of simple triangles, decorated with exaggerated brushstrokes, which were first called *Bizarre*, but the name became an umbrella title, so the factory order books had to refer to it as *Original Bizarre*. These pieces have either a hand-painted *Bizarre* mark, or a large *Bizarre* backstamp

PALM (B) A stylized tree with grass around the base (1934)

PANSIES (B) The *Nasturtium* design in pastel shades with *Delecia* runnings (1932)

PARROT TULIP (B) Freehand tulips painted freehand. Known from the archive factory and one example (1929)

PASSION FRUIT (B & C) A branch heavy with blue, pink and green fruit and flowers (1936)

*PATINA** (U) A range name for ware covered with 'splashes' of pink or grey slip, then honeyglazed and decorated in standard or custom patterns. Freehand designs include *Patina Country*, *Patina Coastal*, and *Patina Tree* (all 1932). Floral examples include *Daisy* and *Tulip* (both 1932). Later the ware was briefly issued in standard patterns *Blue Firs*, *Coral Firs* and *Secrets* (all 1933)

PEBBLES (F) A cluster of multi-coloured circles in panels with zigzag shapes (1928)

PERSIAN (INSPIRATION) (U) Isnic style patterns produced in the *Inspiration* glaze in pinks, mauves and blues (1929)

PERSIAN (ORIGINAL) (U) Isnic designs in hand-painted enamels decorated in the original *Bizarre* style (1928)

PETUNIA (B) A variation of *Canterbury Bells* with freehand flowers which are *not* Petunias (1933)

PICASSO FLOWER (B) A bold coral or orange flower with a blue centre, bisected by a green angular stem. Also known in a blue colourway (1930)

PINE GROVE (B & C) Black and blue fir trees, covered with thin yellow lines, also pattern number 6499 (1935)

PINK PEARLS (B & C) see *Rhodanthe* (1934)

PINK ROOF COTTAGE (F) A pink cottage by a bridge with pastel trees and bushes. See *Orange Roof Cottage* (1932)

POLLEN (F) Simple freehand brown and orange flowers with flying 'pollen' (1932 or 1933)

POPLAR (B) A scene with colourful flowers in the foreground, and a cottage next to orange and blue poplar trees in the distance (1932)

PROPELLER (B) Highly stylized flowers resembling a ship's propeller with blue and green leaves (1931)

RAINBOW (B) Fine edge banding in bright colours on tableware, Newport pattern number 5981 (1931)

RAVEL (B) A tableware motif of simple Cubist flowers and leaves in jade and orange. See also *Brunella* (1929)

RED ROOFS (F) A cottage and trees scene with giant orange flowers on the back (1931)

RED TULIP (F) A bold tulip in coral and yellow with swirling green leaves (1930)

RHODANTHE (B & C) Flowers painted in an etched style in orange, yellow and brown, on sinuous brown stems. Colourways: *Aurea*, green, pink and yellow; *Pink Pearls*, pink and grey; *Viscaria*, blue and green (1934)

RUDYARD (F) A tree with variegated green trunk and pink and blue hanging foliage. See also *Honolulu* (1933)

SANDON (F) A country garden with an etched tree and delphiniums with small yellow and orange flowers. See also *Fragrance* (1935)

SCARLET FLOWER (B) An early floral design featuring thick black outlining of large coral flowers, a small blue one, and green leaves (1928)

SECRETS (F & B) Two half hidden cottages on a hill by an estuary next to a tree with green and yellow foliage. Pattern number 6070 for the full design, 6196 the shoulder pattern. Alternate colourway: *Secrets Orange* (1933–37)

SHARK'S TEETH (B) Curvilinear shapes with 'teeth' in black along the edge (1929)

SILVER BIRCH (C) Trees and bushes executed in broad outlines and stripes, with pink bushes (1937)

SLICED CIRCLE (B) Circles and semi circles against radiating blocks of colour (1929)

SLICED FRUIT (B) Stylized fruit 'sliced' to show their segments amidst small flowers and leaves (1930)

SOLITUDE (F) A coral coloured bridge over a green, yellow and grey sea with an orange tree in the foreground (1933)

SOLOMON'S SEAL (B) A simple printed outline of stylized flowers enamelled in orange, purple and green (1930)

SPEARWORT (B) A design of yellow flowers for *Biarritz* tableware (1934)

SPIRE (C) A distant church with fields and a simple tree in the foreground (1937)

STILE AND TREES (C) A country gate with trees and bushes in naturalistic colours (1937)

ST CLOUD (B) A tableware pattern with green crescents by small flowers (1932)

SUMMER* (U) The range name of ware covered in a pale green glaze on which are painted adaptations of standard designs: *Summer Crocus, Summer Nasturtium* (1934)

SUMMER DAWN (Sand Flower) (B) Freehand orange daisies with blue 'dot' flowers as an edge motif. Produced at Newport before *Bizarre* but then issued with Clarice Cliff markings (1927)

SUMMERHOUSE (F) A pendulous yellow tree with a green trunk and pendant red flowers by a coral hut and black bushes (1931)

SUNBURST (B) A red star shape with yellow, brown and orange triangles (1930)

SUNDEW (B & C) A pink and green colourway of *Honeydew* (1936)

SUNGAY (B) Blue, yellow and green asters, similar to *Gayday* (1932)

SUNGOLD (B) Yellow, orange and amber triangular wedges with shaded banding. See also *Killarney* (1934)

SUNRAY (B) An abstract design depicting skyscrapers, sunrays, a bridge, stars and clouds. Colourway: *Sunray Green* (1929)

SUNRAY LEAVES (F) Panels of jade and orange sunrays, with small stylized flowers (1929)

SUNRISE (F) A sunray motif, wavy lines and spots. Colourways: orange, red and blue (1929)

SUNSHINE (U) Flowers printed in brown outline with green and yellow enamelling (1931)

SUNSPOTS (B) Freehand circles, triangles and dots, and geometric and wavy lines (1930)

SWIRLS (B) Overlapping, multi-coloured, curved forms (1930)

TAORMINA (B & C) A tree with etched foliage, on a cliff top. Colourways: orange, pink and blue (1935)

TARTAN POPPY (C) A tableware motif of a stylized poppy and leaves coloured with fine hatching (1935)

TENNIS (B) Freehand lines and curves in blue, red, grey, green and lilac, with a lilac net (late 1930–31)

TRALLEE (B & C) A garden scene with a thatched cottage with window shutters, and blue *Café-au-lait* sky coming out of the chimney (1935)

TREE (F) A simple stylized tree with blobby pendulous foliage (1928)

TREES AND HOUSE (F) A simple cottage half-hidden by stylized trees and a 'bubble' bush, with lenticular clouds. Colourways: orange, coral, pastel, blue, yellow (1929)

TRIANGLE FLOWER (F) Giant, geometric flowers and leaves outlined in purple, mainly exported to Australia and New Zealand (1929)

TROPIC (Pink Tree) (F) A tree with pink cloud-shaped foliage, by a cottage with a thatched yellow roof (1934)

TULIPS (B) A garden scene with a tree and cottage, and tulips in the distance. The same design with a crinoline lady is called *Idyll* (1934)

UMBRELLAS (F) The 'umbrella' part of the *Umbrellas and Rain* design. Colourways: orange, coral (1929)

UMBRELLAS AND RAIN (F) Alternate abstract panels of stylized umbrellas, and circular raindrops on lines. Colourways: orange, coral (1929)

VISCARIA (B & C) See *Rhodanthe*

WATERMILL (B) Panels of highly stylized sunrays (1930)

WAX FLOWER (B) Abstract blue flowers with curving and straight lines against orange. An alternate version has more colours (1930)

WILD FLOWERS (B) Primitively outlined blue and purple morning glory flowers (1928)

WINDBELLS (F) A tree with sinuous black trunk and blue lenticular foliage, against a wavy background (1933)

WINDFLOWERS (B) Freehand flowers in yellow, blue and brown by a brown *Café-au-lait* ground (Probably 1933)

WINSOME (B) Abstract leaf shapes in panels, an early variation on *Original Bizarre* (1929)

WISHING WELL (C) A hand-painted motif of a wishing well and gilt stars in the sky (1939)

WOMAN'S JOURNAL (U) A printed floral tableware motif with multi-coloured enamelling, offered to readers of this magazine (1931)

WOODLAND (B) A printed design of a tree with orange and green foliage. It was Wilkinson's pattern 8869 but was issued with a *Bizarre* backstamp (1931)

XANTHIC (B) An outlined abstract of square and curved forms in yellow, grey, and orange. See *Xavier* (1932)

XAVIER (B) A freehand version of the *Xanthic* design as a panel on ware covered in yellow *Café-au-lait*. See *Xanthic* (1932)

YELLOW ROSE (B) A simple flower with striped leaves and linear motif found on tableware (1932)

YOO HOO (B) Ware with the body aerographed in black and handles and feet painted in coral (1930)

YUAN (C) Simple cottages and trees painted freehand as a motif, generally on a green glaze (1937)

YUGOSLAVIAN DANCERS (B) Dancers in peasant costumes surrounded by mountains and swirling forms and flowers. Probably a unique exhibition piece (1933 or 1934)

ZAP (B) A mass of overlapping geometric and circular shapes and stylized flowers in orange, yellow and blue (1930)

SHAPE CATALOGUE

The shapes used for *Bizarre* ware were a mixture of old Newport Pottery and Wilkinson's ones, many of which Clarice had modelled, and hundreds of modern shapes she produced from 1928. Pre-1927 shapes such as *Sabots*, *Cauldrons* and various bowls became a popular part of the *Bizarre* range. The *Lotus* jug had originally been part of a jug and bowl set, designed by John Butler in 1919. Clarice issued it with one or two handles, and with no handle as an *Isis* vase.

Confusion is caused by the shapes Clarice worked on between 1922 and 1927. The *Dutch* man and woman, the *Girl* candlestick, the *Viking* boat, the stylized *Duck* figure, the *Arab boy* figure, and the amorous *Friday Night Ducks* were originally issued with just a Wilkinson mark. When she incorporated them into the shape sheets some were given new numbers which imply they were contemporary with the *Bizarre* shapes.

From 1929 some Clarice Cliff *shapes* were decorated at Wilkinson, not in her designs but in simple freehand patterns. The intention was to make ware with the look and shape of *Bizarre* available to smaller dealers, at a lower price. This is why we find *Stamford Early Morning* sets in freehand designs of leaves, or *Daffodil* shape tea ware in all-over aerographed colour. These pieces need to be valued for exactly what they are, Clarice's shapes but *not* her designs.

The original shape sheets that follow were assembled over several years using Clarice's reference photographs of the pieces. Not all the shape numbers were used sequentially. The fact that early designs and later ones appear together does not show that the patterns are all from the same period, the sheets were primarily to illustrate the *shapes*.

There are no shape sheets known from 1932 onwards.

VASE ISIS 2 SIZES 2 HANDLES   ISIS 2 SIZES I HANDLE   ISIS 2 SIZES NO HANDLE   TOILET "ETRUSCAN"   SETS "TOLPHIN"   VASE 73   VASE 14 5 SIZES   119   120

GINGER JAR 132   MINATURE VASES 177 SERIES   186 3 SIZES   194,195 AND 196   204,205 AND 206   217   264 265   268 269   278,279 AND 280   187 3 SIZES   315

FLOWER HOLDER 377   341   VASE 342   LAMP STAND 343 & 344   353, 354 AND 355   VASE 356 AND 371   358   FLOWER HOLDER 359   360   361

362   363   365   370   372   374   375   376   377   386

BOWLS 54ˢ
55ˢ AND 56ˢ

Nº 4 HOLBORN
147, 148 AND 149

OCTAGON
Nºˢ 1, 2, 3, 4 AND 5

HAVRE
6 SIZES

KENDAL ˢ/ˢ

171
172

ROSE BOWL
234

259   260   IVOR

JUNKET OR
PUNCH

"HIAWATHA"

"LOTUS

320

347   357

POPPY
BOWL

EVE

FLOWER BLOCK
225, 2 SIZES

DESSERT
BOWL 9"

FRUIT BOWL
OCTAGON

"DOVER" 6 SIZES

FLOWER
"BOWNESS" 2 SIZES

POTS
"CHIPPENDALE"

373

FLOWER BASKET
"GAIETY"

VIKING
BOAT

SALAD BOWL
AND SERVERS 299

FLOWER BASKET
"ELEGANT"

MATCH HOLDERS
S/S   L/S

ASH TRAYS "503" SHAPE
HIAWATHA 2 SIZES

"SQUARE"

"CIGARETTE BOX"

CAULDRONS
2 SIZES

"FERN"
CHESTER

FERN
169

FERN"HEATH"
4 AND 5

SABOT
2 SIZES

PUFF BOX
339

PUFF BOX
3" & 5"

MUFFINEER
SET

TOAST RACK
2 SIZES

DUCK
EGG SETS

COVERED HONIES "230"
2½", 3", AND 4"

APPLE

ORANGE
2 SIZES

BEEHIVE
2 SIZES

ALMOND
SET

336

BISCUIT JARS
335

HEREFORD

COVERED BUTTER
DUTCH

CHEESES ATHOL
2 SIZES

CRESS AND
STAND

COFFEE POT TANKARD
24ˢ 30ˢ 36ˢ 42ˢ

TEAPOTS
ATHENS

24ˢ 30ˢ 36ˢ 42ˢ
GLOBE

COVERED JUGS
24ˢ 30ˢ 36ˢ

24ˢ 30ˢ 36ˢ 42ˢ
PERTH

CROWN

JUGS
ATHENS

24ˢ 30ˢ 36ˢ
CORONET

DUCK SANDWICH TRAY

MUFFINEER SET
UNITED   SERVICES FIGURES

COVERED HONEY
DUTCH

TEAPOT
"BONES THE BUTCHER"

CREAM
BOY BLUE

SUGAR
HUMPTY

OCTAGONAL
2 SIZES
331
CANDLESTICKS
310
391
392
COMPORT
304
COMPORT
7"
COMPORT
7" & 9"
SUBWAY SADIE
COMPORT

BOOK ENDS

405
406
408
407
NURSERY
409
FRIDAY NIGHT
444

411
412
414
415
FLYING SWAN
FLOWER HOLDER
423

427
428
429
430
431
410
ANGEL FISH
FLOWER HOLDER
424

425
426
433
434
432
435
436
DANCING FIGURES.

VASE
378
VASE
379
380
381
BOWLS
382
383 ⅞s
383 ⅘s

383 ⅗s
384
CANDLESTICK
384
ROSE BOWLS
400
BOWLS
401
SUGAR
INDIVIDUAL
CREAM
CONICAL
TEA & SAUCER
ODILON
TEAPOT
MORNING SET, ODILON

402
BISCUIT JAR

COFFEE POT, 24', 30'
36', CONICAL, ODILON

TEAPOT 24', 30', 36'
CONICAL, ODILON

JUG 24', 30', 36'
ODILON
AND INDIVIDUAL

COVERDISH
ODILON

CREAM CHEESE
ODILON

CREAM 30'
ODILON

VASE
366

BOWL
367

FERN
368

369.

198

199.

200.

FERN 421

TREE 437

PANSIES 438

TULIPS 439
and FERN

DOUBLE
INK 462

INK WELL 457

INK WELL 458

BISCUIT 422

WALL MEDALLION

STAGE COACH 445
CIGARETTE BOX

SERVIETTE HOLDER
OR
CIGARETTES & MATCHES 468

SERVIETTE
RING 556

LIDO S/s.
ASH TRAY
561

LIDO L/s.
ASH TRAY
581

SMOKER'S SET
467

CIGARETTE
& ASH TRAY
420

CIGARETTE &
MATCH HOLDER
463

SHELL CRUET SET 480

MUFFINEER

SET 555

EGG SET, W/H.
551

TEA WARE & MORNING SET

BISCUIT
547

HONEY
557

SUGAR SIFTER
558

GRAPE FRUIT
467

WALL MEDALLION
553
MADE IN TWO SIZES

MARGUERITE

VASE 470

VASE 526

BOWL 473
MADE IN 3 SIZES

BOWL 493
OVAL

VASE 474

VASE 517

SCRAPHITO

COFFEE CAN
& SAUCER

TEACUP &
SAUCER

COFFEE
POT, 36's

B. & B.
PLATE

JUG, 30's

TEAPOT, 30's

TEASIZE
CREAM

TEASIZE
SUGAR

INDIV. SUGAR AND
CREAM ON TRAY
554

DAFFODIL SHAPE

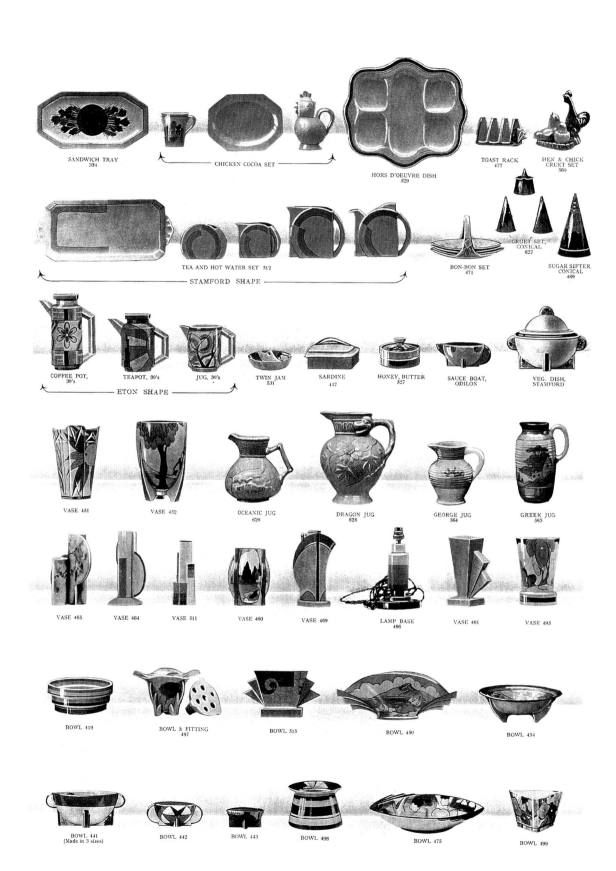

SANDWICH TRAY
334

CHICKEN COCOA SET

HORS D'OEUVRE DISH
529

TOAST RACK
477

HEN & CHICK
CRUET SET
560

TEA AND HOT WATER SET 512

BON-BON SET
471

CRUET SET,
CONICAL
627

SUGAR SIFTER,
CONICAL
489

STAMFORD SHAPE

COFFEE POT,
30's

TEAPOT, 30's

JUG, 30's

TWIN JAM
531

SARDINE
447

HONEY, BUTTER
527

SAUCE BOAT,
ODILON

VEG. DISH,
STAMFORD

ETON SHAPE

VASE 451

VASE 452

OCEANIC JUG
629

DRAGON JUG
628

GEORGE JUG
564

GREEK JUG
563

VASE 465

VASE 464

VASE 511

VASE 460

VASE 469

LAMP BASE
466

VASE 461

VASE 495

BOWL 419

BOWL & FITTING
497

BOWL 515

BOWL 450

BOWL 454

BOWL 441
(Made in 3 sizes)

BOWL 442

BOWL 443

BOWL 498

BOWL 475

BOWL 499

CLARICE'S BIZARRE TEAM

There were hundreds of workers at Newport and Wilkinsons who played a part producing Clarice's ware so it is simply not possible to record them individually. Their skills, which helped create the amazing shapes and bright colours, had very descriptive job titles: fettler, mould runner, saggar-makers, bottom knocker. However, inevitably the focus of our attention is the paintress, whose skills we all identify with. Few people are not tempted to pick up a brush if there is some paint around! Realizing how poor our efforts are, we are full of admiration for their skills.

We are able to list comprehensively the paintresses (plus the few male decorators) because unlike other factories, Clarice nurtured a team spirit and kept all her staff in employment. Although many could band, enamel or outline if needed, the staff are listed by their *main* job. Where they recall a particular range they decorated, this is listed, but many of the staff died before 1981 so these details are lost. All the 'girls' recall being told to 'drop what you're doing', and to 'go on to *Crocus* or *Ravel*' when large orders arrived!

Some of the 'girls' joined Clarice from Wilkinson's so their start date is before they joined the *Bizarre* shop. When Clarice sold the factory to Midwinter's, some 'girls', including Cissy Rhodes and Florrie Winkle stayed, so their 'end' date is after Clarice left. Rosa Rigby, who had joined Clarice in 1935, finally left Midwinter's in 1980!

OUTLINERS: Gladys Scarlett, *Original Bizarre*, 1926 to 1932; Annie Beresford, *Original Bizarre* and *Trees and House*, 1927 to 1934; Nancy Liversage, painted samples and all 'specials', 1928 to 1940; Sadie Maskrey, samples and *Café-au-lait*, 1927 to 1933; Doris Thirlwall, *Original Bizarre* and *Latona*, 1928 to 1936; Tom Stringer, *Broth* and *Autumn*, 1928 to 1933; John Shaw, *Appliqué* and *Fantasque*, also modelling, 1928 to 1936; Harold Walker, *Appliqué* and *Fantasque*, nearly all *Windbells*, also modelling, 1928 to 1936; Ellen Browne, *House and Bridge*, *Circus* ware, 1929 to 1940; Eileen Tharme, *Fantasque*, *Appliqué*, *Chintz*, *Latona*, 1928 to 1941; Kathy Keeling, *Gibraltar* and *Secrets*, 1928 to 1940; Ella Hopkins, *Original Bizarre*, *Trees and House*, 1929 to 1939; Fred Salmon, *Autumn* and *Summerhouse*, 1929 to 1932;

Phoebe Hodgkinson, *Appliqué* and fine detail samples, 1929 to 1938; Gladys Birkin, 1930 to 1940; Rene Dale, *Secrets*, *Gibraltar* and *Crayon Scenes*, 1931 to 1941, then 1947 to 1952; Pru Sharman, 1931 to 1937.

FREEHAND/ENAMELLERS: Ada Cornes, 1928 to 1940; Agnes Durber, 1928 to 1941; Alice Andrews, 1931 to 1942, then just 1946; Annie Elsby, 1929 to 1939; Annie Holland, 1930 to 1937; Audrey Ridgway, 1930 briefly; Beryl Ridgway, 1930 briefly; Betty Dakin, 1929 to 1934 (died in 1934); Betty Henshall, 1929 to 1939; Betty Hollingsworth, 1930 to 1934; Cissy Rhodes, 1928 to 1940, then 1949 to 1967; Connie Hodgkinson, 1935 to 1938; Daisy Seckercon, 1928 to 1932?; Doreen Yates, 1933 to 1940; Doris Bailey, 1929 to early thirties; Doris Beech, 1928 to 1939; Doris Johnson, *Nasturtium* and *Honeydew*, 1934 to 1940; Dorothy Davis, 1933 to 1936; Dorothy Higginson, 1935 to 1939; Edith Pointon, 1930 only; Edith Walton, early thirties; Edna Becket, *Inspiration* and *Café-au-lait*, 1926 to 1939; Edna Cheetham, *Rhodanthe*, 1934 to 1940; Elsie Devon, 1930 to 193?; Elsie Kearns, 1932 to 1941; Ethel Barrow, mainly *Crocus*, 1928 to 1938, then 1948 to 1965; Ethel Cliff (Clarice's sister), 1930 to 1940; Ethel Coates, 1929 to 1939; Ethel Timmis, *Rhodanthe* and *Honeydew*, 1932 to 1937, then 1946 to 1953; Florrie Eardley, 1929 to 1942; Florrie Robinson,

BELOW: Still a team in 1998, original Bizarre *girls May Booth, Doris Johnson, Nora Dabbs and Alice Andrews, at the Gladstone Pottery Museum with author Leonard Griffin*

1930 to 1937; Florrie Winkle, 1928 to 1942, then 1946 to 1970; Gertie Love, 1928 to 1939; Gladys Baggaley, 1931 to 1935; Hilda Peers, 1929 to 1940; Ivy Stringer, *Umbrellas and Rain*, *Inspiration* and *Delecia Poppy*, 1929 to 1941; Kitty Oakes, 1930 to 1933; Laura Bossons, 1929 to 1935; Lily Barrow, *Delecia* and *Nasturtium*, 1930 to 1938; Lily Dabbs (younger sister of Nora), 1932 only; Lucy Moon, 1930 to 1933; Lucy Travis, 1928 to 1936; Mary Moses, shape 973 *Water Lily* bowls, 1928 to 1942, then 1948 to 1952; May Booth, 1937 to 1939; May Keeling, 1928 to 1932; Millie Liversage, early thirties; Nancy Dale, 1929 to 1937; Nancy Flynn, 1930 only; Nancy Lawton, 1929 to early thirties; Nellie Harrison, 1928 to 1930; Nellie Thacker, 1928 to 1939; Nellie Webb, *My Garden*, 1928 to 1941; Patty Shaw, early thirties; Phoebe Hogkinson, 1929 to 1938; Vera Hollins, *Appliqué*, 1928 to 1937; Vera Parr, 1934 to 1942; Vera Rawlinson, 1928 to 1929; Violet Farley, 1929 to 1939; Winnie Pound, 1930 to 1942, then 1945 to 1947; Jessie McKenzie, 1930 to 1935; Phyllis Woodhead, 1928 to 1932.

BANDERS: Mary Brown, 1927 to 1938, then 1956 to 1965; Phyllis Tharme, 1927 to 1939; Marjory Higginson, also *Honiton*, 1929 to 1940, then 1948 to 1956; Annie Cotton, 1929 to 1940; Elsie Nixon, also *Delecia*, 1929 to 1939; Maud Jones, 1929 to 1932; Winnie Smith, 1929 to 1942; Harriet Rhodes, 1929 to early thirties; Nora Dabbs, *Gayday* and *Delecia*, 1930 to 1943; Ivy Tunicliff, 1932 to 1939; Mollie Browne, 1932 to 1940; Katie Hulme, 1933 to 1941; Clara Brindley, 1933 to 1939; Beth Evans, 1929 to 1950; Clara Thomas (Clarice's first bander), 1927 to 1959; Rosa Rigby, 1935 to 1940, then 1946 to 1980; Winnie Davies, 1928 to 1940; Marianne Holcroft, 1939 to 1941; Ray Booth, 1939 to 1946, then 1945 to 1953.

MODELLERS AND DESIGNERS: John Butler, until approximately 1930; Fred Ridgway, until 1938; Ron Birks, 1928 to 1932; Peggy Davies, 1936 to 1939; Nancy Greatrex, 1936 to 1939; Betty Silvester, 1935 to 1940; Aubrey Dunn, 1937 to 1940, then 1946 to 1955; Eric Elliott, 1952 to 1955.

DESIGN NUMBERS

Collectors will find Newport Pottery and Wilkinson's ware with a confusing range of design numbers. In the years 1922 to 1940 the Newport Pottery numbers ran from 5000 to 7200, while at Wilkinson's they were in the range 6100 to 9500. Newport Pottery numbers above 5700 date from after the launch of *Bizarre* ware. Just a few of the more important or significant Newport Pottery numbers are listed, including those from before *Bizarre* was launched.

NEWPORT POTTERY PATTERN NUMBERS

5145 *Countryside* A printed scene of a cottage and windmill with aerographed colour

5388 A black print of bird and flowers with orange lustre aerographing

5436 A black lithograph of dancing Peter Pan figures

5455 *Canton* A print of oranges, blackberries and blackcurrants covered in orange lustre

5576 *Homeland Series Australia/New Zealand/India* Prints with freehand colour, designed by Fred Ridgway

5799 The original pattern number for *Ravel* (May 1929)

5800 *Brunella* A variation on *Ravel* (May 1929)

5802 A banded design, broad orange at the edge with fine black, blue, yellow, black lines inside, found on sandwich sets (1929–31)

5850 (or 5859?) *Peter Pan Crocus*

5851 A variation on 5799 in blue

5887 *Chloris* A printed floral band with hand-painted details (1931–35)

5949 Blocks of red, orange and yellow in the centre of dinnerware plates, by a black and red crescent (1931)

5956 A print of red roses and purple anemones found on *Damask Rose* ware (1932)

5957 A motif based on *Chintz*, of yellow flowers with green and yellow lily pads (1932)

5998 Lilac and purple colouring on *Scraphito* ware (1932)

6042 The *Kew* design hand-painted as a tableware cartouche (1932)

6053–6056 The original pattern numbers for *Cowslip Amber*, *Green*, *Chocolate* and *Blue* (1933)

6070 *Secrets* The design number of this major landscape design (1933)

6083 *Kew* A printed version of 6042 with different colouring (1933)

6138 *Eight o'clock* ware. A clock face on *Bon Jour* teapots, blue and red colourways (1933)

6140 A central landscape with a banded and spotted rim in yellow and brown credited to Harold Walker in the pattern books, but not known (1933)

6153 The *Tulips* landscape design as a cartouche with blue and green lining on tableware (1933)

6194 The pattern number for *Blue Firs* as a *Biarritz* shoulder pattern (1933–34)

6196 The pattern number for *Secrets* as a *Biarritz* shoulder pattern (1933–34)

6198 A pink tree with blue flowers on one side of *Biarritz* tableware (1933–34)

6199 The pattern number for *Coral Firs* as a *Biarritz* shoulder pattern (1933–34)

6311–6314 *Aura* Various colourways (1934)

6394 *Pastel Etching* All over etching in pink, grey and turquoise (1935)

6413–6415 *Opalesque* ware designs (1935)

6450 *Initial* ware. A customer's initials hand-painted in silver and black on *Bon Jour* and *Biarritz* ware (1935)

6485 *Wheat* A printed and enamelled design (1935)

6502 A variation on *Rhodanthe* in pink, grey and blue (1935)

6531 *Eating Apples* (1935)

6614 *Forest Glen/Newlyn* (1935)

6768 *Matana* A printed motif of stylized pastel flowers with blue or green banding (1936)

6932 *Clovelly* (1937)

WILKINSON'S PATTERN NUMBERS

Designs such as 6172, a black print of a chequered motif with pink aerographing, and 6271, a black print of

Japanese blossoms with lilac aerographing, were issued from 1922. Clarice Cliff would have been heavily involved on these as she was working alongside John Butler. In 1924 she is recorded in pattern 7309, a Fred Ridgway design of a dragon and birds, on which she painted the gold. The *Cries of London* were printed, traditional scenes by Fred Ridgway, the *Muffin Man*, *Orange Girl*, *Milkmaid*, and some of Clarice's early figurines were part of this series.

From 1928 Clarice Cliff's own shapes were issued in Wilkinson's printed and enamelled patterns to make them available at a cheaper price to dealers who could not afford to stock *Bizarre* ware. These include:

8699 *Florida* A printed and enamelled leaf design (1929)

8702 *Poppyland* A radial shoulder pattern of black litho print of trees with enamelled poppies (1929)

8716 *Oranges* A freehand pattern of simple oranges with a little black detail and no banding, it seems to have been produced mainly for export (1929–30)

8719 *Lodore* A printed and enamelled Clarice Cliff design (1929–30)

8757 *Lourie* A freehand motif of a brown trellis with a few green leaves (1930)

8827 *Forest Leaves* Orange and brown freehand etched leaves, sometimes with green and yellow detail (1930)

8854 *Solomon's Seal* A printed Clarice Cliff design with hand enamelling (1930)

8876 *Nemesia* A printed Clarice Cliff design with hand enamelling (1930)

8758 *Kylis* A printed motif of flowers by a bridge with hand-painted detail (1930)

9359 *Honeybloom* A floral motif painted in yellow and then enamelled, with a custom *Honeybloom* backstamp (1933–34)

A mass of other patterns followed, sometimes with non-sequential numbers, and production also continued after the War through until December 1964.

GLOSSARY

BANDER AND LINER: A decorator who put fine lines or thicker bands of colour on ware by applying the paint on brushes of different thicknesses whilst rotating the ware on a potter's wheel.

BISCUIT: The name given to ware which has had just one firing to harden it, before it is glazed.

BOTTLE OVENS: Kilns built of brick and fired by coal which were often forty to fifty feet high.

EARLY MORNING SET: A tea set for two comprising teapot, milk and sugar, two cups and saucers, and just one or two plates. Designed to be used in the bedroom for the first cup of tea of the day, they were also popular with housewives for use when a visitor called.

ENAMEL KILN: An oven used to fire ware with enamelled decoration on-glaze.

ENAMELLER: A decorator who applied colour freehand or within another decorator's outline.

FANCIES: Small non-essential items such as cauldrons, sabots, ink wells, bookends, which constituted an important part of Clarice Cliff's range.

FREEHAND: A decorator who applied a design with no existing guidelines, such as on *Crocus* or *Gayday*.

GILDING: Painting fine gold lines on pottery.

GLOST: Ware which has been glazed but is undecorated, this was stored in the glost warehouse.

HONEYGLAZE: The tradename for the clear glaze used on her pottery. This had one per cent iron oxide content, hence the name and colour.

KILNS: Smaller versions of bottle ovens where glazed or enamelled ware was fired.

LITHOGRAPHY: The art of applying printed transfers on ware as the main decoration.

MISSUS: A woman who supervised a decorating shop and trained the workers in the necessary techniques. She was generally an experienced paintress herself.

ON-GLAZE: Decoration applied to the ware after it had been fired and glazed, which was then re-fired in the enamel kiln. This was the main style of decoration used on Clarice's hand-painted ware.

OUTLINER: A skilled decorator who painted the pattern outline directly onto ware.

PÂTE-SUR-PÂTE: Decoration created by applying slip in very fine layers to build the design, originally evolved at Sèvres.

POCHOIR: A printing process, popular in France in the twenties, used to produce fine quality prints in many colours.

POTBANK: The Staffordshire name given to a pottery factory as in the early days they had a 'bank' of clay outside, and made 'pots'.

THE POTTERIES: A collective name for the six Staffordshire towns of Hanley, Tunstall, Longton, Burslem, Fenton and Stoke.

SHARDS: Broken pieces of ware which formed white mounds – shard rucks – covering acres of land adjacent to the factories. This is pronounced 'sherds' in Staffordshire.

SHOP: The Staffordshire term for a room in a factory dedicated to one process, such as a decorating shop or a lithography shop.

SHOULDER PATTERN: A design confined to all or part of the rim of a plate.

SLIP: Liquid clay used for casting ware, and as a form of decoration on Clarice's *Patina* ware.

UNDERGLAZE: Ware decorated in the biscuit state before it was glazed, the traditional way of decorating printed ware, only rarely used by Clarice Cliff in the thirties.

BIBLIOGRAPHY

BOOKS

The Decorative Thirties, Martin Battersby, Studio Vista, 1969

Clarice Cliff, Kay Johnson and Peter Wentworth-Sheilds, L'Odeon, 1976 and 1981

The Shorter Connection, Gordon and Irene Hopwood, Richard Dennis, 1992

Charleston – A Bloomsbury House and Garden, Quentin Bell and Virginia Nicholson, Frances Lincoln, 1997

Potters and Paintresses, Cheryl Buckley, Women's Press, 1990

JOURNALS, MAGAZINES AND EXHIBITION CATALOGUES

Pottery Gazette and Glass Review

Staffordshire Pottery and Glass Record

Mobilier et Décoration, Paris: Editions Edmund Honor, 1929

Susie Cooper Productions (Exhibition), Ann Eatwell, V&A, 1987

Hand-Painted Gray's Pottery (Exhibition), Paul and Kathy Niblett, The Potteries Museum, 1982

Thirties (Exhibition), Jennifer Hawkins, Arts Council, 1980

Clarice Cliff (Exhibition), Betty O'Looney/Martin Battersby, Brighton Museum and Art Gallery, 1972

ACKNOWLEDGEMENTS

IN GREAT BRITAIN: the late Nancy Cliff, the late Marjory Higginson, John B. Shorter, John Oakes, Eric Grindley, Jim Hall, Bryan Havenhand, Mrs Joy Couper, Norman Smith, Esme Bailey, Professor Flavia Swann, Dr Phil Woodward, Sharon Gater, Gaye Blake-Roberts, Andrew Klimecki, Sheila Elliot, Alison Reid, Terry Abbotts, Dave Wallet, Michael Lowe, David and Barbara, Mick and Linda, Shirley and Michael, Gordon and Irene, David and Teresa Latham, Tony and Rachel, Ron and Stephanie, Ron and Teresa, Neil and Shirley Matthew, Roger Hopkins, Muir Hewitt, Ron Knee, Gavin Casey, Peter Peach, Peter Ford, John and Pam Ewen, The Barry Jones Collection, Brian and Marie, David Mobbs, Mary, Maureen and Harold, Sandra and Michael, Iain Everitt, Iris and Sheila, Mark and Michael at Christie's, Mike and Jane, Jill and Neil, David Wilkins, Michael and Robert, Jonathan and Alan of Banana Dance, and particularly to Doreen Jenkins.

IN NEW ZEALAND: Jonathan, Lynley and Georgie Drain, Ishbel Meadows, John Winton, Ken and Beverley, Russell and Erik, Kevin and Bernadette Straka.

IN AUSTRALIA: Sue and George Walters, Shane and Henri, Greg Slater, Kathy King, Carole Hansen, and Dan Hogg

IN NORTH AMERICA: Peter and Kay, Julie and Sandy, Susan Scott, Chris Purkis, Pat Halfpenny, Richard Kutner, Judi and Herb, S and B, Robert Prescott-Walker, and *very* special thanks to Louis and Susan Meisel.

IN SOUTH AFRICA: Hendrik and Ricki.

Archive photographs are courtesy of John B. Shorter, Catherine Humphreys, the *Bizarre* 'girls', the British Museum, the Stoke-on-Trent City Archives and Stoke-on-Trent Archive Service and the Clarice Cliff Collectors Club photograph archive. Particular thanks to Christie's, South Kensington, for the *Circus* and *May Avenue* images. Excerpts from Clarice's letters are courtesy of the Clarice Cliff Collectors' Club.

The *biggest* thanks go to Clarice's marvellous 'girls', an unbeatable team then *and* now, and Mike Slaney, an ever-patient human being, and the light that has guided me through five books. LG

The *Clarice Cliff Collectors Club*, founded in 1982, publishes its *Review* three times a year, and has meetings where members meet the original *Bizarre* 'girls'. Hand-painted Clarice Cliff reproductions, produced by Wedgwood, are available exclusively to members. For details send an s.a.e. to: Subscriptions, C.C.C.C., Fantasque House, Tennis Drive, The Park, Nottingham NG7 1AE; in New Zealand to: C.C.C.C., c/o Burlington Berties, 91 Great South Road, Auckland; in Australia to: c/o Deco Downunder, 24 Parade Street, Albany, Western Australia 6330. The *Clarice Cliff Collectors Club* is on the Internet at: www.claricecliff.com.

'Clarice Cliff' and 'Bizarre' are registered trademarks of Josiah Wedgwood and are used with permission.

INDEX